READERS' GUIDES TO ESSENTIAL CRITICIS

CONSULTANT EDITOR: NICOLAS TREDELL

Published

Readers' Guides to Essential Criticism
Series Standing Order
ISBN 978–1–403–90108–8
(*outside North America only*)

You can receive future titles in this series as they are published by placing a standing order. Please contact your bookseller or, in the case of difficulty, write to us at the address below with your name and address, the title of the series and the ISBN quoted above.

Customer Services Department, Macmillan Distribution Ltd, Houndmills, Basingstoke, Hampshire, RG21 6XS, UK

The Poetry of Ted Hughes

SANDIE BYRNE

Consultant Editor: NICOLAS TREDELL

First published 2014 by
PALGRAVE MACMILLAN

Palgrave Macmillan in the UK is an imprint of Macmillan Publishers Limited,
registered in England, company number 785998, of Houndmills, Basingstoke,
Hampshire RG21 6XS.

Palgrave Macmillan in the US is a division of St Martin's Press LLC,
175 Fifth Avenue, New York, NY 10010.

Palgrave Macmillan is the global academic imprint of the above companies
and has companies and representatives throughout the world.

Palgrave® and Macmillan® are registered trademarks in the United States,
the United Kingdom, Europe and other countries.

ISBN 978-1-137-31092-7   ISBN 978-1-137-31094-1 (eBook)
DOI 10.1007/978-1-137-31094-1

A catalogue record for this book is available from the British Library.

A catalog record for this book is available from the Library of Congress.

Typeset by MPS Limited, Chennai, India.

Contents

of animals; Hughes and Jung; Hughes and shamanism; Hughes and Robert Graves; Hughes and the Goddess; and Hughes and dialect. Criticism by Rand Brandes, Terry Eagleton, Ekbert Faas, Nick Gammage, Terry Gifford and Neil Roberts, Seamus Heaney, Blake Morrison, Craig Robinson, Keith Sagar, Annie Schofield, Michael Sweeting, Daniel Weissbort and Thomas West. Close readings of 'The Thought-Fox', 'Thistles' and 'Fern' by Seamus Heaney, and Blake Morrison on 'Wodwo'.

Whispers and *Capriccios*. Criticism of these works by Paul Bentley, Melvyn Bragg, Neil Corcoran, Jo Gill, John Lucas, Neil Roberts, Sean O'Brien, Tom Paulin, M.G. Ramanan, Anne Skea, Jon Stallworthy, Elizabeth A. Stansell and Marina Warner.

Overviews of Hughes's Achievement

Late and posthumous assessments of Hughes's poetic career, including obituaries, newspaper articles, tributes to Ted Hughes and his achievement and assessments of Hughes's lasting significance, by, among others, Simon Armitage, Douglas Dunn, Terry Gifford, Seamus Heaney, John Kinsella, Sarah Maguire, Andrew Motion, Jeffrey Meyers, Don Paterson, John Redmond and Alan Sillitoe, Keith Sagar, Anthony Thwaite and Boyd Tonkin.

List of Abbreviations

THitR	*The Hawk in the Rain*. London: Faber & Faber, 1957.
L	*Lupercal*. London: Faber & Faber, 1960.
W	*Wodwo*. London: Faber & Faber, 1967.
C	*Crow: From the Life and Songs of the Crow*, illus. Leonard Baskin. London: Faber & Faber, 1970.
CB	*Cave Birds: An Alchemical Cave Drama*, illus. Leonard Baskin. Limited edition. London: Scholar Press, 1975.
G	*Gaudete*. London: Faber & Faber, 1977.
RE	*Remains of Elmet*, illus. photographs Fay Godwin. London: Faber & Faber, 1979. Revised edition published as *Elmet*, 1994.
M	*Moortown*. London: Faber & Faber, 1979.
R	*River*, illus. photographs P. Keen. London and Boston: Faber & Faber in association with James & James, 1983.
MD	*Moortown Diary*. London: Faber & Faber, 1989.
W	*Wolfwatching*. London: Faber & Faber, 1989.
RCD	*Rain-Charm for the Duchy and Other Laureate Poems*. London: Faber & Faber, 1992.
E	Elmet. London: Faber & Faber, 1994.
NSP	*New Selected Poems 1957–1994*. London: Faber & Faber, 1995.
TfO	*Tales from Ovid*. London: Faber & Faber, 1997.
BL	*Birthday Letters*. London: Faber & Faber, 1998.
CP	*Ted Hughes: Collected Poems*, ed Paul Keegan. London: Faber & Faber, 2003.
SPCP	Sylvia Plath, *Collected Poems* (1981); repr. London: Faber & Faber, 1992.

INTRODUCTION

Hughes's Life

Edward James Hughes was born on 17 August 1930 in Mytholmroyd, West Yorkshire, although the family moved to Mexborough, South Yorkshire, when he was 7 years old. After attending Mexborough Grammar School, where he wrote poems for the school magazine, in 1948 Hughes won an open exhibition to Pembroke College, Cambridge, but chose to complete his two years of National Service before going up to read English in 1951.

Though Hughes was a competent analyst of literary texts in the Leavisite style then prevalent at Cambridge, he hated the work. During the two years before he moved from the study of English to that of archaeology and anthropology, he felt that the clinical dismemberment and reassemblage of literary texts was killing part of him, the part that was a poet. That feeling was made manifest in a dream, vividly described in his prose collection, *Winter Pollen* (1994), which has become iconic, of Hughes, his poetic endeavour, and his shamanic status. In the dream, a fox, tall and badly charred, entered Hughes's student room in Cambridge, walking on its hind legs. It put a paw on the papers on the desk, leaving a bloody mark, came over to the bed, looked down at Hughes, and said: 'You're killing us.'[1]

If that feral part of Hughes or his unconscious was stifled or starved by English studies, it was nurtured or allowed release by his work in archaeology and anthropology during his third year at Cambridge. In the month in which he graduated, June 1954, his poem, 'The Little Boys and the Seasons' (*CP*, p. 8), was published in the Cambridge magazine *Granta*, under the pseudonym 'Daniel Hearing'. After graduating, he worked in a zoo, as a gardener, a night-watchman, and as a reader for J. Arthur Rank, the film production company, but continued to publish poems and was co-founder of a poetry magazine, *St Botolph's Review*. It was at the launch party for *St Botolph's* in February 1956 that he met Sylvia Plath, who had come to Newnham College, Cambridge, from America on a Fulbright Scholarship. They married in June that year, and while Plath finished her degree, Hughes taught English and drama in a local secondary school. The next year, they went to live and teach in America: Plath at Smith College; Hughes at the University of Massachusetts in Amherst.

Before leaving for America, Hughes had finished his first collection of poems, *The Hawk in the Rain* (1957). Typed up and sent in by Plath, the poems won the First Publication Award in a contest sponsored by the Poetry Center of the Young Men's and Young Women's Hebrew Association of New York, which was judged by W.H. Auden, Marianne Moore and Stephen Spender. The prize was publication by Harper & Brothers. After a year, Plath decided to give up her teaching job in order to write, but a Guggenheim Fellowship enabled the couple to spend the summer of 1959 travelling and camping throughout the USA, and to spend time at the writers' community at Yaddo. There, Hughes finished his next book, *Lupercal*, which was published in March 1960 and was awarded the Hawthornden Prize. These two collections established Hughes as a significant poet, and a dissenting voice from that associated with Movement poetry. Meanwhile, in December 1959, Hughes and Plath had returned to live in England, briefly in Heptonstall, then Primrose Hill, London (where their first child was born on 1 April 1960) and in Devon (where their second child was born on 17 January 1962). By then, their marriage had become unstable. In August, they separated, and Plath took a flat back in Primrose Hill. On 11 February 1963, she killed herself by gas asphyxiation.

After March 1963, during which he wrote two poems, Hughes published no poetry for three years. He wrote reviews and articles, worked on an adaptation of Johann Valentin Andreae's *The Chemical Wedding of Christian Rosencreutz*,[2] selected and introduced a volume of Keith Douglas's poetry which was published in 1964, and in 1966 became co-founder of the journal *Modern Poetry in Translation*, but the next volume of his own poetry did not appear until 1967. Between publication of *Wodwo* and *Crow* (1970) another tragedy occurred: Assia Wevill, with whom Hughes had a relationship and with whom he had a daughter, Shura, took her own life and that of Shura.

In 1970 Hughes married Carol Orchard and they settled back at Court Green. Soon after they bought a small farm nearby which Hughes worked on with his father-in-law, Jack Orchard, a farming life that is chronicled in *Moortown Diary* (1979), whose poems were taken directly from Hughes's journal notes.

Hughes was an invaluable contributor to the Arvon Foundation, which runs writing schools and offers help and encouragement to new writers, and during the 1970s he was several times a guest speaker in the foundation's Devon Centre. His house, Lumb Bank, near Heptonstall in West Yorkshire, was first leased and then sold to the Foundation, and has become the Arvon northern centre. In addition to his own writing, he continued to translate, edit and collect other poets' work. His own publications from the 1970s and 1980s include *Crow: From the Life and Songs of the Crow* (1970), *Cave Birds: An Alchemical Cave Drama* (1975), *Gaudete* (1977), *Remains of Elmet* (1979), *River* (1983) and *Wolfwatching* (1989). *The Rattle-Bag* (1982), an anthology edited with Seamus Heaney, was followed by *The School Bag* in 1997.

Hughes's love of the countryside led him to be active in protest against its pollution and is evident in an eco-fable, *The Iron Woman* (1993), a sequel to his *The Iron Man: A Story in Five Nights* (1968). In 1984, he succeeded Sir John Betjeman as Poet Laureate, publishing *Rain-Charm for the Duchy and other Laureate Poems* in 1992. In 1998, he became the first poet to be appointed to the Order of Merit since Walter De La Mare (1873–1956) was honoured in 1953. These were added to an impressive list of honours which included the Harper publication contest (1957), the Guinness Poetry Award (1958), a Guggenheim Fellowship (1959), the Somerset Maugham award (1960), the City of Florence International Poetry Prize (1969), the Premio Internazionale Taormina (1973), the Queen's Gold Medal for Poetry (1974), the Whitbread Book of the Year (1998, 1999), the W.H. Smith Literature Award (1998), the Forward Prize for Poetry (1998), the T.S. Eliot Prize for Poetry (1998) and the South Bank Award for Literature (1999). Hughes's *Collected Animal Poems* (1984) for children won both the *Guardian* Children's Fiction Award and the Signal Poetry Award.

POSTHUMOUS ACCLAIM FOR TED HUGHES

The death of Ted Hughes on 28 October 1998 was reported on television and radio news, and in the national and international broadsheets and periodicals, which ran lengthy testimonials and obituaries. To those who knew Ted Hughes personally, the news was, of course, earth-stopping, and responses to the announcement by those who did not know him personally suggested that the shock was nonetheless great and the loss profound. In his Editor's Note to *The Epic Poise* (1999), Nick Gammage wrote of a shock-wave that followed the announcement, and of the sense readers had had of Hughes as a weighty, permanent fixture; a landmark from which we could take bearings and a repository of the 'wisdom of ages'.[3] As often in evaluations of Hughes's work, the weight and stature of the achievement is seen as inseparable from the nature and stature of the man. Gammage found nothing either peripheral or fleeting about either, but did find that the physical stature of the poet gave an impression of permanence, so that the loss was irreparable.

It is a testament to Hughes's status and achievement that his death was so widely reported and the loss to Britain, to readers and to literature, so widely mourned during a decade when the status of poetry was at best ambivalent, when Oxford University Press closed its poetry list and sales of poetry in the UK were relatively low (in spite of poetry being proclaimed as the new rock and roll).

At the memorial service for Hughes in May 1999, Seamus Heaney described his feelings when, at Hughes's funeral in November 1998, he had watched his friend being borne along what seemed to be a living stream of air and water, and into the realm of myth and heroic stature. What came into his mind, Heaney reported, was Wilfred Owen's poem 'Hospital Barge', which in turn was influenced by that poet's reading of Tennyson's reference to the barge that carried King Arthur to Avalon. The image that came to mind was of the hero of epic stature, translated and transfigured into memory and fame.[4] Again, Hughes is described in terms of permanence, here as a figure in the tapestry of legend, fittingly housed in Westminster Abbey with kings and poets whose lives and works are eternally renewed and reshaped in story. This process had begun in Hughes's lifetime, and many memoirs that were to follow continued his translation and reification. Heaney suggests that Hughes would have been as much at home with the Anglo-Saxon poet Caedmon in the Whitby monastery as with Wilfred Owen in the trenches of the Somme. In this way, Heaney celebrated Hughes not only for his own work but as a 'genius of the shore', that is, as a guardian spirit of both the land and the language.

The sense of guardian spirit bound up with the land persisted in Heaney's double-edged comparison of Hughes to a merlin in his fly-casting and Merlin in his presence. Heaney's comparison of Hughes to Caedmon was developed in his assertion that Hughes's first impulse was to give glory to creation, and through that glorification to allow it to be more abundantly itself. Heaney also stressed, however, that Hughes was also a 'made poet', deeply learned in the art of poetry, marked by sorrow both personal and historical, possessed of a soothsayer's awareness of his own destiny, and of knowledge that facing a destiny would involve his undergoing an ordeal.[5]

Heaney had been an advocate of Hughes's work since at least 1967. The powerful presence that he celebrated and that others, including

Philip Larkin, had derided or reviled has been as much the subject of critical discussion as Hughes's powerful poetry. Leonard M. Scigaj notes that before Hughes's death critical reception of Hughes's poetry had been lethargic, and that Hughes remained an undiscovered country to most American readers. Scigaj argues that this was largely because Americans often find Hughes's poetry difficult, even forbidding, and because Hughes's changes of style and subject matter leave them 'wondering if his interests are very eccentric'.[6] An alternative explanation for the relative lack in the USA, during some periods, of critical interest in Hughes's work, as opposed to Hughes's life, is the overshadowing of his poetry by the accounts of his relationship with Sylvia Plath. (Critical views of this are discussed in Chapter 4.)

Hughes's attitude to success as measured by sales and fame seems to have been ambivalent. In a poem 'Ouija' (*BL, CP*, p. 1076), a ouija board is asked: 'Shall we be famous?' Plath's sudden tears suggest that she has received an answer prophetic of both her fame and the price she will pay for it. While protesting his own lack of ambition, and attributing his quest for public recognition to compliance with the drives of his wife and mother-in-law, without whose ambitions he might be 'fishing off a rock/In Western Australia', Hughes seems to accept the fame as predestined. In another poem, written more than forty years before the publication of *Birthday Letters*, and before he became famous, Hughes invites the reader to look at an imaginary poet who has achieved fame. The eye cast on the subject is cold; the famous poet, a 'monster', is accused not only of losing his fire, but also of continuing to produce poems, or sham-poems to order, without it ('Famous Poet', *THITR, CP*, p. 23). The represented poet may be guilty of falsity and obscurity, but the poem also accuses the audience, the public, for always wanting an artist to repeat his or her successes.

In 'Famous Poet', a simile of a funeral with drums, coffin and mourners, and the couplet 'tread/dead' have echoes of Auden's 'Song IX' ('Stop all the Clocks') (though Auden uses 'overhead/dead').[7] Auden was 50 when Hughes's poem was published and had been elected Oxford Professor of Poetry the year before, but he was not a spent force; one of his most acclaimed collections, *The Shield of Achilles*, had been published in 1955. The subject of 'Famous Poet' is, of course, any and no particular poet, but the lines must have had an ironic resonance for Hughes when he became famous for the wrong reasons in 1963, and as Poet Laureate in 1984.

More echoes might have sounded with the awarding of other prizes, such as the Whitbread and the T.S. Eliot. Some critics, such as Neil Corcoran, suggested that Hughes's acceptance of the accolade of the

Laureateship was unexpected. It is perhaps significant that there are no pieces on the Laureate collection, *Rain-Charm for the Duchy*, in a number of posthumous celebrations of Hughes's work such as *Epic Poise* and *Lire Ted Hughes*,[8] and some reviewers of the collection were lukewarm, though others, such as Sean O'Brien, noted the seriousness with which Hughes approached the role (discussed in Chapter 5).[9]

However ambivalent Hughes was, then, he did become a 'famous poet', and his work and life therefore were opened to the concomitant critical scrutiny, part of which, that of his work, this study discusses.

CRITICAL APPROACHES TO HUGHES'S WORK

Relatively few Derridean, post-colonial or Marxist critics have interrogated Hughes's work, though Paul Bentley offers a poststructuralist reading in his full-length study,[10] and Adolphe Haberer reads 'Mayday in Holderness' through Lacanian theory.[11] Critical debates about Hughes's work have been focused on the nature of the violence, the abstraction and metaphysics of poem sequences such as *Cave Birds*, and the influence of, for example, Jung, Heidegger, Nietzsche and Schopenhauer. Whereas there has been debate about the intersection between the personal and the political in Heaney's poetry, conducted by, among others, Seamus Deane, John Wilson Foster, Mark Patrick Hederman, Richard Kearney and Edna Longley, the debate about Hughes's work has been whether it is political at all, in the sense of overtly concerned with social structures and events. The personal has received critical attention, but the focus has often been on autobiographical and biographical information not necessarily present in the poetry, at least before publication of the poems collected in *Birthday Letters*. There are many full-length studies, articles and reviews devoted to Hughes's writing, many of those insightful works of close critical analysis, but also a number of the biographical or exegetical kind, and the dominant note of the latter has been Jungian. Not all criticism has seen Hughes as an apolitical poet of nature, however; Tom Paulin, for example, writes of Hughes as like an itinerant street preacher, and a chronicler of working-class struggle.[12]

Though his poetry has always achieved respectable sales and commanded critical respect and admiration, that which – other than the Laureateship – brought Hughes into the public spotlight and his poetry under the media microscope and scalpel was his personal life, or rather its tragedies. Two suicides cast a shadow over Hughes's private life and public utterance from which he could not emerge in his lifetime and from which his poems, perhaps, never will emerge. However much Hughes refused to discuss his first marriage and its ending, however much he exercised editorial control over Sylvia Plath's published poems, however much he wished to deflect interest from the life to the work, some critics, whose work is summarised by James Fenton in a review discussed in Chapter 4, seemed to be unable or unwilling to expunge knowledge of one while reading the other.[13] The guarded openness of the *Birthday Letters* poems (serialised in *The Times* from January 1998) was certain to resurrect the interest, and rather than offering the end to speculation, provided matter for more. The poems were touching, poignant, agonised; but they were poems, not straightforward autobiography. They were also deemed to be very good poems and, in judging them to be so, critics have written about *Birthday Letters*, often in conjunction with *Tales from Ovid*, as a return to a form that had been, if not lost, perhaps occluded.[14] Hughes's appointment to the Laureateship revitalised sales of his work; thousands of copies of his *New Selected Poems 1957–1994* were sold on the day the news was announced, and later the same week Faber & Faber produced a printing of 15,000 copies. That *Birthday Letters* has so far outsold any of Hughes's other works, however, perhaps demonstrates a continued interest in his relationship with his first wife as great as that in his poetry.

A number of critics have found complexities, even obscurities, in some of Hughes's collections. Others explain perceived difficulties of understanding and assessment as consequences of deficiencies in the reader rather than in Hughes's texts. Leonard Scigaj, for example, suggests that the problem for the average critic is the sheer size of Hughes's output, his stylistic changes, and his varied reading interests, which Scigaj records as ranging from North American Indian folklore and the mythology of primitive cultures to Sufi fables, Tamil *vacanas* and Indian and Chinese mysticism. Scigaj accuses reviewers and academic critics (those who do not admit outright bafflement) of glossing over the content of new volumes with 'glib catchwords', or restricting their commentary to superficial points about language or taste. The extent of the influences incorporated in Hughes's poetry means that the critic must limit the focus to specifying only a few of the most significant patterns in 'a very richly woven carpet'.[15]

Keith Sagar, the most prolific and consistent apologist and interpreter of Hughes's work, saw a consistency in those patterns, and set himself the task of tracing the ways in which Hughes's poems relate 'to each other, to the tradition, to the work of other contemporary and recent writers'. Sagar argues that this is important because, although ever since the appearance of *The Hawk in the Rain* in 1957 large claims have

been made for Hughes, there was still no consensus about his importance, because there was no consensus about 'the nature, meaning and
relative value of his poems'.[16] Some such consensus is implicit in the
statement on the inner flap of the dust jacket of a collection of essays
edited by Sagar, *The Achievement of Ted Hughes*, which states unequivocally that few people would disagree that Ted Hughes is the 'greatest living English poet'.[17] Though this latter claim about the 'relative
value' of Hughes's work is likely to have been a consensus, even after
the publication of *Achievement* in 1983, critical disagreements about the
nature and meaning of the poems remain.

AIM OF THE GUIDE

This guide sets out to answer the question of why we should remember Ted Hughes by reference to the evaluative judgements of a range
of critics from the 1950s to the 2010s. Since the volume and range of
both Hughes's poetry and criticism of that poetry can seem daunting,
especially to readers looking for consistent themes and subjects, this
work also aims to guide readers through the many approaches to and
different readings of Hughes's work and the concomitant assessments
of its worth. Approaches range from those that classify Hughes as a
late Modernist, and focus on the form and surface of his writing, to
those that suggest we need a library of background material in order
to understand the poems. Others place Hughes in a line of descent
through Blake, Lawrence and Graves, or Leavis and Ransom, or group
him with Lowell or Eliot or Gunn, or place him in opposition to The
Movement or enlightenment rationalism, or place him in the context
of Ecopoetics.

   Any scheme of categorisation and subcategorisation of Hughes's work
and the criticism of that work will inevitably find overlaps, exceptions
and anomalies, but the guide is organised roughly thematically and
chronologically. Chapters 1 and 2 introduce some of the early responses
to Hughes's poetry, and representative samples of the enormous body
of writing about Hughes's nature poetry, from the early reception of
The Hawk in the Rain onwards. Chapter 2 focuses particularly on criticism which looks at Hughes's use of mythology, and which makes reference to philosophical works. Chapter 3 looks at critical reaction to
the later themed collections and sequences, such as *Crow, Remains of
Elmet, Cave Birds* and *River*. Chapter 4 looks at critical works that have
discussed the mutual influence of Hughes and Plath on each other's
poetry, and the effect the personal attacks on Hughes for his handling

of the Plath Estate may have had on his writing. Chapter 5 compares responses to Hughes's appointment as Laureate, and to his Laureate poems, *Rain-Charm for the Duchy*. The Conclusion includes evaluations of Hughes's lasting literary legacy.

Though this guide is concerned solely with criticism of Hughes's poetry, the select bibliography lists his major critical, children's and prose fiction publications. For Hughes's poetry, readers are directed to his *Collected Poems* (ed. Paul Keegan, London: Faber & Faber, 2003).

CHAPTER ONE

Early Work

The poetry of Ted Hughes elicited strong responses from the beginning of his career as a published poet, though opinions about its merits and meanings were divided. This chapter looks at responses to Hughes's early poetry, broadly categorised as 'nature poetry' in the sense of having animals, landscapes and the elements as its subjects. Criticism which looks at Hughes's poems about the natural world in terms of psychology, anthropology or philosophy is discussed in Chapter 2.

BACKGROUND

In his eulogy for Ted Hughes, Seamus Heaney associated his friend with the first known English poet, the seventh-century Saxon herdsman Caedmon, who sang the glory of Creation as one indivisible whole. 'He was the born poet in so far as his first impulse was to give glory to creation and through his glorification allow it to be more abundantly itself.'[1] While Hughes might have accepted the mantle of *scop* (the Old English equivalent of a bard; genealogist and historian as well as occasional poet of the clan or tribe), and may have appreciated the association of his poetry with that of a man indissolubly connected to the earth and its animal life, the analogy can only be maintained so far. Caedmon's hymn is to the glory of the creator, God, and envisages the Earth and all its bounty as created for humankind, which, in keeping with orthodox Christian tradition, stands at the centre and apex of creation. That arrogant anthropocentric assumption could by no means be derived from Hughes's poems, though they do not advocate animal rights in the sense of condemning the killing of animals for food, 'sport', research or other reasons.

That Hughes's poetry is not anthropocentric but biocentric (that is, it places at the centre of the universe not humankind but the bio-system of Nature of which humanity is just one part of a complex system of interrelations) is argued in an essay by Leonard Scigaj which traces Hughes's interest in ecology and finds in his poetry an indictment of the anthropocentrism of the post-Enlightenment grand discourses of (for example) science and religion.[2] The extent to which Hughes's poems glorify nature is debatable; they are not odes to the west wind, nor dithyrambs called forth by the beauty of a landscape. Seamus Heaney rarely uses words lightly or inaccurately, however, and perhaps the aspects of animal behaviour which readers might find disturbing or even horrific are precisely found glorious in their rightness, that is, their truthfulness to the animals' nature, and to the truth of Nature in its endless drama of struggle, death and rebirth.

Much of Hughes's early work is nature poetry (that is, in some way about the natural world of landscape, the elements, flora and fauna), but most critics agree that it is not traditional pastoral (that is, art which offers the countryside, usually a gentle and fertile landscape, as a place of refuge, especially from urban life, and of spiritual replenishment), or neo-Georgian (that is, in the manner of the group of writers in the reign of George V (1910–36) including Rupert Brooke, John Masefield and W.H. Davies, much of whose work appeared in the series *Georgian Poetry* published between 1912 and 1922, and which was criticised as both pastoral and escapist). An early advocate of Hughes's work discussed in this chapter, A. Alvarez, cited Hughes's 'A Dream of Horses' (*L*, *CP*, pp. 65–6) as rescuing English representations of nature from 'gentility'.[3] An exception to this view, also discussed in this chapter, is Ian Hamilton.[4] When Hughes's subject is agricultural land and domesticated animals, there is always the sense of struggle and tension, of the wild harnessed but not held by the enclosure walls and dykes of husbandry, and likely at any minute to twitch, roll, and shake them off. There are, however, elements of the continuation of a strand of Romantic nature poetry in that Hughes's imagery often opposes the elemental forces of the natural world and the instinctual drives of animals against the rationality of the human, seemingly favouring the former over the latter. Antony Easthope, in an article also discussed in this chapter, sees Hughes's work as in some respects entrenched in pre-Modernist and Romantic ideas.[5]

Hughes does not assert that his poems can themselves heal the wasteland of the modern world or the dissociation of humanity from the natural world, but nonetheless, Heaney suggests, 'there was something homoeopathic about his celebration of plants and creatures, since the poems were reminders that we are all part of the same fabric, woven out of and into the palpable, mysterious universe'.[6] While humanity is often absent from Hughes's landscapes, it is indissolubly, if tenuously and invisibly, connected to the wild which it has smothered both outside and within itself. The animals in Hughes's poetry are often those that have in a way remained totems, in Western and other mythologies, and even for twenty-first-century city-dwellers, as emblems of the wild beyond or behind, or perhaps within us. This theme, fundamental to Hughes's poetry and discussed by, among others, Keith Sagar and Leonard Scigaj in a number of publications, is touched on in this chapter and more fully developed in the next.

RESPONSES TO VIOLENCE IN HUGHES'S WORK

THITR was recognised in several reviews as introducing an important and vigorous force into English poetry of the mid-century. Graham Hough in *Encounter* found a 'poetic intelligence' running all the way through the collection, and remarked that Hughes gave the impression of being 'a poet by nature and instinct' and that though this did not exclude echoes of Hopkins and Dylan Thomas, the point was that a 'rich, even a turbulent life of feeling and observation' seemed to Hough to transfer itself immediately to Hughes's words, 'without diminution or impairment'.[7] A.E. Dyson found it the 'most distinguished volume of verse' by a poet of Hughes's generation, and noted that it 'escapes the various poetic labels' (Movement, Maverick) of the previous ten years.[8] Dyson ended by predicting that Hughes would be one of the select few poets who would still be read in a hundred years. Edwin Muir, writing in the *New Statesman*, judged that Hughes was clearly a remarkable poet who seemed to be 'quite outside the currents of his time'. Muir judged Hughes's 'distinguishing power' as at best a fusing of the sensuous, the verbal and the imaginative. He found *THITR* 'a most surprising first book', but in raising the topic of the violence of Hughes's imagery, though he found it 'admirable', Muir anticipated the focus of a number of less admiring reviews.[9]

The dominant strain in English poetry when Hughes began to publish was represented by D.J. Enright's anthology *Poets of the 1950s*, and by *New Lines* (1956),[10] the first of two anthologies edited and introduced by Robert Conquest, which brought together the work of poets associated with 'The Movement', a term used in 1954 by the literary editor of the *Spectator* of a group of writers including Kingsley Amis, Robert Conquest, Donald Davie, D.J. Enright, Philip Larkin and John Wain, though not all of those poets were pleased to be included in that grouping. Movement poems were characteristically rational and ironic in tone, austere in language and anti-Romantic in theme.

Reviewing Hughes's first two collections in 1961, J.M. Newton suggested that if anything, the poet had gone too far in the opposite direction from the *New Lines* restraint, and recommended that Hughes cultivate 'a greater inner stillness' to counteract his youthful vitality, and, rather than 'snatch at his inspiration', let 'its fruit come quietly, with all its apparent fragility and incompleteness, of its own accord'.[11] Alan Brownjohn, however, deplored the 'raw sex-and-violence imagery', 'self-consciously turbulent diction' and melodramatic and 'slapdash' hyperbole that he perceived in the poems.[12] Observing that Hughes had received considerable praise from reviewers, and that *THITR* had been given the First Publication Award of the New York Poetry Center, Brownjohn wonders how this could have happened, given that the book 'turns out to be of a dismaying badness'. Calvin Bedient found that in *THITR* everything – 'war, childbirth, the weather, laughter, love' – was 'galvanised into the improbable' so that 'even the prodigious wears a fright wig'. Bedient saw Hughes's characteristic parallel structures as 'welded in a series like brass knuckles' and the underlying attitudes that he infers from the poems as stale and crude. The language 'attempts to squeeze every thrill out of its subjects and yet to be priggishly superior to them'.[13] Bedient suggested that Hughes did not celebrate violence so much as the will to live and 'energy too strong for death', and in admiring animals, the more terrible, the more admired, showed contempt for humankind. These comments set the tone for a subsequent strain in Hughes criticism which deplored the poet's representation of the violence latent in nature.

Reviewing Hughes's second collection, *L*, John Press suggested that the poems had a preoccupation with 'power and violence' which were 'regarded almost as ends-in-themselves'.[14] For Bedient, in *L* Hughes has become 'a fearful lover of the will to live', which is far more profound. Hughes, '[w]ading out at last beyond the froth of violent escapism', is 'abruptly stunned by the elemental severity of his subject'. Bedient suggests that now Hughes knows what before 'he had been too glutted with sensation to enquire' – that 'the tooth is the clue to existence'. Hughes 'hardens himself, he prepares for battle' and tells himself that 'it is better to speak of this subject', 'in a style as sharp and as naked as an incisor'.[15]

A 1960 *Times* round-up review of new poetry collections found Hughes to be a 'rhetorical poet' in the sense that his language was designed 'to have a powerful effect on the reader', and it notes that

L had confirmed the aptness of the 'acclamation' with which *THITR* was received. The reviewer finds Hughes to be a 'beautiful technician' who can 'change his tone at will from the precise calculation' of Marianne Moore to 'a kind of harsh balladry'. His verse is 'doubly charged with music and meaning'. The section on Hughes concludes that when assessment is made, Hughes may be seen as the Auden of his generation: 'a formative, brilliantly equipped, and representative poet'.[16]

Keith Sagar summarises the early critical response to Hughes's work by saying that on the whole, reviews of *THITR* did the reviewers credit, and that Robin Skelton, writing in the *Manchester Guardian*, spoke for the majority when he declared that everyone 'looking for the emergence of a major poet' must buy the collection.[17] Some reviewers, however, pointed to alleged faults of stridency and bravado, whilst others said that there were some bad poems which they did not specify. Sagar adds that among the few who did specify, there was little consensus, and gives the example of the poem 'The Martyrdom of Bishop Ferrar' (*THITR, CP*, pp. 48–9), which was listed with both the best and the worst poems in the book.[18]

HUGHES AND *THE NEW POETRY*

Seminal in the development of the reputation of Hughes's poetry was its appearance in A. Alvarez's *The New Poetry* anthology in 1962, and, even more, in Alvarez's introduction.[19] Alvarez used Hughes's 'A Dream of Horses' to contrast with Philip Larkin's poem 'At Grass'[20] in order to illustrate what Alvarez saw as a failing of much contemporary poetry. Hughes's poem is offered as a shining example not of fully realised technique, but of potential; it demonstrates a hope for what poetry might become if the poets of the mid-century could learn to reconcile the diverse influences of D.H. Lawrence and T.S. Eliot. Alvarez asserts that poetry needs a new seriousness, a willingness and ability on the part of the poet to 'face the full range of his experience with his full intelligence' and not to take the conventional response of 'choking incoherence'.[21] He writes of a new generation of poets who arose in the USA in the 1940s, most important of whom were Robert Lowell and John Berryman. These poets had assimilated the lesson of T.S. Eliot and the critical 1930s, and assumed that poets must be skilful, original and intelligent, but did not assume that this required the concomitant Eliotesque impersonality. This meant that they could write poetry which coped with the 'quick of their experience, experience sometimes on the edge of disintegration and breakdown'. Alvarez cites the example of Lowell, who, he says, was no longer attempting to 'externalize his disturbances theologically in Catholicism and rhetorically in certain mannerisms of language and rhythm', but was coping with them 'nakedly, and without evasion', though to walk naked is, 'of course, no guarantee of achievement in the arts – often the contrary'.[22] Alvarez contrasts this with the common sense and understatement of the Movement poets, among whom he includes Philip Larkin. At their best, he argues, Movement poets command a self-contained strength and discipline which is vital if poetry is to remain public, but he questions the kind of success which this style allows. Whilst 'At Grass' is elegant, unpretentious and even beautiful, it nostalgically re-creates an idea (which Alvarez calls Platonic or New Yorker) of a part-pastoral, part-sporting English scene.[23] Larkin's horses, he says, are the social creatures of 'fashionable race meetings and high style', and emotionally they come from the world of the RSPCA. Whilst the poem is more skilful, it is less urgent than Hughes's. Although Hughes's is not as controlled as Larkin's poem, and has romantic and 'quasi-medieval trappings which verge on the pretentious', 'A Dream of Horses' is 'unquestionably about something' and is a 'serious attempt to re-create and so clarify, unfalsified and in the strongest imaginative terms possible, a powerful complex of emotion and sensation'.[24] Sharp details bring the violent presence of the horses threateningly to life, reaching back, 'as in a dream, into a nexus of fear and sensation'. Anticipating later criticism of Hughes's animal poems, Alvarez finds the brute world of the horses part physical, part state of mind. In suggesting the horses which terrorise Ursula Brangwen in D.H. Lawrence's *The Rainbow* (1915), Hughes's horses indicate their wider significance. Although, Alvarez notes, F.R. Leavis believes that D.H. Lawrence and T.S. Eliot represent two 'warring and unreconcilable poles of modern writing', Alvarez asserts that the best contemporary English poetry, which he calls the 'new depth poetry', indicates that these disparate influences can be reconciled; Lawrence's psychological insight and integrity and Eliot's technical skill and formal intelligence.[25] That Alvarez proclaims Hughes as in the vanguard of the new depth poetry perhaps responds to Brownjohn's astringent warning to Hughes in his earlier review to beware of being made into a Lambert Simnel by a set of kingmakers.[26]

Hughes is represented in Alvarez's *The New Poetry* by eighteen poems, more than any other poet,[27] so presumably he is counted among the 'good deal of poetic talent [which] exists in England at the moment' whose chance of coming to anything 'largely depends not on the machinations of any literary racket but on the degree to which the poets can remain immune to the disease so often found in English culture: gentility'.[28] Alvarez's preface to the revised edition of 1965, however, suggests that the first *New Poetry* selection was not entirely representative of such work. He writes that he would have liked to have included more of Sylvia Plath's work, but that Plath's literary executors 'felt, reasonably enough, that this might interfere with the sale of her first posthumous collection, *Ariel*', so he took only four poems from that collection, while three of Hughes's poems were removed at Hughes's request.[29]

Initially reviewing *L*, Alvarez had declared that Hughes had 'found his own voice, created his own artistic world and has emerged as a poet of the first importance'. Writing of the occasion thirty-eight years later, Alvarez goes further: 'I was then in the middle of what turned out to be ten years as poetry critic and editor of *The Observer* and *Lupercal* struck me as the best book by an English poet that I had read since I started my stint.'[30] Although his writing about Sylvia Plath in works such as *The Savage God* (1971) had subsequently alienated him from Hughes, Alvarez professed a consistent admiration for the poetry. He also further justifies the association he makes between Hughes and D.H. Lawrence in the preface to *The New Poetry*. Alvarez notes that the two writers shared a northern and working-class background (though a British person would be more likely to categorise Lawrence's Nottingham as East Midlands), and asserts that Hughes was profoundly influenced by his predecessor. For Alvarez, Hughes's work is that of Lawrence without the 'nerves and preaching' but also without 'the flowers and the tenderness'.[31] He suggests that whereas Lawrence was always in dialogue with his creatures – snake, mountain lion, tortoise, stallion and mosquito – letting them both voice his preoccupations and argue back, vehemently, Hughes's creatures are different, irredeemably alien, and that it was the otherness, their 'world of instincts and threat and incipient violence', that interested Hughes. For Alvarez, Hughes's water-lilies ('To Paint a Water Lily' (*L*, *CP*, pp. 70–1) are nothing like those at Giverny as painted by Monet. Hughes's flower is 'suspended between horror and horror, between an air shimmering with murderous insects and the pond's bed where "Prehistoric bedragonned times/Crawl that darkness with Latin names"'. Alvarez finds that in the 'domain of Hughes's unforgiving imagination, beauty existed but always perilously, as an act of will, and the forces ranged against it were terrible'. Anticipating some of the work discussed in Chapter 2, Alvarez continues: 'Wild creatures, for him, were like dreams; they were his way through to hidden parts of his mind.'[32]

OPPOSING RESPONSES TO HUGHES'S EARLY WORK

Published in the same year as Alvarez's anthology, an article by J.D. Hainsworth takes a quite different perspective. Hainsworth refuses to see any depth or sophistication in Hughes's poetry. Whilst suggesting that Hughes's intended meaning was allegorical, Hainsworth alleges that Hughes became too involved in each animal, and therefore distracted; his poems are brutish rather than intellectual.[33]

By 1965, enough of Hughes's work had been published to merit a reappraisal by Claude Rawson in *Essays in Criticism*. This could confidently state that everyone would agree that Hughes's subject was violence,[34] written in a form of 'amoral, unmoralized factuality'. Forestalling psychological and Jungian analysis of Hughes's work, Rawson asserted that the poems did not read as 'compulsive surfacing of dark undergrowths' or as 'allegories of states of mind', but only as the 'factual solidity of things seen'.[35] Two years later, Hughes was included in another set of 'new poets', this time chosen by M.L. Rosenthal, who describes Hughes as the 'most striking figure to emerge among British poets since the last war'.[36] Rosenthal admires the 'authority that stamps this poet's work', and praises the power of Hughes's 'exuberantly horrid imagination' in a discussion of 'Vampire' (*THITR, CP*, p. 39).[37] Rosenthal finds in Hughes's work an 'ultimate terror and fascination at the gross brutality of nature, and of man in his more unreflective animal aspect and in the savagery of his wars, which makes itself felt in this poet as it did in the writing of his wife, Sylvia Plath'. No other poet has, like Hughes, managed to internalise 'the murderousness of nature through such brilliantly objective means, and with such economy as Hughes'.[38]

Geoffrey Thurley takes issue with Alvarez's changing attitude to Hughes's poetry in a section on Hughes in his *The Ironic Harvest: English Poetry of the Twentieth Century* (1975). Indeed, Thurley recalls that Hughes was 'an immediate embarrassment' to the critical establishment.[39] He suggests that Alvarez's 'adjustment' of critical views about the early Hughes would not have given the poet 'unqualified satisfaction', since Hughes had progressed beyond 'the essentialist tradition from which he so clearly derived'. That he did so with 'an arrogant consciousness of role' was, Thurley states, as disturbing to Alvarez as to Hughes's Cambridge contemporaries. Hughes's 'showing-off' would have been easy to place for Cambridge, as would have been 'the fairly clear derivation of the style or styles on display' in Hughes's poetry: 'the Dylan Thomas bohemianism, along with a clear verbal debt to Hopkins and Donne'. Rather than classifying Hughes as plagiarist or his writing as derivative, however, Thurley asserts that Hughes's language had 'that body, that "strength of the English language," Dr Leavis had always been so concerned to preserve'. Though Hughes's 'Macaw and Little Miss' 'comes straight out of the later Dylan Thomas' and Hughes's technique 'brilliantly recalls the flamboyant metaphysical exuberance of English Marinism, of Crawshaw, and Góngora himself', these influences 'release, they do not imprison'. The principles by which Hughes's language is organised are Hughes's own.[40]

HUGHES AND THE MOVEMENT

Hughes himself suggested that poets of the generation before his own had been left with a kind of fatigue. The *New Lines* poets, he wrote, shared the post-war mood of having had enough: 'enough rhetoric, enough overweening push of any kind, enough of the dark gods, enough of the id, enough of the Angelic powers and the heroic efforts to make new worlds. They'd seen it all turn back into death camps and atomic bombs.' The Second World War sent them recoiling 'to some essential English strengths' and 'set them dead against negotiation with anything outside the cosiest arrangement of society'. Hughes, however, 'hadn't had enough. I was all for opening negotiations with whatever happened to be out there.'[41]

Sean O'Brien argues that Hughes's first collection was published in a poetic climate which did not encourage political engagement. He notes that the survivors from the 1930s had moved away from 'the political here-and-now', and their concerns had come to seem remote to poets emerging in the 1950s and 1960s.[42] While the Cold War brought new terrors, including fear of nuclear war, the Eisenhower era had a symptomatic narcosis described by Robert Lowell. O'Brien detects in Movement poetry the 'anxieties and paradoxes' which befitted the 'uncertainties of Britain confronted by the 1956 Suez Crisis', and finds that with the exception of the poems of Thom Gunn and Ted Hughes, the publications of 1957 suggested an emphasis on 'a blend of formal scruple and modest ambitions'. The regret and melancholy of Donald Davie's poem 'Remembering the Thirties', and, in his discussion of that poem in *Encounter*, Davie's 'acceptance of imaginative defeat at the hands of "the scheme of things"',[43] O'Brien says, reflect the political quietism and neutrality of Movement thinking, which, for some Movement writers who were assimilated into the literary establishment, became an aggressive adoption of conservative attitudes.[44] O'Brien asserts that the exhaustion of ideology in 'Butskellism' (a term which combined the names of the Labour Chancellor, Hugh Gaitskell

(1950–51 – later Leader of the Opposition) and his Conservative successor (1951–55), Richard Austen Butler, 'Rab', and referred to the alleged indistinguishable politics of the British left and right) in Britain and retrenchment abroad was matched by 'moral miniaturism' in literature, which O'Brien sees as a 'hoarding of meagre resources in the absence of any compelling ideal or political project'.[45] He argues that relative affluence combined with the stagnation of class politics at that time helped to drive the imagination inwards, or out of the urban towards the pastoral. O'Brien quotes Zbigniew Herbert's 1956 poem on the Hungarian Uprising: 'we stand at the border called reason and we look into the fire and admire death',[46] and notes that in 1950s Britain there was neither need nor opportunity for that kind of historical commentary, since realpolitik was something practised under different, oppressive regimes, and 'endured by, among others, poets' who were 'accorded an importance denied their Western peers'.[47]

In such an environment, therefore, the shock of Hughes's originality was enormous, and that originality was supported by a strong appeal to the English sense that nature and the countryside were the home ground of poetry. Not for Hughes, O'Brien writes, were the hopes and fears, friends and incipient memories of the Welfare State. Instead, came poems from Hughes's native Yorkshire, from feral nature, and from a 'highly specialised sense of history', which, like that of Thom Gunn, could leap between the sixteenth and twentieth centuries.[48] O'Brien associates what he sees as the apolitical quality in Hughes's poetry with Hughes's use of mythic structures from *W* on, which is discussed in the next chapter.

Thomas West doubts whether anyone would challenge the assertion that 'Hughes has been one of our most important poets since the appearance of *Crow* in 1970.'[49] He goes on, however, to suggest that even though none would deny that Hughes is one of the most important of recent poets, some readers dislike his work. He attributes this to a distrust of Hughes's vatic view of poetry and to suspicion of Hughes's 'gratuitous violence' and 'apparent refusal of complicity with the world as it exists'. For those who do not dislike but on the contrary admire Hughes, however, the same qualities, West asserts, are seen in an opposite light; Hughes becomes a 'nature poet' or an 'animal poet' who turned for inspiration to an untamed and unsocial world.

The vatic quality in Hughes's work could be expected to have elicited disapproval from American New Critics and exponents of close reading and practical criticism looking for complex ambiguity, and approving the understated urbanity of The Movement. So it would not be surprising if Hughes's early and middle publications had their detractors.

Hughes was best known as a nature poet during a time when it was very hard to write about birds, beasts and flowers without irony or without being categorised as Wordsworthian, reactionary, Luddite, naïve, or, later, New Age. Ian Hamilton recollects literary gossip, after Hughes's 'bestiary' was complete following publication of *L*, wondering where, '[b]eastless', Hughes would go next.[50] Would Hughes allow reassertion of the 'fevered apocalyptic rhetoric that had been ominously omnipresent' in *THITR*? Would he develop the 'naïve, generalizing commentaries on human conduct' that had appeared in *L*? Hamilton writes that the 'justified suspicion' was that, in a phase of 'tame, chatty, effortlessly rationalistic verse', it would be easy to overrate any poet who 'possessed even the beginnings of vigour' and in the case of Hughes, to mistake 'a souped-up, ripplingly muscular neo-Georgianism' for writing that was 'much more wise and novel'.

Whilst Hamilton concedes that Hughes has a gift for 'fierce and thrilling natural observation', he also cites striking faults: 'flailingly portentous verbiage'; 'indulged relish for the violent and the painful'; a 'deep authorial evasiveness' and 'the skimped and shallow dealings with the human world'.[51] He suggests that Hughes solved the problem of having run out of animals by inventing new kinds or 'revamping old favourites' such as the jaguar. The central problem, for Hamilton, is an absence of engagement with the world of the human, and he finds in the 'bursts of Gothickry' in *W* a suggestion that Hughes, 'far from looking for a way of directing his linguistic gifts back to the human world', sought 'an area in which those gifts could be exercised even more randomly than hitherto'.

'NOT NEW ENOUGH': ANTHONY EASTHOPE

Further critique of Hughes's work was made by the cultural materialist Antony Easthope. In 'The Poetry of Ted Hughes: Some Reservations' (1999), Easthope contradicts received wisdom about Ted Hughes's originality and vitality by finding that his writing is 'not new enough'; it has not altered poetic expression or significantly transformed the tradition.[52] Easthope had already advanced his hypothesis about the dominant and enduring strain of English Romanticism in modern poetry, and its consequences for the relationship between expression and empiricism, in an article on Jacqueline Rose's commentary on Sylvia Plath's 1962 poem 'Daddy', and thus applied to Plath's work some of the criticisms that he later made of Hughes's. Rose had responded to accusations that in deploying Holocaust imagery, Plath lacked 'objective correlatives' in poems such as 'Daddy', by saying that in Plath's work there was a 'preliminary privileging of the personal'.[53] Easthope uses that defence as the starting-point for an analysis of Plath's modes and conditions of representation. For Easthope, 'Daddy' failed to challenge the lyric-confessional mode it inherited, and remains an old-fashioned poem which invites comparison with Robert Lowell's 'The Quaker Graveyard in Nantucket'. The problem with such poetry, that puts a dramatisation of the unified self at the centre of writing, is that it conforms to a humanist ideology in which 'the self' is the sole author of history and of the literary text.[54]

Writing of Hughes's work five years later, Easthope similarly finds Hughes wanting in true originality.[55] His premiss is that unless poetry enacts the contemporary in its deepest structures, it will be read only by its contemporaries, since, as T.S. Eliot wrote (in 1930), 'sensibility alters from generation to generation in everybody, whether we will or not; but expression is only altered by a man of genius'.[56] Lasting force in poetry, Easthope asserts, comes from its ability to alter expression. He asks whether Hughes alters poetry and significantly transforms the tradition. To assess this, Easthope sets out three contexts: the English tradition, the specific conditions of the English high-cultural poetic inheritance (the canon), and the changes in sensibility 'rippling out from the advent of the nineteen-sixties in the United Kingdom'.[57]

Describing 'The English Tradition', Easthope contrasts two forms of 'European' and 'English Romanticism'; a 'European tradition' of passion and intensity represented by Goethe and Victor Hugo, Byron, Shelley and Keats, and a differently inflected English tradition at whose centre 'like a rock' is Wordsworth. Although Romantic, this poetry conforms to the English empiricist tradition (which posits that truth can be derived from direct experience of reality), and is often in the form of a visionary perception of an external event or object that is internalised and remembered by the poem's 'I'. Easthope suggests that the division persists; while Tennyson and Gerard Manley Hopkins can be aligned with European Romanticism, Thomas Hardy follows Wordsworth. Citing as examples of the different tenor of the two kinds of poetry 'some of the most erotic lines in the language' from Tennyson's *The Princess*, and Hardy's 'At Castle Boterel', Easthope affirms the continuance of this Hardyesque poetry of individuals and their experiences. His examples are from Blake Morrison and Andrew Motion's *Contemporary British Poetry* (1982): Motion's 'In the Attic' and Paul Muldoon's 'Quoof'. Both traditions, Wordsworth to Hardy and Keats to Tennyson and Hopkins, Easthope says, should have been long superseded by 1930. He defines Modernism as bringing three things with it: a disruption of a fixed opposition between subject and object, a crisis for the supposedly transcendental subject, and the return of the signifier. From these three radical innovations, he argues, the poetry of Hughes takes just enough to have a 'veneer of up-to-dateness', but steps aside from the unsettling challenges, epistemological and linguistic, which are made inescapable by 'Cubism, Dada, Surrealism and the rest'. Hughes's poetry, like too much of contemporary English culture, Easthope says, hopes to take 'the scenic route' around Modernism's alien, polluted city, to the green fields of an outworn pastoral vision.[58]

Whereas Alvarez took Hughes's poem 'The Horses' as an example of writing that breaks 'the gentility principle' and 'makes new', Easthope sees the structure of the same poem as contrasting dramatically with that of Modernist works, in which 'subject and object, speaker and experienced perception, remain disconcertingly disjunct'. In Modernist poetry, language, floating free of any supposed referent, becomes an objective correlative for feelings which are subjective but which can claim no more than an 'arbitrary purchase on what is outside that subjectivity'. Thus, textuality is thrown into prominence as the reader is forced to become aware of the poem *as poem*, but 'not so with Hughes'.[59]

Like several critics, Easthope takes Hughes's relatively early poem 'Pike' as his example, comparing Hughes's fish with that of Edmund Blunden in Blunden's poem 'The Pike'.[60] Blunden's is 'a classic Georgian poem in that it seeks to resuscitate and preserve a country way of life which was rapidly giving way to modernisation across England at the time', and Blunden's pike makes sense as a pike. Blunden's metaphors aggrandise the animal without losing touch with it, so that although the pike is said to be a 'glutted tyrant', with 'gorgon eyes', these are pathetic fallacies (attribution of human characteristics to nature) deliberately imagining the fish as other than it is known to be. Easthope suggests that Hughes uses metaphor in a very different way, pushing the pike 'towards something no fish ever was'. Applying a more literal interpretation, Easthope notes that though Hughes's pikes are said to 'spare nobody', in fact they only eat perch and ruffe. That Hughes's pike lives in a pond of 'Stilled legendary depth ... as deep as England' (*L, CP*, pp. 84–6) is of crucial importance. The symbolic and atavistic pond holds an equally ancient symbolic pike which evokes a feeling of fierce, unconscious aggression, 'even in the middle of England'. In Easthope's view, then, Hughes's 'Pike' moves far beyond Blunden's 'conscientious natural description' with the aim, he suggests, of saying 'something about the dark forces the history of the twentieth century has reminded us are present in what people can do to each other'. Yet he sees the pike, 'hung in an amber cavern of weeds', as phallic, and Hughes as getting beyond Blunden's 'timid suburbanism' only 'along a line anticipated by Lawrence, Hopkins and indeed the whole Romantic tradition'.[61]

Articulating this Romantic theme, however, Easthope finds Modernist-influenced language, stripped of 'stilted archaisms'. He notes that instead of Blunden's 'polite and sustained syntax, a paratactic movement allows intonation and line ending to match meaning' in the lines beginning 'Pike, three inches ...' and ending '... from the egg'. This informality, however, Easthope finds is at the service of more forceful expression. Far from a Modernist or post-Modern trope of signifier drawing attention to its own materiality, 'sound is subordinated to sense as it has been in the English canon since Shakespeare'. Easthope observes that 'Pike' is not composed in free verse but in 'a loose, four-beat line, which shows its basic adherence to the inherited metric by returning every now and then to syllabic rhythms', and gives the example of 'They dance on the surface among the flies' as almost perfectly anapaestic.[62]

Easthope cites S.T. Coleridge to argue that the most traditional feature of 'Pike' is in its figurative language. He quotes: 'a Poet's *Heart & Intellect* should be *combined, intimately* combined *and unified* with the great appearances in Nature', and not merely mixed with them through 'formal Similies'.[63] This requires poets to avoid shared conventional comparisons, and to seek out those which have no obvious precedent. Examples he gives of these are the description of the pike's scales as 'green tigering the gold', its jaw as a 'hooked clamp and fangs', its gills as 'kneading quietly'; it is 'Jungled' among the weeds it inhabits. In this way 'formal trope [that is, device or artistic convention] is made over into an expression of personal feeling, each verbal detail symbolic in de Man's sense that experience becomes elided with its representation'. Easthope points out that language is always language, and can never be anything else, but he asserts the possibility of creating a poetic effect in which 'the phonetic force of the signifier is held so tightly onto the meaning that it seems to be contained by it'.[64]

Easthope argues that in the work of poets from Coleridge via Hopkins and Dylan Thomas to Hughes, 'the natural object ascends immediately to the status of symbol', so that there is not much difference between poems ostensibly narrated by a speaker who is represented in relation to an object, and poems in which the symbol is represented alone. Though 'The Horses' has a speaker, an 'I', other poems by Hughes offer the natural object alone, suppressing any sense of a perceiving speaker. Whereas in 'The Hawk in the Rain' a man ploughing looks up at a hawk, in 'Hawk Roosting' there is no focaliser but only the hawk, and 'individualised agency is displaced from a speaker to the natural object'.

What differentiates Hughes from the Movement poets, for Easthope, is Hughes's 'more sensational awareness of violent possibilities in the human unconscious', but he finds ample antecedents of that awareness in Brecht and D.H. Lawrence. Thus, though the vocabulary and diction suggest a Modernist influence, significant aspects of the formative properties of Hughes's poems are 'indelibly pre-Modernist'. In particular, Hughes's alleged 'attempt to render the natural object as though it participated in some supposedly pre-given symbolic reality' seemingly endows his words with 'an essential transparency to meaning so that text – writing – is made over into the approximation of a voice'. Hughes's metaphors are 'contrived to give a sense of objects and ideas being personally experienced', in accordance with conventions established by Wordsworth and Coleridge. Easthope concludes that Hughes's language 'seeks to be expressive'.[65]

Easthope suggests that Hughes's later poetry has not moved on. He cites 'A Visit' as exemplifying Hughes's failure to develop the Modernist enterprise in the way that alternative avant-garde poets such as Jeremy Prynne and Tom Raworth have. Quoting from 'Suddenly I read' to 'where's Mummy' (Birthday Letters, p. 7), he asserts that the poem affirms the transparency of language, and asks: 'Sensibility has been altering rapidly since the start of this century. How much has Hughes' expression altered?'[66]

HUGHES AND THE SPIRIT OF PLACE: KEITH SAGAR

Keith Sagar classifies Hughes's wildlife as both of the real and of the unconscious: the life which has been killed off and now marauds in the underworld of the unconscious is the wolf; the life making a last stand in remote fastnesses is adder and otter; the life that humankind tries to kill but which, somehow, survives, is stoat and fox. He also points out that the landscape itself is a huge animal, harnessed and apparently tamed, but breaking loose.[67] Sagar stresses the importance to Hughes's work of the geography of Hughes's childhood, which gave him his earliest metaphors and whose interplay of elements gave him his sense of the creating and destroying processes of the world. Not only the landscape, but its local species shaped Hughes's distinctive way of looking at the world; the local animals became Hughes's theriomorphic archetypes. (Theriomorphism is the belief in gods who have the form of animals, which evokes the image of an Egyptian pantheon of crocodile-headed or hawk-headed gods who have the bodies of men and women but are remote from, and often indifferent to, human-kind.) Even when the powers at work in the poems are not those of destruction and death but the surge and thrust of the planet through geological time, or the imperceptible but irresistible oncoming of the season, there is something terrifying about the scale, the implacability, the otherness of it all.

Sagar suggests that Hughes takes animals for metaphors because they enact the primary struggles, particularly the struggle between death and vitality, in naked extremity. Animals 'roar or bellow the evidence which men warp in sophistry or turn a blind eye to'. The unwavering killing instinct of Hughes's thrushes becomes a lesson in the vital difference between humans and animals: animals live according to one categorical imperative, humankind has the 'doom' of consciousness and choice, which becomes the burden of not knowing what to do, and therefore of perpetually questioning, and peering into the darkness for a sign. The gulf between humanity and animals, however, is also the gulf between the individual and the animal self, which Sagar calls also the angelic or demonic self and the only self capable of recognising a divinity in the darkness beyond the little area lit by consciousness and desk lamp, and being at one with it.[68]

Hughes's hawks, thrushes and pikes are minimalist killers with no redundancy. They have neither sophistry nor distraction, but they are not without human characteristics. There is no vanity in his hawk's arrogance; in the lovely cadences of its catalogue of its own precisions. In a sense, the whole of creation, the whole of evolution, has gone into the perfect coincidence of hawk's talon and prey's flesh, but is the hawk's undistracted, streamlined single-mindedness (or lack of self-consciousness) clouded when its interior monologue develops an outside interest and complete confidence in its powers develops into solipsism? 'My eye has permitted no change./I am going to keep things like this' ('Hawk Roosting', L, *CP*, pp. 68–9).

Sagar sees Hughes as poet as a vehicle for the transmission of messages from the non-human to the psyche and from there to consciousness, and borrows the concept of *duende* from the Spanish poet and dramatist Federico García Lorca to describe Hughes's representation of landscape. He acclaims Hughes as the archetype of poet-priest-magician, the poet of *duende*, the spirit of life, the life-force which constantly opposes death, and which is primarily manifested in the wild places of the earth. For Sagar, poetry must be religious or it is nothing, and its claim to be taken more seriously than other forms of art or language comes from its ability to maintain the connections between 'the depths of the human psyche and the hidden sources of everything in the non-human world'. In this view, the poet is the medium which transmits 'an occult charge' from the non-human to the psyche and thence into consciousness. Sagar asserts that Celtic poets know this in their blood, but, echoing other critics of poetry of the mid-twentieth century, finds that most English poets, having drifted into a 'rational humanism', then 'arrogantly expect' readers to value their 'measured musings'. This rational humanism makes their poetry lacking in Lorca's *duende*. For Sagar, much of the history of civilisation has been characterised by the effort to mutilate or kill one of the primary manifestations of *duende*, the spirit of place, and the surest way to kill it in the psyche is to learn to ignore it, to sentimentalise it, or to prettify it. 'It is emphatically not the loving mother of post-Wordsworthian English Nature poetry.' Aware of this spirit of place, the Celt takes as given that the poet is shaped by the landscape. Whilst much of the landscape of England is 'relatively bland', parts of the country have just as much character 'as anywhere over the border'.[69]

Clearly, the poet need not remain in the landscape which retains the spirit of place in order to write about it and to be the medium of the occult charge, since although Hughes was born in the Pennines, he wrote most of his poetry elsewhere. Sagar quotes from a 1961 radio interview in which Hughes said that move away from Mytholmroyd to Mexborough when he was 8 years old 'sealed off my first seven years so that now my first seven years seems almost half my life. I've remembered almost everything because it was sealed off in that particular way and became a sort of brain – another subsidiary brain for me.'[70] Sagar asserts that that landscape was imprinted on Hughes's soul, that in a sense all of his poems are about it, and that, when the poems are 'overtly, literally, about it, the magical change from description to metaphor to myth is enacted before our eyes, as in *Remains of Elmet*'. From those and earlier works, Sagar argues, the reader can trace 'the evolution of the most penetrating, authentic and all-embracing poetic vision of our time'.

HUGHES, JUNG AND LACAN: PAUL BENTLEY

Paul Bentley's approach to Hughes's in some ways the reverse of that of Sagar. In another analysis of 'Pike' Bentley observes that the seemingly factual naming-of-parts description of the opening has a potential for imaginative disturbance signalled by use of the noun-as-verb 'tigering' as the only verb in the initial noun-phrase, and that there is an imaginative participation in the statement that the pike move 'stunned by their own grandeur'.[71] He finds in the last line of the stanza an anarchic suggestiveness: the fish are dancing 'on the surface' of the water 'among the flies', thus 'defying their empirical confines and anticipating the disorienting perspectives of the final stanza'. Terms of factual measurement are counterpointed by others, so that a register of empirical observation is in dialectic with the imagination, whose measurements are primordial or mythical: a three-inch-long pike is a hundred feet long in its world; the pond, fifty feet by one measure, is 'deep as England'.[72]

Bentley traces the influence of Jung here and elsewhere in Hughes's poetry. He finds that the echo of Blake in 'The Jaguar' (*THITR, CP*, pp. 19–20) highlights Hughes's neo-Romantic conception of the creative and regenerative faculties of the imagination, a conception which is, however, subject to a post-Freudian sense of the failings of language and to the human capacity for self-delusion. The echo of Jung's concept of 'illimitable unconscious' in 'Pike', Bentley argues, enables the poem to develop an intuition similar to that of 'The Jaguar', but with more subtlety and irony. Here, Bentley uses Jung's assertion that though we may be able to indicate the limits of consciousness, the unconscious is the unknown psyche, and illimitable because indeterminable. Jung states that empirical manifestations of the contents of the unconscious are likely to bear the marks of the illimitable, of things not determined by space and time. That quality is numinous and therefore alarming, especially to a cautious mind that knows the value of precisely delimited concepts.

Bentley suggests that the 'illimitable unconscious' remains undefined in 'Pike' because the pike is not caught but slips the net of number and measurement. Those empirical calculations come to nothing; all that is left is the knowing grin of the pike. Bentley quotes Hughes's 'Myth and Education' (*Children's Literature in Education* 1 (March 1970) 55–70, 57) to show that objective scientific fact-watching is useless in the activity that he saw as most vital, the activity of understanding ourselves.[73]

For Bentley, the awed imagination of the poem finds its apotheosis in a dreamlike subversion of the quotidian world which is evoked in the image of owls 'hushing' the 'floating woods'. He finds that the line's 'nervous, shuddering assonance' brings with it a decentring of the rational self, pointed up by the paradox of intentionality contained in 'I dared not cast/But silently cast' and the confusion of the hunter and the hunted in the final stanza. Bentley states that the gerund form of 'watching', a menacingly non-finite end to the poem, leaves the I poised on the threshold of Jung's illimitable, a realm whose edges 'evade fixity', in which 'aggressive, primordial phantoms' threaten the empirical ground upon which the rational part of the self is standing.[74]

Bentley agrees with Leonard Scigaj that 'Pike' is saved from portentousness by the tone of the poem. Knowledgeable overstatement becomes comic understatement as the narrator loses his empirical bearings and the pike come into their own. He finds that the language of 'Pike' is therefore more careful and tentative than that of earlier poems such as 'The Jaguar'; the primordial thing resists embodiment in human terms.

Some of Hughes's animal metaphors have been taken as standing for the real world of nature and humankind's relationship with it; others as aspects of the psyche or the self, offered as both individual and archetypal. The fox is perhaps both: a representation of a projection from the speaker's psyche demanding that he abandon the arid pursuit of English literature and turn to the archaeology of his own unconscious, and an archetype or essence of Fox demanding attention in its own right as one of the wild things at the edges of, and underneath, civilisation. Critics have seen this duality as central to the poems of L. Bentley refers to it as the emergence of supplanting energies within the self, and to the animals of the volume as mirrors in which the inner drama can, to some degree, be apprehended. He does not deny the focus on the animals as animals, however; on the contrary, he asserts that the poems register the aspects of animal being that remain beyond human appropriation. He cites the bull in 'The Bull Moses' (L, CP, pp. 74–5), which is too deep in itself to offer any reflection of our human light; the material otherness of the animal resisting the human ego's narcissistic desire to see itself reflected; and the otter in 'An Otter' (L, CP, p. 79), whose slipperiness (neither a fish nor a beast) aligns animals with 'something slippery and indefinite in the self'.[75]

Bentley continues with a discussion of 'View of a Pig' (L, CP, pp. 75–6), noting that though the speaker repeatedly attempts to frame the disturbing sight of the dead pig, to assign it meaning and thus 'assimilate it to consciousness', those attempts fail, as the pig becomes further off even than death. What might seem to be an idle thought, the wondering how the pig might be moved, is for Bentley the key to the poem's own 'meaning': the dead pig, for him, here embodies 'what is *intractable* (it cannot be "moved" within or by language)', and is thus disturbing for the speaker; for the consciousness that constitutes itself through its ability to assign meaning and represent the world to itself.[76]

Bentley writes that he set out to do otherwise than interpret the poems through biography, or summarise their themes, motifs and *dramatis personae*. He suggests that much criticism of Hughes's work has overlooked how Hughes's language works, 'what makes the poems tick *as poems*, over and above what they appear to be saying'. Since 'poetry does something with language that other forms of language do not', 'it is Hughes's distinctive handling of language' that is Bentley's 'primary concern'.[77]

When Hughes's lines have not been picked over for the bones of his marriage to Sylvia Plath, they have been read all too often, Bentley suggests, 'for their referential content: the word is taken to be transparent, a window onto what is being described or depicted (the world of nature, for example)'. Hughes, however, draws on 'the energies of dialect' as a rebellion against the contemporary poetic ethic and to emphasise the social, cultural and regional context of their production. Bentley asserts that if the poems attempt to '"call out for more", in Heaney's words, they do so with their hands loaded down with the contingencies of language and culture'.[78] Bentley contrasts Hughes's 'slippery, makeshift, unstable' language with the 'rational, comprehensible language' applauded by Robert Conquest. He finds that Hughes's distancing himself from the rational voice of the Movement poets delineates 'a self split between a centripetal contract of linguistic, social and cultural norms and taboos and the centrifugal pull of pre-linguistic, unconscious drives inherited from the infant's world of maternal dependency'. Bentley argues that Hughes makes concrete the 'material conditions (unconscious, linguistic, cultural) that structure and determine the way we perceive the world'. The self in this view is less an autonomous, metaphysical entity than 'an effect of certain deep-seated ways of perceiving and representing'.[79]

Whereas Hughes approaches psychoanalytical insights through myth, Bentley proposes to do the reverse, through a theoretical reading. Whilst analogies can be drawn between the 'shamanistic motifs of flight/descent/dismemberment/death/return' and some motifs of Hughes's work, that does not help with the question of how the language of a poet might be deemed to function shamanistically.[80] Using Claude Lévi-Strauss's and Jacques Lacan's theory of the 'Symbolic' in opposition to the 'Real' solves this problem, since for the human mind the Real, resisting symbolisation, is inaccessible, but the shaman has the ability to enter the Real.

Bentley looks at Hughes's poems as encrypted messages from Hughes's shamanic subconscious which he can decode through attention to imagery and pronoun-shift, and as Hughes's consciously 'playful' anthropomorphism; his plundering of the myth-shaped symbolism of his imagination in order to illustrate the illusory nature of reality by insinuating that the phenomenal world is shaped by consciousness. He traces Hughes's dramatisation of Lacan's substitution of the subject-position for the stable ego, and thus problematisation of the boundaries of the real, the imaginary and the illusory. As one of the few analyses of Hughes's writing to offer poststructuralist readings of the poems, *The Poetry of Ted Hughes: Language, Illusion and Beyond* is refreshing and challenging.

LACANIAN ANALYSIS OF 'MAYDAY ON HOLDERNESS': ADOLPHE HABERER

Lacanian and other poststructuralist concepts enable Adolphe Haberer to examine qualities he regards as transgressive in the themes of Hughes's early, and for him central, poem, 'Mayday on Holderness' (*L, CP*, pp. 60–1). Haberer finds that the poem initially seems 'obscure and difficult', which is characteristic of the extent to which Hughes's poetry, rather than giving pleasure, affects readers differently. It implicates them in 'the multiple layers of its own impenetrableness, unsettles them, and forces them to pose unanswerable questions concerning life, death, sex and, significantly, origin'. That 'Mayday on Holderness' was the first of Hughes's early poems to be included in his *Selected Poems 1957–1981*, and that the Lupercal was the cave where Romulus and Remus, founders of Rome, were suckled by a wolf, introduces, Haberer says, the theme of 'origin represented in relation to animality', a theme that can be deemed transgressive.[81]

Haberer notes that D.H. Lawrence in 'Poetry of the Present' (1918) defined free verse as '"direct utterance from the instant whole man", something produced in the body without any mediation, a spasm-like expression of "the insurgent naked throb of the instant moment"', and added that, 'for this type of poetry, "any externally applied law would be mere shackles and death. The law must come new each time from within."' Although the form of 'Mayday on Holderness' is not obviously transgressing, Haberer finds that Hughes has an affinity with Lawrence.

Using Lacan, Haberer reads 'Mayday on Holderness' as the written trace

■ of a phantasy that insistently articulates a desire to represent, even at the risk of horror, an origin outside the Law and an impossible as much as prohibited return to the real of the maternal body. The phantasy originates in a transgressive orality, involving a mouth that is no longer connected to *parole.* Such transgressive orality is evident in the recurring emergence of a whole bestiary of devouring predators accompanied by a procession of images of violence and death. These images signal the truth of a desire that, in its transgression of the Law, can only be a desire for death.[82] □

Haberer concludes that the title of the poem can be understood only after working through the poem, in relation to and opposition with the calls for help it contains. One of those calls, the dying soldier's 'Mother, Mother!', signifies 'the dominant desire in the poem for a return to the maternal origin'. On the other hand, however, 'Mayday' (*m'aidez*), sited as 'introduction and endword, programme and   conclusion', is coded as a distress signal, another cry for help which makes the poem a plea to the Other. Another such plea is addressed 'with the una-voidable metalingual reference made by the poem *as poem* to the code of language'. In this respect, Haberer argues, the poem is a 'symbolic mediation, the trace of an enunciation in which the subject is always absent from that which is enunciated, irreducible to the phantasy rep-resented therein'. That is why the poem can be read at all; it

■ offers the reader a verbal space in which his own structure as subject (as subject of desire and *parole)* can come into play. It offers him a space that allows him to glimpse the unspeakable horror of madness and death *from a distance*, through the signifying texture of a highly structured, unyielding and powerfully articulated poem. □

Reading the poem in this way allows the reader 'to grasp the fact that meaning, in poetry, is always connected to non-sense (or ab-sence) breaking through'.[83]

HUGHES'S 'NATURE THINKING': TERRY GIFFORD AND NEIL ROBERTS

Discussion in Chapter 2 of analyses of Hughes's animal poems in terms of mythic and psychic archetypes includes work by Terry Gifford and Neil Roberts. The same authors explore Hughes's representation of ani-mals in a different way in a penetrating discussion of 'Hawk Roosting'. Like other critics, they quote from the interview given by Hughes to the *London Magazine*,[84] but their subsequent analysis does not depend solely on the author's reported intention. Hughes recalled that the hawk in his poem had been accused of being a fascist, a symbol of a genocidal dictator, but that what he had in mind had been that in the hawk he had represented Nature thinking. Gifford and Roberts respond by saying that for Nature thinking, Hughes had found a language quite different from that of poems such as 'Jaguar' and 'Thrushes' (L, CP, pp. 82–3) in which, in his own voice, he had attempted to 'perform an empathy' with the animals. Instead of that earlier style, which they describe as extravagant, energetic and fusing, they find a cool, self-possessed, distanced language. The tone is established by words 'surprisingly' but 'wittily' and 'elegantly' abstract, such as 'rehearse', 'convenience', 'advantage', 'inspection', 'manners', 'allotment' and 'permitted'. Apparently incongruous with hawkish thoughts as these words might seem, given in short elliptical phrases they contribute to the overall effect of brutal hardness, as if each were 'a robbery from some human rational context', and their confident placement emphasises the hawk's physical splendour without need for direct description.

For Gifford and Roberts, Hughes's claim that the poem is 'Nature thinking' is most strongly supported by the assurance of the hawk that it is at the centre of things. Its poise, serenity and contemplative ease mean that unlike Hughes's thrushes it is not all 'bounce and stab', but nonetheless, every line of the poem is tense with a predator's ferocity. The use of the first-person singular, however, is said to carry with it an inevitable irony. Nature thinking cannot be conceived without the consequence of the loss of the ability to say 'I'. The last three lines of the poem, the authors suggest, exploit this paradox, as Nature and the hawk both think the same but mean different things. Nature articulates the knowledge that it maintains itself; the hawk 'is rehearsing its own necessary blindness: what the hawk sees as a straight line with himself intact at each end of it is really, of course, a cycle that includes his own death'.[85] The inevitable irony, however, is not at the expense of the hawk. The necessary blindness is Nature, Nature dwelling in the individual creature, so that the 'magnificent structure of Creation is built upon ignorance of death'. The assertion, then, is that the poem is dramatic, and that what it enacts is the writer's engagement with the non-human reality that is both enticing and threatening. Whilst it does not moralise, the hawk is not offered as a model for imitation.

'Skylarks' (W, CP, pp. 173–6), the authors suggest, is one of a number of the W poems that explore the paradoxes of living with the limit of intensity; the vigorous vital energy and its cost.[86] The analysis reveals Hughes's economy and power in representing a nature that, as Gifford and Roberts say, makes the skylark almost a predator of itself. The first five lines of the final section of the poem are at the very edge of the human ability to make a register for the signification of non-human life, but that representation cannot be sustained. The authors find that anthropomorphic empathy comes into the description of the skylarks' descent. Whereas earlier sections of the poem represented the birds as more like forces than creatures, words such as 'relax' and 'relief' carry human connotations, and Hughes's phrase 'the earth gives them the O.K.' is said to remind one irresistibly of 'a pilot receiving instructions'.[87]

If the empathic quality of this section and its human register allow the reader to relax, however, he or she is likely to be jolted by 'The plummeting dead drop/with long cutting screams buckling like razors'. Only material metaphors, Gifford and Roberts say, are adequate for this phase of the skylarks' being. They find the return to anthropomorphism in the last line bewildering, suggesting that it is as if, under the finality, the birds are mocking both the poet and his readers. That mockery is in the birds' 'perfect imitation of a familiar human feeling, but as the outcome of a terrifying departure from the normal human range'. Gifford and Roberts read this not as an attack on anthropomorphism, but as a 'remarkable investigation' of both the inevitability and the limits of that trope.

Whereas in the extract considered above Paul Bentley focuses on the unknowable otherness of Hughes's animals, and the slipperiness of their being, Gifford and Roberts find the term 'otherness' unhelpful. They note that it was D.H. Lawrence's achievement 'to honour the animal creation by asserting its independence of human ideas'; that Hughes frequently does not 'honour' his animal subjects offended some critics.[88] His poems, they acknowledge, sometimes seem like an invasion of their subjects' being. It is in discussion of this that they find the term 'other' particularly unhelpful. For them, Hughes's animals are other in that they present a shock and a challenge to the poet, but they are never as impenetrably alien as the fish and bat of Lawrence's writing. Of his fish, D.H. Lawrence says: 'I didn't know him .../I didn't know his God', and 'I .../said to my heart, there are limits/ ... Fish are beyond me.'[89] Gifford and Roberts suggest that Hughes's poems, however, come out of the conviction that he does know the god of the hawk, jaguar or pike; not in the sense of 'being able to define, but of being intimately acquainted with'.[90]

Gifford and Roberts examine Hughes's treatment of that indivisible whole on which all life is founded. Hughes's conception they see as an interdependence of creation and destruction, in which the relationship of consciousness to natural processes is of paramount importance. In a discussion of the exciting effect of the poem 'Jaguar', they find readers' awareness that the poet is identifying himself with the animal, and that it is a poem not just of observation but also of longing

and affirmation. The final lines of the poem offer an enticing possibility, but one that entails preserving intact aspects of our own nature:
predatory ferocity, rage, blindness and deafness. This they find implicit
in the way that the poem's most intense life is concentrated in the
'undeviating thrust of the jaguar's being'.

The authors' close critical analysis of 'Jaguar' offers insights into
Hughes's lexical and metrical choices.[91] The word 'drills' represents the
animal's field of vision, narrow and narrowly focused, but also places
his predatory power in his very eyesight, suggesting that he bores holes
in his prey even before he reaches it. They find in the poem's penul-
timate line a 'superbly mimetic juxtaposition' of long stressed sylla-
bles, which makes the reader imagine both that the jaguar's energy
is turning the world and that the same action spurns the world, as he
relentlessly pursues the horizons. They find that the power of the final
line derives from the sense that the vision of the horizons has been
transferred to the poet through his 'unquestioning absorption in the
jaguar's being'. The caged jaguar, they assert, is a natural representative of a man's imprisoned animal energies. The jaguar is objectively
caged, but subjectively he is free, since he has no means of concep-
tualising imprisonment. They state that the jaguar is an example to
the man who longs to live fully in those energies, but then ask: 'Or is
he?' 'A man is not only conscious of his prison, but his consciousness
forms the very bars of his cell.' The authors note that in the last three
lines of the poem, it is the conscious longing of the poet that 'attributes freedom to the jaguar'. The animal in a sense 'only plays back the
wishfulness that the poet feeds into it'. At the same time, 'in this blind
heroic commitment to the source of his own vitality', Hughes does
create 'a genuine embodiment of his animal subject'. For Gifford and
Roberts, then, this poem 'inaugurates the great quest' of Ted Hughes's
work, but his perseverance in that quest was to take him 'beyond blind
identification'.

BIOGRAPHICAL READINGS: KEITH SAGAR

Keith Sagar finds significance in Hughes's birthplace having been
neither an isolated rural nor built-up metropolitan area, 'but in the
very frontier where the two were engaged in a "fight to the death"'.[92]
In moving to a South Yorkshire town, Hughes 'suffered in childhood
the crisis of our civilisation in a very pure form' which forced him
into a double life, one with the town boys, the other in his bolt-holes
of nearby farms and estates, and into 'a fiercely dualistic attitude to

life'. This attitude, Sagar believes, released the 'amazing energies' of Hughes's first three collections, and the subsequent collections represent a 'gradual healing of that split'.[93]

Like other critics, Sagar points out that through Hughes's father, William Hughes, Ted Hughes was also exposed to another crisis of our civilisation, the trauma of the First World War, a trauma that Sagar sees as having acted directly on Hughes himself, even more so than the war that he lived through, and which also contributed to his development as a poet of dislocation and loss, as well as nature. In this view, Hughes conflates the 'natural' violence of animals and landscape and the man-made violence of war; the images of war 'superimposed in perfect register' on the images 'impressed on him by the surrounding landscape'.[94] This echoes a prescient statement about Hughes and war made in response to Hughes's first two collections by Rosenthal, whose section on Hughes in *The New Poets* is discussed above. In this view, Hughes is the 'legitimate heir to the young British poets of World War I' and Hughes's 'sensibility exists in some sort of continuum with theirs, but far beyond the Georgian context'. Rosenthal observes that Hughes's introduction to the *Selected Poems of Keith Douglas* (1964), who was killed in the Second World War, 'underlines this affinity'.[95]

Paul Bentley effectively summarises the early response to Hughes's alleged 'poetry of violence', and explains the apparent lack of comprehension of some of its critics.[96] He points out that the mediated status of nature means that is no longer simple. Refracted 'through religion, myth and ideology, nature, in effect becomes culture'. In assuming that Hughes's hawks and thrushes represented birds and birds alone, and illustrated the 'natural' or 'inevitable' violence' of nature, critics both missed the point and rendered the poems mere sketches of observed behaviour. Arguing from Hughes's response to accusations that he depicts and endorses gratuitous violence, or fascistic attitudes, Bentley suggests that the violence depicted is positive in opposition to negative violence which is 'an oppressive and violating force'.[97] That force 'is the culture that shapes the response' of the affronted readers; the poems are critiques of the attitude which Hughes describes as recoiling from the poems in a sentimental way, the same way in which those readers would recoil from visual recordings of animals killing other animals. That disapproval, he argues, masks the reader's implication in the process and denies his guilt, since he is effacing the 'unspoken abattoir between the bullock in the field and the steak on his plate'.[98] Hughes's representation of the positive violence of nature was presented as 'a counterpoint' to the invisible 'negative' violence inherent in 'customary social and humanitarian values; it implies a critique of those values, of the very reaction the poems provoked', and is, as Bentley convincingly argues, in a dialectical relationship with them.[99]

The early assessments of Hughes's work discussed in this chapter, then, though diverse in approach and conclusion, were agreed that Hughes, writing against the grain of contemporary poetry, made a striking debut and a powerful impact. Many focused on the violence represented in the poems, some finding it gratuitous, others simply clear-eyed. The next chapter of this work looks at those critics who explored Hughes's animals and landscapes as both referential of creatures and places in the real world and as figures from the psyche and from myth.

CHAPTER TWO

Nature Poetry

As has been seen, critical evaluation and even categorisation of Hughes's work has been varied. There is, however, some critical consensus about the importance in Hughes's writing of certain concepts, one of which is 'Truth', a concept significant enough to be figured in Hughes's writing about poetry and writing for children,[1] as well as in his poems. Daniel Weissbort, writing about Hughes's co-foundation of the periodical *Modern Poetry in Translation*, stated that 'Hughes was looking for the Truth. That which underlies language and survives translation.'[2] His children's fable, *What is the Truth?*, depicted characters who in their sleep came most close to describing animals in a way that captured each creature's essence, but the story does more than that, interrogating poetry, Hughes, and the kind of poet that he has been and was still capable of being. Weissbort concludes that the Truth cannot be contained in description, 'however mimetically powerful'.[3]

For Adolphe Haberer, reading Hughes through Lacan (see Chapter 1), the true or the real is in opposition to the symbolic; for Joanny Moulin, it is synonymous with the *mythos* and opposed to the *logos* (see below); Keith Sagar relates the search for truth to the reconciliation of inner and outer realities, and to a visionary and healing function in the urgent communication of the symbolism of myth.[4] However it is defined, the use of the concept suggests a belief in a serious or transcendent function of poetry; a message to be conveyed, a story to be told, whether in a realist or non-realist mode, through metaphors, Jungian archetypes, or *mythoi*. This chapter looks at criticism which examines Hughes's use of archetypes and his adaptation and creation of myths, which reads into his nature poetry anthropological or psychological or religious significance, and which brings to the analysis of Hughes's poetry philosophical concepts from, among others, Heidegger and Nietzsche. It also discusses works which find sources for Hughes's poetry in religion and war. Some works included in this chapter touch on Hughes's longer poem sequences, criticism of which is examined in Chapter 3.

NATURE, THE PAGAN AND THE SHAMANIC IN HUGHES'S POETRY

By 1981, Terry Gifford and Neil Roberts, who have between them covered most of Hughes's writing from a variety of perspectives in illuminating and insightful analyses, could confidently describe Ted Hughes as a great poet on the basis that he had developed 'from an early reliance on external nature to a greater metaphysical assurance and the creation of a distinctive imaginative world', though, they add, 'there have inevitably been many critics who have regretted this development'.[5] They suggest that while the early poems describe the natural world, and may use it to describe the inner world of humankind, *C* and subsequent volumes depict an entirely imaginary world, a mythic landscape populated by mythic animals of Hughes's creating. This does not entail a radical reorientation or rejection of the earlier poems. Hughes's subject, the relationship between humankind and nature, remains constant. For Gifford and Roberts, however, this categorising of Hughes's work, though fair, does not convey the intensity of the poet's imaginative endeavour, nor do justice to the nuances of the relationship Hughes portrays. They argue that the endeavour is to gain access to and give expression to a level of being in which there is a continuity between the processes of the experience of nature within and the processes of nature observed without, unimpeded by consciousness. In this, they say, is the source of all energy, creativity and delight. The individual consciousness which insists on its separateness is the source of destructive alienation from this inner life, and the unhappiness of many of the human protagonists of Hughes's poetry. Consciousness, however, is inescapable, and poems are acts of consciousness. The subterranean world explored in Hughes's work 'can never be completely projected into language, nor can anyone permanently live in it'.[6] Didactic elements are therefore suspect; the poems cannot be final statements, but they can mediate or reconcile.

Gifford and Roberts regard Hughes's 'Second Glance at a Jaguar', collected ten years after 'Jaguar', in *W* (*CP*, pp. 151–2), as expressing second thoughts, now suggesting that the jaguar's freedom was the poet's illusion. They find that though the jaguar is of course unconscious, he does not transcend his cage: 'imprisonment has penetrated his body'.[7] Hughes's achievement in this poem is to maintain over thirty-three lines 'a relentless, threatening momentum that expresses the animal's unyielding ferocity yet carries a rhythmic embodiment of his tragic loss of grace in every line'. The jaguar is compared to Milton's devils, having traces of his angelic nature which fill the reader with awe, but emphasise the calamity of his fall. Gifford and Roberts suggests that the animal is perhaps, 'in Hughes's words, "a symbol of man's baser nature shoved down into the id and growing cannibal murderous with deprivation"'.[8] Even so, they add, this does not entail a recantation of Hughes's earlier poetry. The initial response to the jaguar in 'Jaguar' perhaps expressed an illusion or fantasy, but, they assert, that is all the more reason for, somehow, giving him a real freedom.[9]

Seamus Heaney suggests that Hughes's sensibility is pagan, in the original sense of the word; he is a haunter of the *pagus*, the Latin for rural area; he is a heathen, a heath-dweller moving by instinct 'in the thickets beyond the *urbs*, neither urban nor urbane', and his poetry is 'as redolent of the lair as it is of the library'.[10]

Heaney notes that the titles of Hughes's books 'are casts made into the outback of our animal recognitions', such as *Lupercal*, a word 'infested with wolfish stinks' yet coming from Shakespeare's *Julius Caesar*: 'You all did see that on the Lupercal/I thrice presented him a kingly crown' (3.2.74–5), and before that, passing into the Lupercal cave beyond the Western corner of Rome's Palatine Hill, and the Lupercal festival of 15 February. After the festival's sacrifices, young men wearing the skins of the victims ran about hitting people, particularly women, with strips of goatskin. According to Heaney this was both a beating of the bounds of the city and a fertility rite, as, in a way, is Hughes's language. The 'sensuous fetch' of that language, 'its redolence of blood and gland and grass and water, recalled English poetry in the fifties from a too suburban aversion of the attention from the elemental; and the poems beat the bounds of a hidden England in streams and trees, on moors and in byres'.[11]

For Heaney, Hughes's enterprise is 'to make vocal the inner life, the simple being-thereness, "the substance, nature and consequence of life" in sea, stone, wind and tree'.[12] Heaney's acute ear links this theme and the subject matter of Hughes's writing to its language and form. The rock in the Calder Valley whose significance Hughes explains in 'The Rock' and to which a number of critics refer, is, in Heaney's interpretation, both the imaginary and the linguistic foundation of Hughes's poems: 'the equivalent in its poetic landscape of dialect in his poetic speech'. Heaney finds that the rock survives and endures and informs Hughes's imagination, and forms the bedrock of the language upon which Hughes's version of survival and endurance is founded.

That English language of Hughes's foundation is 'the northern deposits of English', the Old English that became the Middle English alliterative tradition 'and then went underground to sustain the folk poetry, the ballads, and the ebullience of Shakespeare and the Elizabethans'.[13] The England of Hughes's mind that Heaney describes is primeval, inhabited by the elements with religious force, a landscape in which stones cry out and horizons endure. It is a place of monoliths and lintels, which is menaced by demonic protean crow-shapes and God's voice in the wind. In that landscape the poet wanders among ruins, cut off from consolation by catastrophe.[14]

Paganism, animals, the wild and religion come together in the figure of the shaman, a figure associated with Hughes by several critics. Gifford and Roberts define the shaman as anthropologists' 'preferred term for what is more properly called a sorcerer or witch-doctor, a function found predominantly in herding societies'.[15] The authors quote from Mircea Eliade's *Shamanism* (1951): "'Each time a shaman succeeds in sharing in the animal mode of being, he in a manner re-establishes the situation that existed in *illo tempore*, in mythical times, when the divorce between man and the animal world had not yet occurred.'"[16]

Keith Sagar, also quoting from Eliade's *Shamanism*, notes that the process of making a shaman requires the surrender of the initiate's consciousness, with its stable sense of self and reality, through sleep deprivation, fasting or the use of narcotic substances.[17] The shamanic self that results from this has radically altered perceptions which are open to or may enter the worlds of spirits and of animals. As well as communicating with animal spirits, the shaman may share their mode of being. Before communing with, or taking on, the human-animal/spirit form, shamans undergo an arduous and terrifying experience of death and rebirth, which might involve dismemberment of the old to facilitate the creation of the new body which returns to consciousness and the material world transformed by knowledge of the other one.

The shaman summons spirit helpers by drumming and speaking a secret animal language, and obtains a 'second state' that 'provides the impetus for linguistic creation and the rhythms of lyric poetry'.[18] Eliade argues that every poetic language begins as a secret language, and the most pure poetic act seems to re-create language from an inner experience that, like religious ecstasy or divine inspiration, reveals the essence of things. From linguistic creations made possible by pre-ecstatic inspiration derive the secret languages of mystics and traditional allegorical languages. Hughes, in Sagar's view, performs a function analogous to 'that performed in more "primitive" cultures by the shaman': 'to make the dangerous journey, on behalf of his society, into the spirit world, which is to say into his own unconscious'.[19] From the beginning, Sagar finds, Hughes aimed to find a way to reconcile human vision with the 'energies, powers, presences, of the non-human cosmos'. At first, the task was to identify those energies and describe them in both human and their own, that is, Nature's terms. Then the task was to find whether negotiations between humanity and Nature may be possible, and if so, why they have collapsed, and what are the consequences of that collapse.[20]

Hughes's poems share some of the archetypes and forms of shamanic belief and ritual. In *Gaudete* (*CP*, pp. 357–74), Lumb descends to an underworld or innerworld where he encounters the Goddess of life and undergoes a terrifying alteration before returning in a different state. That an otter comes from a lough at his call suggests that Lumb has achieved communication, or even union, with the animal world, but the episode occurs almost as an afterword at the end of a long narrative mostly concerned with the doings of the creature created, from an oak tree, to replace Lumb in the material world while he was in the world of the spirit. Gifford and Roberts provide a characteristically insightful analysis of this complex poem in the light of Hughes's 'Myth and Education' and Euripides's *The Bacchae*,[21] Neil Roberts develops the work in an outstanding contribution to Sagar's *Challenge of Ted Hughes*,[22] and Michael Sweeting discusses the development of 'a shamanistic formula' in 'Hughes and Shamanism'.[23]

For Sweeting, Hughes received a shamanic call in the dream about the burned fox described in Chapter 1.[24] He writes that the song of the shaman has three factors – 'the energy or ecstasy, the myth, expressed in some form of ritual, and a resulting catharsis or abreaction' – and that these combine 'to produce healing, reintegration and answers to spiritual questions'.[25] In the best of Hughes's writing, Sweeting argues, the experience is lived by the poet, but initially, the poems are separate from that which they describe; Hughes 'has not yet dealt with a tendency towards curious metaphysical enquiry and a corresponding distancing of the subject from the healing power of the myth'. In *G*, the mythic element is made more accessible by the human perspective, and Hughes is 'now intent upon a poetic living-out of the ritual'.[26] This, Sweeting writes, is because Hughes believes that if the 'shaman/ poet/reader can get as far as to ask the vital question of the divine being, that might constitute an answer in itself'. In *W*, Hughes attains a proper understanding of his aims, and takes up the shamanic call fully. In explanation of the 'delay', Sweeting quotes Hughes's point that most poets refuse this call on the basis that how could a poet become a medicine man, fly to the source and return to pronounce oracles or heal?[27]

HUGHES AND ROBERT GRAVES

The shaman is one ancestor of the bard, the powerful figure combining the functions of priest, genealogist, historian, prophet, visionary and poet so important in Celtic culture and, imaginatively, to Romantic literature. An early source of Hughes's knowledge of shamanism and bardic poetry, and perhaps an early model for his own writing, acknowledged by critics such as Sagar and Gifford and Roberts, was Robert Graves's *The White Goddess* (1946), which was given to Hughes as a prize when he left Mexborough Grammar School. Subtitled 'a historical grammar of poetic myth', the work locates the origin of the slant of Western metaphysics (which Graves refers to as 'Greek Olympianism' or 'Socratic intellectual homosexuality') in Judaism, and traces the 'tampering' of the language of poetic myth back through Mycenaean patriarchal imperialism, Classical philosophy, Enlightenment rationalism, Protestantism and Puritanism to twentieth-century scepticism and logic. For Graves, patriarchal religions, with their hierarchical binary division of soul (or mind) and body, male and female, rationality and myth, supplanted and suppressed knowledge of the existence of an older, matriarchal religion, and instituted philosophical dualism. In the old religion the poet had a special place as the champion and lover of the triple goddess (maiden, mother and crone), and poetry had a special, magical function. *The White Goddess* examines the history of the language of myth (that is, the units of meaning or signifiers of myth which combine to encode the meaning of a myth beyond that of its surface story) and the history of the recording of language itself, of literacy, which, according to Graves, was one of the great mysteries, reserved in ancient societies for initiates such as the Celtic *olaves*.

Graves's thesis is that in the ancient Mediterranean and northern Europe there was a language of poetic myth related to a widespread cult of the Moon Goddess, and that this language remains the true language of poetry: '"*true*" in the nostalgic modern sense of "the unimproved original, not a synthetic substitute"'.[28] That language was marginalised, repressed and replaced by successive waves of patrilinear and patriarchal cultures, but initially derived from the inspiration of the Moon Goddess, who demanded that man should pay homage, both sexually and spiritually, to woman, and that her poet, the true poet, should devote his life to her worship and the telling of the one true poetic theme. The dedicatory poem of *The White Goddess* describes her.[29]

Graves's insistence on inspiration from the Goddess or Muse as the source of poetry and the function of poetry as invocation, and his remark that poetry 'of a magical quality' is written in modern industrialised Europe always as a result of 'an inspired, almost pathological, reversion to the original language – a wild Pentecostal "speaking with tongues" – rather than from a conscientious study of its grammar and vocabulary',[30] is taken by a number of critics as shedding light on Hughes's description of poetic method in *Poetry in the Making* and elsewhere, and on Hughes's use of the Goddess myth and his relationship with nature. Graves writes that mankind was warned to keep in harmony with the 'family of living creatures among which he was born, by obedience to the wishes of the lady of the house', but that he has 'disregarded the warning, turned the house upside down by capricious experiments in philosophy, science and industry, and brought ruin on himself and his family'.[31]

For Graves's true poet, there is only one story worthy of telling in the true poetic language, as he demonstrates in a haunting poem to his son, 'To Juan at the Winter Solstice'.[32] Graves states that the poet was originally 'the leader of a totem-society of religious dancers', and that 'all the totem-societies in ancient Europe were under the dominion of the Great Goddess, the Lady of the Wild Things'. The religious dances 'fitted into an annual pattern from which gradually emerges the single grand theme of poetry: the life, death and resurrection of the Spirit of the Year, the Goddess's son and lover'.[33]

Nick Gammage, in his piece for Patrick J. Quinn's *New Perspectives on Robert Graves* (1999), suggests that war was a trauma for both Graves and Hughes, and led them both to protect the vigorous life of the spirit that had been assaulted by the unimaginable horrors of trench warfare. He finds that though the focus of Graves and Hughes may be the same in some poems, in that both associated the life-force of the spirit with sexual energy, there are 'fundamental differences' in the way the two evoke and describe the energy', and that the nature of this difference illustrates the tension between the 'male impulse to control and rationalize and the female irrepressible intuitiveness'.[34] Whereas Graves's evocation of the Goddess is cool and polished, detached and distancing, reverential but cautious, above all controlling, the mimetic rhythms of Hughes's poetry (an example given is from *M*) work both to evoke and control the energies and the expression of tenderness. Hughes's enterprise, for Gammage, is to balance unbounded female sexual energy and male control.

Ekbert Faas describes the widening of the Goddess theme in Hughes's work in a section on the 'shared mythologies' of Hughes and Plath.[35] Faas notes that, though Hughes's 'poetic quest for the rescue of the desecrated female' remained unfulfilled, the theme widened in significance for Hughes from 1970, in which year Hughes is found 'pondering the "subtly apotheosised misogyny of Reformed Christianity" and its "fanatic rejection of Nature" in a review of Max Nicholson's *The Environmental Revolution* (1970), as well as prophesying something "unthinkable only ten years ago, except as a poetic dream: the re-emergence of Nature as the Great Goddess of mankind, and the Mother of all life"'.[36] The following year, in his *Shakespeare and the Goddess of Complete Being* (1993), Hughes is said to have diagnosed Shakespeare's 'knot of obsessions' as reflecting the major psychic conflict of his time, 'the struggle between Calvinistic witch-hunt misogyny and the Celtic pre-Christian Mother worship surviving in the cult of the Queen'.[37] Faas sees in *G* the Reverend Lumb's continuation of Hughes's poetic quest to resurrect the Great Mother and bring about a renovation 'of women and therefore of life in general' in a 'postholocaust North England town turned mass grave'.[38] That mission ends in failure: the women he hoped to save are all abused, murdered, or driven to suicide. Faas recalls a letter from Hughes in 1977 in which he replies to the question of whether the 'débâcle' reflected his own pessimism. Hughes wrote that the pessismism of G was 'an inevitable part of the working out of the theme'. Faas also asked the poet 'whether what was symbolically implied in the rebirth of the baboon woman might become reality or whether a solution to the problem was as unattainable as a phantasmagorical mirage'. The reply was that Faas was asking for an explanation to Hughes's riddle, which Hughes would refrain from giving.[39]

Faas asserts that though Lumb fails, *G* ends on a note which, for all its obvious irony, seems to be more in tune with the title. The 'bride of [Lumb's] and the poet's devotions survives in the Epilogue poems'. Faas also find that other poems go beyond Lumb's failures. In 1970, Hughes told Faas about a 'search for a new divinity' which '"won't be under the rubble when the churches collapse"'.[40] Faas suggests that 'Churches Topple' (*G*, *CP*, p. 368), in conflating religious with sexual imagery in a new kind of pun-riddled symbolism, points towards the fulfilment of the quest.[41] In contrast with the patriarchal Christian god, this female divinity 'unites the creator and destroyer in one, and in "Who are you?" (*G*, *CP*, p. 358), in response to Lumb's question, "Who are you?" the implacable cruelty of life spells out the answers.'

Faas quotes from 'The spider clamps the bluefly' to 'Who watches the skylines fixedly', and argues that in spite of this implacable cycle of death, the Goddess mostly appears as comforter and protectress whose kiss of life resurrects the dead and whose kiss of death frees us from the 'veils of wrinkle and shawls of ache'. He concludes that we are not allowed to forget that Lumb, 'as much as his Doppelgänger, has proved to be a mere "veteran of negatives"'. The role-reversal between saviour and victim adds a final touch of both irony and wisdom to the story of failure. Lumb does not save the desecrated female; instead, the Goddess rescues her helpless would-be champion.[42]

HUGHES, MYTHOLOGY AND MYTHIC ARCHETYPES: ANNIE SCHOFIELD

Analyses of Hughes's work through its mythology and, more spe-cifically, through the deployment of its mythic archetypes, have sometimes treated the poems as thinly disguised messages from Hughes's psyche and the actions of characters such as Crow as symp-toms of Hughes's psychic disorder. Ian Hamilton's 'Ted Hughes' Crow', in *A Poetry Chronicle* (1973), for example, psychoanalyses Hughes through his writing. Annie Schofield, also writing in Sagar's *Achievement of Ted Hughes*, points out the dangers in this enterprise and offers Jungian theory as more productive to bring to the read-ing of Hughes's work.[43] She argues that Hamilton finds in Hughes an 'authorial evasiveness' devised to help Hughes to find 'a territory and a device which would enable him to unload his obsessions without requiring that he test them out, in any precise way, against reality'.[44] The cause of statements such as this, Schofield argues, is the 'small psychology' ('Witches', *L, CP*, p. 80) of Freud, which 'generalises from facts which are relevant to neurotic states of mind only, and reduces everything to the personal'. Jung's 'larger' psychology 'must suggest a new stance towards Hughes and towards reality'. Schofield cites Jung's essay 'Psychology and Literature', in which he defines two modes of artistic creation, the psychological and the visionary.[45] The psychological deals with materials from the conscious life of man, 'raised from the commonplace to the level of poetic experi-ence'. However varied this is, and however far it seems to be removed from the level of everyday life, this material 'never transcends the bounds of psychological intelligibility', whereas the materials of the visionary artist 'are vastly more inaccessible'. Jung finds that the differences between the first and second parts of Goethe's *Faust* mark the difference between 'psychological' and 'visionary' modes of artistic creation.

> ■ The latter reverses all the conditions of the former. The experience that furnishes the material for artistic expression is no longer familiar. It is a strange something that derives its existence from the hinterland of man's mind – that suggests the abyss of time separating us from the pre-human ages, or evokes a super-human world of contrasting light and darkness. It is a primordial experience which surpasses man's understanding, and to which he is therefore in danger of succumbing. The value and force of the experience are given by its economy. It arises from timeless depths; it is foreign and cold, many-sided, demonic and grotesque.[46] □

These materials provided by 'the primordial experiences of the visionary artist' are, Schofield states, more volatile than those of the psychological mode, and their source can be as obscure to the artist as to his audience.[47] She notes that Jung holds that it is this very obscurity which leads to accusations of authorial evasiveness. Quoting from Jung, she makes the point that Freudian psychology encourages us to suppose that some highly personal experience underlies 'this grotesque darkness'. Therefore we hope in that way to explain glimpses of chaos, and to understand why poets seek to conceal that experience from us. 'It is only a step from this way of looking at the matter to the statement that we are here dealing with a pathological and neurotic art.'[48]

Schofield notes that Hughes is often accused of other evasions, and that Hamilton accuses him of 'skimped and shallow dealings with the human world',[49] and of escaping into anachronistic use of myth. For Jung myth is the only adequate means of expression to the visionary artist. 'The primordial experience is the source of his creativeness; it cannot be fathomed, and therefore requires mythological imagery to give form.'[50] Schofield speculates that perhaps in an effort to rescue her work from the 'reductive effects of Freudian criticism', Hughes has offered a Jungian account of the background of Sylvia Plath's poems. These are described as 'emblematic visionary events' which Hughes sees as parts of 'one long poem', as 'chapters in a mythology where the plot, seen as a whole and in retrospect is strong and clear – even if the dramatis personae are at bottom enigmatic'.[51]

For Schofield, Hughes's poems can be seen in the same way, 'as emblematic visionary chapters in a developing mythology', in which Hughes at first 'uses the figures of established myth' but subsequently evolves his material. She finds that when Hughes is able to write of the mother, in *W* and in subsequent works, what emerges is not evidence of an 'Oedipus complex' but awareness of a 'Universal dilemma'.

She again quotes from Jung, who asks why one should risk saying too much that is false and inadequate about, and why put the weight of so much responsibility and load of meaning upon, the human mother. Sensitive people, she argues, will know that the mother 'carries for us that inborn image of the *mater natura* and *mater spiritualis* of the totality of life'. We should not hesitate, she insists, 'to relieve the human mother of this appalling burden'. The 'mother-complex' is not disposed of by 'blindly reducing the mother to human proportions', and 'we can run the risk of dissolving the experience "Mother" to atoms'.[52]

In Schofield's view, Hughes is not dealing with a familial mother and son, nor even with the wider theme of his emergence from the dark womb of the Calder Valley, but with the archetypal love-myth of Mother and Son. She notes that the central theme of the 'love-myth' of Mother–Son concerns the union of opposites: 'matter and spirit, body and soul, feminine and masculine, instinct and reason', and she cites Jung's study of this theme in his *Mysterium Coniunctionis*. For Jung, the symbolism of this myth was appropriated by Christian 'ecclesiastical allegory in the mystic marriage of sponsus (Christ) and sponsa (Church), and by the alchemists in the *mysterium coniunctionis* – the alchemical marriage – which was the goal of the alchemical opus. In both of these the dilemma has been brought to a dubious resolution.'[53] In Christian myth, the resolution of this conflict is 'purely pneumatic, the physical relations of the sexes being turned into allegory or – quite illegitimately – into a sin that perpetuates and even intensifies the most heinous transgression of the law, namely incest, into a symbol of the union of opposites, hoping in this way to bring back the golden age'. Jung writes that for both trends, 'the solution lay in extrapolating the union of the sexes into matter. But neither of them located the problem in the place where it arose – the soul of man.'

Schofield sees in Hughes's work an attempt at this task, the undertaking of that psychic journey. This would entail placing the Oedipus myth at the centre of the Western psyche. She notes that in the anecdotes about Crow which accompany Hughes's poetry-readings, Hughes indicates this. He tells of Crow starting to write plays – rewriting everybody else's plays – because that, it seems, is what everybody else has done. Finding a story retold by Sophocles, Seneca and Freud, Crow thinks that there is room for another, and writes 'Song for a Phallus' (*C, CP*, pp. 248–50). For Schofield, 'Hughes's use of the myth starts with Seneca, but does not end there.'[54]

Examining Hughes's comment on *Hamlet*, in *A Choice of Shakespeare's Verse* (1971), Schofield finds herself aware that what Hughes says about Shakespeare may equally apply to Hughes, because he regards himself as answering the 'ancient Universal shamanistic call to the poetic or holy life'.[55] He, too, has a preoccupying concern with the resolution of the conflict between the 'biological polarity of the life of the body and archaic nervous system and the life of the reflective cortex', that 'flying malevolent custard', the conflict between the beast and the angel in man. Its resolution will be to live – to reach a satisfactory 'state of negotiation' with 'his idea of the Creator'. Schofield sees this theme running through Hughes's work as surely as Hughes sees the theme in Shakespeare's. Poles of energy in *Venus and Adonis* become, in Hughes's work, Oedipus and Jocasta. Schofield quotes from *A Choice of Shakespeare's Verse*, in which Hughes writes that Jocasta is the mother and nature, the blood-root and love, whereas Oedipus, the opposite pole, is Spirit, intellect, reason and rigid moral law; the suppressor of that which answers the call of the Goddess. This 'overwhelming, powerful multiple, primaeval being, was dragged into court by the young Puritan Jehovah'.[56]

Like Gammage and others, discussing the influence of Robert Graves's *The White Goddess* on Hughes's poetry and Hughes's readings of Shakespeare's poetry, Schofield points out that Graves traces a genealogy of increasingly repressive Puritanism and increasing resistance to and detestation of material creation from Ezekiel to Calvin via the Essenes and Christ. Hughes sees the attempt of Calvin's Puritan Jehovah to dethrone the Goddess in Shakespeare's England as the source of Shakespeare's poem. Schofield quotes Hughes: '"this suppressed Nature goddess erupts, possessing the man who denied her, and creating this king-killing man of chaos"' (p. 194). This man in Shakespeare's work is Hamlet, Macbeth, Othello and Lear; in Hughes's work, Schofield sees his correspondence in Oedipus, 'though he also uses Tolstoy and St. George as the arch-puritan oppressor'.[57]

Schofield regards Othello as 'indistinguishable from Tolstoy' in the 'Kreutzer Sonata'; Hamlet and Lear 'unambiguously linked with Oedipus' in 'Prospero and Sycorax'. The latter poem, she argues, is the latest overt reference to the Oedipus myth in Hughes's writing. Though the character of Oedipus does not appear, she finds the Oedipal dilemma present in Hughes's later poems, but with a difference. The newly integrated psyche that Schofield sees in Hughes's poetry is evident in *Prometheus on His Crag* (1973). In 'Prometheus 20' (*CP*, pp. 295–6), Prometheus' creation of a mandala from images of the nature of his tormentor comes too suddenly for Schofield; she finds that the language of the poem indicates that the horror has not been truly assimilated; Prometheus is, 'perhaps, as he imagines, "mutilated towards alignment"'. In the process of individuation – the creation of an integrated self from a divided psyche – "every experience must be lived through. There is no feat of interpretation or any other trick by which to circumvent this difficulty, for the union of conscious and unconscious can only be achieved step by step."[58]

The Mother–Son love-myth, then, is the story of the reconciliation of binary opposites – matter/spirit; male/female; conscious/unconscious – and of the divided self. Jung's process of individuation is the alchemical marriage (*unio mystica*), the creation of a whole self from the separate halves of the psyche. Schofield warns that Hughes does not offer solutions to the problems of Western civilisation; rather, his Oedipus myth is, like *The Waste Land* of T.S. Eliot (1922), a chart of his own condition, and a record of a quest for a lost wholeness. Hughes does not, she asserts, even offer an answer to his own Sphinx; the dilemma question that the Sphinx poses has no final answer. 'We go on writing poems because one poem never gets the whole of the account right. There is always something missed. At the end of the ritual comes up a goblin' ('Finale', *CB*, *CP*, p. 440). This goblin, Schofield notes, appears at the end of *CB*, but 'in this mystery play of sorts, Hughes has reached a new stage in his negotiations with his "idea of the Creator"'.[59]

Sagar disagrees about the significance of the *CB* goblin, asserting that it is the 'Old Adam, the spark of unquenchable life in the flesh'; he cites Joseph Campbell's reference to '"that pushing, self-protective, malodorous, carnivorous, lecherous fever which is the very nature of the organic cell"'.[60] Sagar concludes that nature 'will never allow us to become wholly spirit. And all rituals designed to achieve that will fail.'[61]

CRITIQUE OF HUGHES'S MYTHICAL FORMS: TERRY EAGLETON

More critical of Hughes's mythical forms is Terry Eagleton's 'Myth and History in Recent Poetry' in Michael Schmidt and Grevel Lindop's *British Poetry Since 1960*.[62] Eagleton argues that the defects of myth are that it 'strips the individual of his social specificity' and of his 'contingency, his social nullity'. In myth, the individual is 'invested with a freshly representative significance, as the node in which natural forces, historical strands, metaphysical pre-occupations converge'. Myth enables 'that centripetal unity centred in a single figure, but also ... a free-ranging liberty, spanning diverse dimensions of time and space'. The triumph of Hughes's Crow over 'the alienating causalities of history' is, for Eagleton, bought cheaply: 'the inviolable security of myth has replaced, rather than confronted, the contingency of history, as simple compensation'.[63]

Whilst Eagleton acknowledges that Jonathan Raban has put forward a persuasive argument for the value of *C*, Eagleton's impression is that this is not enough; 'it doesn't sufficiently qualify the seriousness of Hughes's commitment to a world-view in which history can have value only in negative and caricatured form'.[64]

HUGHES AND ANTHROPOLOGY: RAND BRANDES

Rand Brandes makes the important point that Hughes's studies in anthropology, at Cambridge and afterwards, provided a vast library of sources for his poetry.[65] He notes that Hughes was not alone in employing myths and mythic archetypes in his work, but with the publication of *C* was 'riding on a new wave of world poetry'. Ancient oral traditions, songs, and myths and rituals once 'buried in the notes of anthropologists and ethnographers' were being transcribed and translated. The 'Otherness of the world', Brandes writes, 'was suddenly made manifest and offered a spiritual alternative to the chaos and confusion' of the 1950s to 1970s.[66] Hughes, Brandes argues, internalised the 'primitivist worldview' in which the 'non-Western mythic past' and the indigenous peoples who seemed connected to that past through 'dances and trances, dreams and drugs, singers and shamans' were the pre-lapsarian Adams and Eves. Unlike W.B. Yeats, however, Hughes does not employ a prepared structural framework, a 'mythic method', for his poetry; 'what makes Hughes's myths so powerful is their intense spontaneity'. For Brandes, Hughes does with his anthropological knowledge what Yeats said that poets should do with philosophy: it should be learned and forgotten.

Quoting from the anthropologist Marvin Harris's discussion of the importance of 'the supposed natural life of primitive peoples' in counter-culture, Brandes accepts that some of Harris's charges echo those of Hughes's critics.[67] A central belief of counter-culture, Harris writes, is that to make people better what you have to do is to change what goes on in their minds. By better is meant more spontaneous, imaginative and feeling; counter-culture members boast of 'fleeing "objectivity" as if from a place inhabited by plagues'.[68] These members associate the qualities of spontaneity, non-materialism and being in touch with 'occult sources of enchantment' with 'the supposed life of primitive peoples', whom they imitate. Primitive consciousness 'is epitomized by the shaman, a figure who has light and power but never pays electric bills'. Counter-culture admires the shaman because he is 'adept at "cultivating exotic states of awareness" and at "roving among the hidden powers of the universe"'. The shaman, Harris states, 'possesses superconsciousness'.[69]

Whilst Hughes does not blindly accept these principles, being a student of history and 'in touch with the objective realities of his time', Brandes observes that reviewers and critics have distrusted Hughes's mythic vision. The myth is trans-historical, transcultural and transgressive, in 'operating the same way in men and women'. This last is 'at the heart of Hughes's mythic sensibility as a result of his preoccupation with the Goddess'. Although from Hughes's perspective the Goddess embodies the '(pro)creative, harmonizing and unifying feminine principle', Brandes notes that critics have argued that there is a 'serious dishonest, even destructive, disconnect between Hughes's worship of a mythic feminine principle and the realities of Hughes's life and the omen in them'.[70] The example Brandes cites is Jacqueline Rose, *The Haunting of Sylvia Plath* (London: Virago, 1991).

HUGHES AND THE LAND

Other critical writing, for example, V.T. Usha's *Modern English Literature: The Real and the Imagined: The Poetic World of Ted Hughes* (1998), finds Hughes's representation of the feminine associated with his advocacy of environmental concerns. In 'Hughes's Social Ecology' in *The Cambridge Companion to Ted Hughes*,[71] Terry Gifford links the 'greening' of Ted Hughes to his reading about marine pollution in *The Nation* (1959) and to Rachel Carson's warning about the effect of pesticides in *Silent Spring* (1962), so that Hughes's 'sense of social ecology came to be focused on the issue of water quality and its implications for human responsibility for all the life – human and non-human – that depended on it'.[72] Gifford notes that the first of Hughes's Laureate poems was about water, Devon rivers, and was originally intended for the collection *R*. Similarly, Keith Sagar brings together rivers, the feminine and the Goddess in his analyses of Hughes's later poetry, discussed in Chapter 5.

The ancient English landscape and the early English language give Hughes's poetry much of its vitality, power and intensity, and some of its myths. Great tracts of that unspoiled landscape, densely forested and inhabited by wolves and wild boar, which still existed in the Middle Ages, are evocatively described in the source of the epigraph to *W* (*CP*, p. 146).

■ Sumwhyle wyth wormez he werreʒ, and wyth wolues als,
Sumwhyle wyth wodwos, þat woned in þe knarreʒ,
Boþe wyth bulleʒ and bereʒ, and boreʒ oþerquyle,
And etayneʒ, þat hym anelede of þe heʒe felle. □

(11.720–4)

The lines come from *Sir Gawain and the Green Knight,* an alliterative poem of over 2500 lines written in the dialect of the north-west midlands of the mid- to late fourteenth century. The quotation is taken from the second 'fitt' (section of narrative) in which Sir Gawain, having accepted a challenge from the mysterious Green Knight, sets off from King Arthur's court to make a long and difficult winter's journey through North Wales and the Wirral to the perilous green chapel. It can be translated as:

■ Sometimes he warred with worms [dragons] and with wolves,
Sometimes with wodwos that lived in the crags,
Both with bulls and bears, and boars at other times
And giants that followed him out of the high fells. □

The beasts that Gawain encounters come out of a fabulous rather than a real landscape. Wodwos were usually depicted as stocky, hirsute wild men armed with clubs.

THE LANGUAGE OF HUGHES'S NATURE POETRY: SEAMUS HEANEY

Heaney finds in Hughes's poetry the same clear outline and inner richness as that of *Gawain*. Attentive to sound, he describes Hughes's language in solid, material terms: consonantal diction which 'snicks through the air' like a blade, carving out shapes within which are hints of mysteries and rituals.[73] Those consonants take the measure of the vowels 'like calipers' or 'stud' a line 'like rivets'. They are 'the Norsemen, the Normans, the Roundheads in the world of his vocables, hacking and hedging and hammering down the abundance and luxury and possible lasciviousness of the vowels'. The example given by Heaney is the first line of Hughes's 'The Thought-Fox' (*THITR, CP*, p. 21), whose hush is achieved by 'the quelling, battening-down action of the m's and d's and t's: I iMagine this MiDnighT MoMenT's foresT'.[74] Heaney asserts that Hughes's aspiration in his early poems is to command the elements and bring them under the jurisdiction of his 'authoritative voice'. In this poem, the thing that lives beyond his jurisdiction is 'characteristically fluid and vowelling and sibilant'. Heaney finds in the phrase 'something else is alive' a movement of that something from mysterious and indeterminate to presence to an epiphany enacted in 'full vowel music'.

Heaney quotes from 'Something more near' to 'the loneliness' and writes that this is granted

■ this dilation of its mystery before it is conjured into the possession of the poet-warden, the vowel-keeper, and its final emergence in the fully sounded i's and e's of 'an eye,/A widening deepening greenness', is gradually mastered by the breaking action of 'brilliantly, concentratedly', and by the shooting of the monosyllabic consonantal bolts in the last stanza of the poem.[75] □

Heaney returns from *THITR* to *W* to consider 'Fern' (*CP*, p. 153), 'whose subject might be expected to woo the tender pious vowels rather than the disciplining consonants from a poet'. He finds, however, that the first line of the poem has the characteristic four strong stresses of Old English poetry, 'three of them picked out by alliteration; and although the frosty grip of those f's thaws out, the fern is still subsumed into images of control and discipline and regal authority'.[76] When, in another poem from the same volume, Hughes turns his attention to 'vegetation more kindred to his spirit than the pliant fern', the thistles become reincarnations of Vikings ('The Warriors of the North', *CP*, p. 167). Heaney suggests that Hughes imagines the Vikings resurrected in 'all their arctic mail' into 'the iron arteries of Calvin', and into the poem. For Heaney, the thistles are emblems of Hughes's voice as he sees it, born of 'an original vigour' and fighting back 'over the same ground'. Quoting from 'Every one' to 'plume of blood', Heaney points out that Hughes himself represents the thistles as images of speech 'uttering itself in gutturals from behind the sloped arms of consonants'.

The gutturals of dialect, which Hughes here connects with the Nordic stratum of English speech, he elsewhere identifies as the germinal secret of his own voice. Heaney quotes from an interview published in the *London Magazine* in January 1971, in which Hughes suggests that one's dialect stays alive 'in a sort of inner freedom', whatever other kind of speech one grows into. For Hughes that first dialect is 'your childhood self there inside the dialect and that is possibly your real self or the core of it'. He asserts that without his dialect he doubts that he 'would ever have written verse'. He adds that 'in the case of the West Yorkshire dialect, of course, it connects you directly and in your most intimate self to Middle English poetry'.[77]

Thus history, language and nature are intertwined in both the poet and his poetry. In Hughes's commentary on the poetry of Keith Douglas, Heaney finds an insight into Hughes's own poetic method: 'of the way his language and his imagination alerted themselves when the hunt for the poem in the adult world became synonymous with the hunt for the animal in the world of childhood, the world of dialect'.[78]

HUGHES'S 'I': THOMAS WEST

Thomas West, writing in 1985, reads '[s]ensual nature' in Hughes's poems of the 1950s and 1960s as 'a set of counters for an inner drama which is the poet's real concern'.[79] Like many critics, West quotes from Hughes's 'The Rock': 'I have heard' to 'definite hurdle'.[80]

West finds striking not only the attribution of a brooding eye to Scout Rock, but also the way in which the 'sinister charmed summit' is seen as demanding a response.[81] The possible 'conflicting roles' in this 'mental drama, either suicide or counter-attack', he writes, were 'vividly apprehended by the young Hughes'. West finds 'a quite complex reaction, in the form of mental repression or censure, which one recognizes in a number of staring or intimidating things in the early writings'. That reaction entails the assimilation of the poet to the rebel, the mountaineer, who chooses to counter-attack the charm of the precipice, rather than to commit suicide, and who sends his thoughts or his body 'over against the oppressive and aggressive limits of the staring natural world'. Poetry therefore becomes a kind of 'mountaineering against the evil eye of the precipice'; it is offered as a combative and liberating force.[82]

For West, the 'I' in poems such as 'The Hawk in the Rain' belongs to a dramatic fiction and is identified with the poet only indirectly, but becomes an actor in a drama akin to that of 'Scout Rock'. The 'I' momentarily takes on the role of victim and 'commits a kind of suicide within the imagination'. This is the 'poetic equivalent of sending one's thoughts into the precipice beneath the rock, against the evil eye'. West finds that the final lines of the poem offer a different perspective and a switch of voices. The narrative voice has become quite distant, almost an omniscient narrator, which steps back 'from both the bloodily dazed "I" and the intimidating hawk'. This voice seems to predict the destruction of the hawk, 'and thus to align itself with the superior powers which became momentarily apparent to the "grabbed" and "dazed" "I"'. One way to interpret this, West says, is as an attempt to usurp the 'threatening stare of the natural world by imaginative means'.[83]

The switch of voices, for West, is evident in the changing tone of the poem and in the 'extreme ambiguity of the syntax and punctuation'. An example given is the full stop which follows 'hangs still', which has no grammatical purpose but instead indicates a pause 'before we enter the prophetic relative clause in the subjunctive mood, "That maybe in his own time ..."'. West suggests that this shift in mood and speaker reveals the dramatic function of the drowning victim's voice, which is replaced by a 'much more prescient, much more authoritative voice, knowledgeable about the ways of the wind and of the hawk'. Perspectives and voices are in tension in the poem, then, and 'sensual nature' acts as a set of counters for the real subject, the inner drama. Though in some storms rain may 'hack' one's 'head to the bone', and 'banging wind' may kill 'stubborn hedges', these images should be seen in the context of the dramatic encounter of the two selves, the victim, and the self that understands the hawk's powers.[84]

Approaching the 'I' of Hughes's 'The Jaguar' and 'The Thought-Fox' as divided *personae*, West offers readings which differ from those of Sagar and other critics. He relates the staring of the crowd at the jaguar to the role of drowning narrator; the stare of the jaguar to the 'outer observer's or the crowd's perception of a great natural force with which they have no direct contact'. West finds this indicated 'in the analogy between a child following his dream and a mesmerized crowd following the jaguar'. Further, the encounter enacts civilised man, in reality a 'fallen' natural creature, looking at his own superior self, in existence outside himself in the jaguar. The stare of the jaguar, an energetic animal above all, is a refusal to acknowledge or to be fettered by the external, surface world. 'The eye is "satisfied to be blind in fire".' This energy, West finds, exists already, beyond the bars, in the awareness of the crowd, mesmerised by the jaguar.[85]

In the final six lines of the poem West finds a celebration of the remarkable perspective of the jaguar through the casting off of 'all tokens of sensual imprisonment'. The narrating voice of the poem makes clear the truth about the jaguar; his movements are not indicative of boredom, he 'spins from the bars', since 'there's no cage for him'. He spins the earth under his feet 'like a ball or a prayer wheel'. From the perspective of the viewer, new lands sweep into view, but from the perspective of the jaguar, it is he who is moving, not the earth. For West, this moves the poem into a 'strangely anti-sensory point of view', and towards 'the perspective of the jaguar's otherness'.[86]

What West calls the radical subjectivity of the jaguar's experience, lying beyond the senses and almost beyond the imagination, is used to dramatise the animal's power. The metaphors employed in the poem 'challenge the reader to identify with a hyperbole which makes the role of victim in the poem (the witness or the crowd that only half-consciously knows of the jaguar's power) almost invisible'. The reader is left with an 'inner' reality and 'a set of external facts which we can no longer appeal to (the jaguar is *not* what the eye can see, *not* what the ear can hear, etc.)'.[87]

HUGHES AND RELIGION: THOMAS WEST

In the stare or gaze depicted in several of Hughes's poems, then, West traces a variety of encounters 'which all seem to begin with the evil eye and Scout Rock'.[88] He suggests that the pervasive feeling of unease which Hughes's narrative *personae* feel when they encounter that stare comes from a complex, powerful fiction or interpretation of nature. He reads Hughes's short story 'Sunday' (1960) in this light, interpreting the central character's attraction yet revulsion to 'Billy Red', who kills rats with his teeth, as a fear of the natural world as it has been presented to him by religion, in the form of his home valley's powerful Methodist chapel.[89] What he fears in Billy Red's 'sparrow-hawk eyes' is 'directly related to a prohibition erected by his chapel'. The evil eye in Hughes's writing is not just 'a dizzying void that excites imaginings of what lies beyond experience but a fictionalized natural world which draws its power to mesmerize from the sublimation of physical power which a body-hating religion has brought about'. West argues that this earlier fiction has already made the body and the physical world taboo and thus, for the perceiving self, has effectively split mind and body into two opposing realities, which is why the normal self 'sees the physical or natural world as something insinuating, monstrous and grotesque'.[90]

In this reading, religion is opposed to the natural world just as spirit is opposed to body. West quotes from 'Mount Zion' (*CP*, pp. 480–1), which, in *RE*, is printed opposite a photograph of a sooty brick chapel, saying that through this we can understand more about why the young Hughes felt that the precipice under Scout Rock or the screech of the rat in Billy Red's mouth 'was aimed directly *at him*'. It was because in the beginning the 'blackness' in the poem was a 'building blocking the moon' and its wall the 'first world-direction' of the poem's narrator, 'Mount Zion's gravestone slab'.

West finds that religion has separated body from spirit, Wesleyanism represents 'a noose around the neck, and the word made flesh, according to the Apostle John, has been turned by Mount Zion religion into "only a naked bleeding worm/Who had given up the ghost"'. That is, the 'word made flesh' has been stripped of its Word and become a 'mindless gnawing worm: a terrible, brute nature'.[91]

Religion, specifically Calvinist-inflected Protestantism, thus affects Hughes ambivalently. He may have campaigned against the destructive anti-life force of modern organised religion in his verse, but he was also 'oriented by certain deep assumptions of Methodism or radical Protestantism'. In a sense, West asserts, Mount Zion Protestantism produced the powerful poet of nature. It gave him an inner certainty and wilfulness which are manifest in a preternatural knowledge of 'what nature and natural energy *really* are', and therefore what humanity must strive to emulate. Hughes's 'dramatically anti-human knowledge' is said to derive not just through Calvin or Knox or Zwingli, but from the same conditions of 'revelation, tragedy and interiorization' that characterise the Pietist tradition. Just as Saul, on the road to Damascus, became able to see only when blinded by light, so, West says, Hughes asserts a visionary's ability to see things unavailable to ordinary human eyes, which are conditioned to rely upon sensory impressions and empirical and deductive processes. Hughes can thus see 'the powers and motor forces of a Nature-God present invisibly both "out there" and "inside", in the mystery of the body itself'.[92]

HUGHES AND HEIDEGGER: CRAIG ROBINSON

While Tom Paulin uses Nietzsche's unhistorical animal and Protestant man of individual conscience for his model of the poet (see Chapter 5), Craig Robinson takes Heidegger's ideal of the poet as 'shepherd of Being' for his approach to Hughes's work.[93] Dissenting from the reading of Hughes's natural world as a critique of, and perhaps fantasy alternative to, a compromised world in which humankind combines the barbarity of murderous behaviour with the narrow cerebration of enlightenment rationalism and in which human behaviour is inevitably inferior to animal, Robinson finds optimism about the possibility of human development. His depiction of Hughes as a Heideggerian 'shepherd of Being' is the basis of an important and revealing reading not only of Hughes's nature poetry but also of his use of myth and, perhaps, the theory of language supporting the poetry.[94]

Robinson argues that though some 'detractors' gave Hughes a reputation for proposing the resignation of the mind's capacity for reason
in favour of 'unbridled licence for the instincts', Hughes was never
an anti-rationalist.[95] Rather, Hughes stood against 'the tyranny of a
diminished reason over the psyche, always seeking an augmentation,
harmonising and attunement of its faculties'. For Robinson, the 'battle
is not for or against reason', but 'over what the word reason should be
taken to include'. The example he takes is 'Tiger-Psalm' (*Earth-Numb*,
CP, pp. 201–3). Though later poems express a more complex view, he
finds in both this and earlier poems 'an espousal of a relatively simple
vitalism which prefers the physically durable to the cerebrally over-
complicated'. Even so, Robinson argues, Hughes sought in the human
world an equivalent of that which he admired in the animal, a sensitive 'attunement to the environment' which he felt had been lost 'in
the evasions, complacencies and proud posturings' of human society.

Hughes attacks the rigidly rationalist outlook, then, from his sense of
the 'blunting of sensitivity it has produced in excluding other aspects of
us from participation in a fuller being'.[96] His work attempts to 'bridge
the gap between an otter, "alert from tip to tail", and the human dispo-
sition so succinctly evoked in the image from the HITR poem "October
Dawn" of "A glass half full of wine left out/To the dark heaven all
night"' (*CP*, p. 37). Thus the poems' characteristic movement is from
'closure to openness, from the rigid to the flexible, from the merely
human to the fully human'. For Robinson, this makes Hughes like Carl
Jung, 'whose writings are frequently concerned with a pattern of development which proceeds by means of the death of a dry, rigid, one-sided
and closed ego and an irrigation by the contents of the unconscious in
a process of imaginative amplification, until the psyche bears the fruit
of a new, balanced and flexible self'.

Jung's belief in the health-bringing capacity of the artistic imagination was shared by Martin Heidegger, whose work, Robinson suggests,
may have been similarly important in the development of Hughes's
vision of humanity and nature, and particularly in furnishing
that vision with a particular concept of 'Being'. Robinson acknowledges that he knows of no evidence that Hughes was familiar with
Heidegger's writing, and that there are many areas, particularly of
politics, in which there is dissonance between the work of the two.[97]
Heidegger's work, however, may provide a vocabulary which could
make possible the explication of Hughes's meanings and suggest their
implications and unity, in a way that Jung alone cannot. The elements
of Hughes's beliefs, priorities and aims for which Heidegger's work
could provide tools for the commentator are

■ the sense of the role of the poet, the confrontation with death, the critique of science and technology, the deprecation of television, the attack on the Socratic heritage, the recurrence of a goddess who is triple in a new sense (having natural, religious and human aspects), the respect for Heraclitus and for myth.[98] □

Robinson finds both Heidegger and Hughes 'incorrigibly optimistic'.[99] This optimism has two forms, 'their belief that error is the source of salvation, and that Nothing is a positive; and, second, in the nature of their key terms'. The key term Being is for both 'the ultimate foundation, the deepest layer of reality, it encompasses and underpins even all deviations from itself and can never be defeated by rational-technological thinking'. Hughes's view of cultural history reflects this optimism partly in 'the master time-scale' of *RE*, partly in the 'hope of a reversal of the seventeenth-century dissociation of sensibility and descent towards the wasteland' which he suggests *CB* encourages, as in Heidegger it is reflected in the concept of 'the Turn, a grand reversal of our long drift from being, initiated now in the attempt at making a new era propitious for the return of the god'. Robinson suggests that perhaps a work of art must always have this kind of optimism, and cites the appeal to 'Children of the Future Age' of William Blake's 'A Little Girl Lost' (from *Songs of Experience* (1794)), which he sees as exemplifying Heidegger's 'truth ... thrown toward the coming preservers'. Heidegger's 'indictment of contemporary error is made in the sure hope that things were not and will not always be thus', and for Robinson, Hughes, who he says has 'often enough been portrayed as a dark pessimist, shares this faith'.[100]

THE VITALITY OF CREATIVE–DESTRUCTIVE NATURE: GIFFORD AND ROBERTS

How the optimism that Robinson finds in Hughes's work might be present in the depictions of violence is discussed to an extent by Gifford and Roberts, who suggest that Hughes associates the term with 'vehement activity' and who prefer the terms 'vitality' or 'energies'.[101] They find that the themes which predominate in almost all of Hughes's work are 'the sustained attempt of the conscious mind to articulate the continuities between the human self and the animal world; and an exploration of the creative-destructive nature of the material reality on which all life is founded'.[102] Though the themes are constant, the artistic strategies for exploring them change. In *G*, *C* and *CB*, Hughes

finds a new use of myth to explore the subterranean world, and relations between the animal self and the rest of the natural world which
perhaps reflects 'a sense that the poet has reached the limit of what he
can do with the short lyric poem focused on a particular animal'.[103]

Gifford and Roberts also consider a fundamental question about
Hughes's work, the extent to which he is a religious poet, and whether
his work implies the existence of a 'reality other than our own' in which
there is a source of divine power.[104] Both this question and the question
of the alleged violence of Hughes's poetry are illuminated, the authors
state, by looking at Hughes's relation to Manichaeism. This, deriving
from the religion of Mani, which originated in Mesopotamia in the
third century AD, envisaged a war between 'spirit and matter, light
and darkness, good and evil' which explains 'the present mixed state
of things as the result of a partially successful assault by the darkness
on the light'. Gifford and Roberts explain that the duty of humanity is
to restore the separation, largely by ascetic practices. A major figure in
its mythology is 'Primaeval Man, a warrior of the forces of light' (they
quote from Geo Widengren, *Mani and Manichaeism*, 1965, pp. 49–50):

■ who clad himself in his armour and set forth to do battle with the
cohorts of matter, of darkness, of evil. The armour consisted of his five
light elements and in sum they constituted not merely his armour but his
own being, his proper 'self', his 'soul'.[105] □

The authors note that Hughes has used the figure of the knight in 'Gog'
(*W, CP*, pp. 161–4) and 'The Knight' (*CB, CP*, pp. 426–7). They find
that 'The Knight' has the 'solemn and reverential tone of a devotional
poem', but that it would be difficult to see it as religious in the usually
accepted sense. It is, however, 'just this combination of religious awe
and surrender with a refusal to look beyond the processes of material
nature that constitutes the distinctive heart of Hughes's vision'.[106]

The authors summarise the theme of Part 1 of *Orghast* as 'the crime
against material nature, the Creatress, source of life and light, by the
Violator, the mental tyrant Holdfast, and her revenge'. The central
perception is relevant beyond *Orghast*. This is that 'the world of spirit
and the material world are the same; that the reality "beyond" our life
whose beckoning prompts religious devotion and theology is that of
material objects and processes, of which we are objectively a part but
feel ourselves to be in some way outside'. For Gifford and Roberts, this
is not a negation of the search for a religious dimension but, on the
contrary, its only possible complete satisfaction: 'the state of oneness
that the great religions in their various ways posit as their *telos* is the

recognition of a literal truth, but the religious sense is always at the mercy of "the mental tyrant Holdfast" and his armed warrior'.[107]

Gifford and Roberts find a parallel to this perception in Mircea Eliade's interpretation of primitive religion, which can also give a clue to the nature of Hughes's own interest in anthropology and the primitive: 'The hardness, ruggedness and permanence of matter was in itself a hierophany in the religious consciousness of the primitive. And nothing was more direct and autonomous in the completeness of its strength, nothing more noble or more awe-inspiring, than a majestic rock, or a boldly-standing block of granite. Above all, stone *is*.'[108]

Just as 'the great religions are drama as well as dogma', so this central perception of Hughes's poetry cannot 'be held fast in any formulation', and Gifford and Roberts find in Hughes's poetry both horror at the material creation and protest against man's place in it.[109] For them, Hughes's work is not a series of statements but of 're-enacted encounters and adventures'. They note that this presence of horror and protest has led Peter Porter, for example, to see Hughes's work as itself Manichaean. Porter points out that the imaginative world of *C* makes a stark opposition between darkness and light, includes a battle between Crown and Stone, and has two Gods. Although the myth of 'God's nightmare' that underlies the book might seem to support this argument, Gifford and Roberts find it too simplistic. They argue, however, that this is mistaken, and that the character of the mythical world of *C* (and consequently of Hughes's whole imaginative world) could rather be clarified by comparison with two myths of the kind on which part of that imaginative world is based. They cite the pre-Christian version of the myth related in Joseph Campbell's *The Masks of God: Primitive Mythology* (1959–68).[110] In this myth, the Great Spirit commands a waterfowl to dive into the water and bring up earth and clay which the Great Spirit uses to create the land, and he blesses the bird. In the Christianised version of this myth, God challenges Satan, who dives into the water. Christ blesses the mud that Satan brings up, and creates a flat, smooth earth. Satan has concealed some of the mud, and out of this the mountains are made.[111]

Gifford and Roberts note that Joseph Campbell identifies the contrast between the innocence of the one version and the 'ethical dualism' of the other, which assigns creation of the 'rugged parts of nature to an evil creator'.[112] They summarise the section of *C* in which God has a nightmare about a voice and a hand which mock his creation and which he challenges to do better, at which point the nightmare 'plunges into matter and creates Crow'. They find that Hughes's version occupies a place between the two 'genuine' myths. The nightmare has a suggestion of 'the devil, of evil and mischief', and none of the innocence of the pre-Christian version. The ethical dualism of the Christianised version is broken down; God is shown as 'fallible and impotent' and 'incapable of breathing life into his own creatures'; the thing created by the nightmare, Crow, is capable of both good and evil. This means that the reader is given 'room to manoeuvre and judge'.

WODWO: BLAKE MORRISON

Blake Morrison recalls that it is often said, 'disparagingly, that Hughes can't do people. But he does, with great authority, the trials people have to face – including the threat of death, and the threat of being bored to death'.[113] Even if 'people didn't loom as large as they might in his work, a certain under-populatedness is apt for evoking the area where he grew up, which had been more populous once, before the mills closed and the jobs went'.

With characteristic frankness, Morrison admits to having misjudged Hughes's poetry for a number of years. He writes that in thrall 'to Alvarez, and his thesis of romantic risk and agony, I saw Hughes as a misanthrope whose sense of life as stony waste and animal horror had been compounded by the suicide of his wife. The humour, stoicism, loving detail – these I hardly saw at all.'[114] Even so, 'wildly' though Morrison misread the work, *W* made a deep impression on him, and he asserts that it marks the point when Hughes found his mature voice. Innocent of the characteristics of modern humanity, a new-made creature, the wodwo has no frame of reference; it does not know what anything is, what things are for, how it should interact with them, but it does know that it is. For Morrison, the human aspect of the wodwo is its intelligence and its self-consciousness; it tries to understand 'why it does what it does even while doing it'.[115] Morrison compares the effect of reading the wodwo's untainted observations with the effect of William Golding's defamiliarisation in *The Inheritors* (1955). The difference is that 'Wodwo' is not a puzzle whose answer can be divined; the wodwo's nature remains a mystery.[116]

The wodwo shares the problem of all defamiliarising vehicles of animal, alien or pre-human kind. It asks itself about the things it does, the things it thinks, the concepts it employs (invents, like Adam?) and the, for the wodwo, nameless things it encounters, but employs human concepts and words ('What am I?'; 'What am I doing ... ?'; 'Do these weeds/know me ...?') to show us that it lacks those concepts and words ('Wodwo' (*W, CP*, p. 183). Though it is impossible to convey the prelinguistic or thought-without-words in language, or, language being a social construct, to depict the first and only speaker, Hughes has still managed to convey a sense of the wodwo's movement, through time, through the trees, through the world; not precisely questing, for he has no object, but looking for something to look for, like a dog snuffling through a wood. It is a powerfully arresting and haunting poem. Morrison suggests that Hughes found a new freedom in these poems, a freedom which was partly stylistic, shown in both the verse form and the syntax: the loose blank verse with its 'minimal punctuation, enjambement, lower-case line beginnings', and the syntactical ambiguity which blurs the ending of one sentence and the beginning of another.[117] These features are appropriate in that they express the wodwo's uncertainty about the limits of its own self. In contrast to the creatures in *THITR* and *L*, '[w]hether hawks roosting or pike stunned by their own grandeur', which are 'violent, imperious, in control', Morrison finds that 'Wodwo' represents a humble and chastened creature. Instead of confident end-stops 'Wodwo' offers tentative questions; rather than 'assertions of authority' there are 'confessions of ignorance'.[118]

Morrison notes that some readers who are looking for 'easy, autobiographical readings' skip *W* in favour of *C*, and find in the 'cartoon violence and blackness' of that collection a representation of Hughes's life in turmoil. The title poem of *W*, however, contains a more 'subtly personal subtext'. For Morrison, whereas the insights into the darker side of nature found in Hughes's early poems can be 'thrilling but also easy and callow', by the time he wrote *W*, having lived in darkness, the poet has lost his 'youthful swagger'. The earlier poems assert that he has looked and seen and has the key, but the later poems say that he has 'looked, and seen, but is no longer sure how to describe what he has found'.[119]

Far from knowing all the answers, Morrison says, the Hughes of *W* treats poetry as a form of quest. '"I'll go on looking" means: To be continued. There is no full stop. It also implies a curiosity and perseverance, which we meet again in the irrepressible crow of *Crow*.' Morrison asserts that however hard the knocks, and however yawning the chasms, Hughes's hero never abandons his quest. 'You don't give up. You go on looking. It's the tale of a wodwo, but it's also the story of Ted Hughes.'[120]

W, although in three sections, one of which is composed of short stories, is described by its author as a single adventure,[121] and constitutes a single narrative, a shamanic journey, in which animals are encountered, but in ways other than those of *THITR* and *L*. *W* thus bridges the early collections of nature poetry and the poetic sequences and linked collections, responses to which are considered in Chapter 3.

CHAPTER THREE

The Sequences

The middle phase of Hughes's poetic career was in part characterised by a movement from external phenomenological reality to internal and metaphysical landscapes in themed collections and sequences. Animals do not disappear from the poems, but they are increasingly less observed object and more protagonist. The Crow poems and *CB* feature figures which are and are not simply birds. These were not Hughes's only modes of writing during this period; the *M* poems, for example, are firmly located in the daily life of a farm, and Hughes continued to write for children and to produce translation and adaptation.

A number of writers have discussed the influence on Hughes's poetry of the work of eastern European poets. In his article in Keith Sagar's *The Achievement of Ted Hughes* (1983), Michael Parker sees the 'brave experimentation', 'drive towards an ur-language' and the 'compassion and humility' which pervade the work of Vasco Popa, Zbigniew Herbert and Miroslav Holub as having helped Hughes to lift himself out of the abyss into which he had been hurled in 1963 and 1969.[1] Hughes's poems, Parker argues, particularly in *W* and *C*, owe much to those poets in their exposure of 'the blackest, innermost recesses of Man's being' and their questioning of the way endless, purposeless suffering seems to be ordained by the metaphysical structure of the universe.

HUGHES'S CRITIQUE OF HUMANITY: NEIL CORCORAN

Neil Corcoran sees Hughes as among the poets of 'post-war European catastrophe', faced with the 'two realities' most formative of modern historical consciousness and conscience: the Nazi concentration camps and the atomic bomb.[2] He argues that inherited memory of, and implication within, specifically European catastrophes may be the originating impulse behind Hughes's involvement with modern European poets such as János Pilinszky and Vasko Popa. Though he lived through the Second World War, Hughes's imagination, Corcoran says, was haunted by the First World War, in which his father fought, and which does duty for the rest of the horrors of the twentieth century.

Corcoran argues that violence in Hughes's poetry is displaced on to the animal in order to criticise the human world, and is a manifestation of Hughes's 'apparent admiration of the energy of animal instinctual violence as an alternative to what he appears to read as a debased contemporary culture'.[3] For Corcoran, Hughes's writing has a quality of 'hard pathos', which derives from 'the way Hughes's celebration *of* natural vitality is crossed with his appalled, fascinated, occasionally apparently near-fetishistic sense of mortality'. In some of Hughes's poems the evocation of natural energy or effort has a kind of desperation, an 'anguished acknowledgement' that the present moment cannot survive for long, no matter how intense it might be. This makes it notable that elegy, especially in *W* and *M*, is 'a generic constant' in Hughes's work. Corcoran finds this quality in 'The Rat's Dance' ('Song of a Rat', *W*, *CP*, pp. 169–70), which, unbearably, 'evokes *a rat* caught and dying in a trap, and dying against everything in his nature ... until "The rat understands suddenly. It bows and is still,/With a little beseeching of blood on its nose-end"' (*NSP*, p. 176). Corcoran sees in these lines one of Hughes's characteristic procedures on display: 'unexpected anthropomorphisms' which give a human pathos to the death of the rat. The animal '"understands", in a word which, suddenly, alarmingly transforms an effort of instinct into an apparent effort of will or moral intelligence, just as the phrase "beseeching of blood" appears to give the rat a power of prayer to this force stronger than itself'.[4]

Corcoran finds two characteristic forms in Hughes's poetry: the critique of humanity and human intellect through animal poetry (seen in Chapters 1 and 2) and the sequence with mythical or metaphysical significance which, Corcoran suggests, could have been encouraged by Vasko Popa's long poem-cycles, *Earth Erect* and *Wolf Salt*. On these latter sequences, Corcoran asserts, Hughes's reputation is justly based. He finds a large ambition in *W*, *C* and *CB*. In these, human meaning is speculatively metaphysical, and assumes an expression which is theological or is parodic of theological expression, and the speculations are supported by the 'driven, wild eloquence' of Hughes's contemporary prose and interviews.[5]

Corcoran notes that this kind of visionary poetry can seen as rather 'late in time', speculating that the work of Hughes's middle period might be the last appearance in English of that kind of vatic poetry, and noting that unlike Blake or Yeats, Hughes did not codify the visionary intimations of his longer poems and sequences into a coherent system.

The close of the *CB* poems in this view acknowledges that there can be no grand finale or closure, since 'At the end of the ritual/up comes a goblin'; another possible myth-cycle.[6]

THE IMPACT OF *CROW*

The impact of *C*, the collection which in some ways heralded the beginning of Hughes's sequences of fully unified narratives, can be judged from the diversity of critical response, particularly during the 1970s. Roy Fuller finds it strange that 'so few critics would think it right to deal with the pathological violence of its language, its anti-human ideas, its sadistic imagery', when 'moral judgement' should have been paramount. Fuller judges that Hughes is prepared to say farewell to the civilisation which gave rise to such forms of judgements, and has 'succumbed (as Nietzsche and Spengler succumbed) to the fallacy that the worse the age the more men must adapt to it'.[7]

Conversely, in the same year, J.M. Newton, who had deplored *THITR*, rescinds his earlier opinion of Hughes's work in 'Some Notes on *Crow*'.[8] Newton discovers that in *C* Hughes's voice sounds more clearly than ever and finds that 'there are now fewer and fewer poems in his earlier volumes that I want to reject as simply as in the past I'm afraid I have'.[9] Newton writes that his breath is taken away not by the power of the poems, but the power in the poems; their source. The poet does not seem to be present, making any kind of fuss or effort, and 'certainly isn't having to grit his teeth' for the poems to become as 'hard and relentless as they are'. Rather than accusing Hughes of delighting in violence or cruelty, Newton argues that the ferocity is not the poet's; Hughes remains 'whole and sensitive and impassive' so that the subject appears 'as the nature of things, the zest of life itself'.[10]

Newton deals with the problem of the identity and significance of the central figure of *C* by saying that it is less important to ask who Crow is than to listen to the crow-voice and the crow-music.[11] That voice is matter-of-fact, colloquial, harsh and abrupt, 'but level, almost toneless, only in that way humorous or fierce'. That music is 'music-by-pauses, and the rhythm of thought'. The most likely mistakes to be made in reading *C* are allowing the simplicity of the syntax to draw us into reading too fast, so that we do not observe the pauses properly, or reading too reverently and slowly so that the sound ceases to be bluntly energetic enough. The former can cause a misapprehension, that the strong shaping of the poems towards epiphanic moments is all-important, whereas the climaxes of the poems are not their only truths or surprises.[12]

Hughes's critique of humanity and human intellect in both the early animal poems and in *C* is itself criticised by David Holbrook in 1977. Holbrook sees Alvarez's advocacy as disastrous for Hughes's development because it urged Hughes towards 'false solutions of hate' and destroyed 'belief in poetry'.[13] The word 'vitalist' applied to Hughes's poetry, Holbrook says, suggests that Hughes tells us something philosophically profound about life, nature and creatures, and there is in 'Thrushes' (*L, CP,* pp. 82–3) a 'natural philosophizing'. Initially, the poem is 'a genuine response to the natural savagery of the bird', but as it proceeds, vague philosophising and forms of moralising take over, dominated by a philosophical biology. These, Holbrook argues, belong to an orthodoxy of 'unmodified natural scepticism' and lame philosophy couched in clumsy and awkward language. Hughes's poetry represents the futility of lost meaning in the world, but the solution it offers is false: 'the dynamics of hate that go with a schizoid response to a schizoid world'.[14] Holbrook defines 'the schizoid problem' as weakness of identity, of 'emptiness and meaninglessness'. The schizoid individual has not experienced love from his mother, so feels a vacancy of identity or feels himself to be a mechanism. He concludes that it is wrong to love because it is dangerous, and so it is better to live by hate, and get some pleasure from that.[15] Holbrook sees this futility in *C*.

In *C*, sexual relations 'are reduced to grotesque acts of meaningless violence, in which every word is exploited for the juice of repulsiveness, or hate, which it can yield'. Holbrook finds that 'primitive schizoid fears of mutual incorporation are evoked', which means that 'under the "excuse" of a reference to the nuclear bomb, there can be an "acting out" indulgence in a primitive vision of the Primal Scene'.[16]

Viewing the criticism of the 1970s from the following decade, Leonard M. Scigaj, *in The Poetry of Ted Hughes: Form and Imagination* (1986),[17] finds the work of critics such as Holbrook, Calvin Bedient and Ian Hamilton, which neglects 'the heart of Hughes's poetry' in favour of its diction and 'a narrow referentiality', fruitless.[18] He suggests that these found *C* exasperating in spite of its 'finely wrought and very purposive formal organization', because they were, 'metaphorically speaking, attempting to evaluate the school of John Donne with critical precepts derived from the school of Ben Jonson'. He adds that the results of this misapplication were 'too often severely limited and irrelevant'.

These difficulties notwithstanding, *C* was chosen by John Carey as one of his books of the century.[19] Seamus Heaney finds Hughes modulating his vital, loud, epic voice into a lyric strain even in the violence of *C*, and sees 'Littleblood' (*C, CP,* p. 258), the last song Crow sings, as the most tender of the poems, and prophetic of Sagar's vision of Hughes's progression from 'the river of blood' to the 'river of light'.[20] (See below, pp. 80–7.) For Heaney, reading 'Littleblood' after the 'Bessemer glare' of the rest of *C* 'is like being exposed to some kind of healing ray'. Like 'eating the medical earth' and finding in it at least 'a memory of its pre-atomic-age goodness'. Heaney relates this to the way Hughes would read the poem, with 'particular delicacy and intensity', articulating 'the *t* of "eating" and the *d* and hard *c* of "medical" so finely and distinctly they were like the small twig-bones of a bird's skeleton, a robin's, say'.[21] Whilst Heaney notes that the poem is clearly set 'in the aftermath of traumatic, even cataclysmic events' when 'the reapers of the whirlwind have prayed for the mountains to fall upon them', and they are now '"hiding from the mountains in the mountains"', there is something stirring 'in the eyehole of a cow's skull, a kind of post-nuclear fledgling, something as frail as the second coming of pity, that "naked new-born babe/Striding the blast"'. This is an image from Macbeth (1.6.21) which Hughes reads, in *Shakespeare and the Goddess of Complete Being*, as 'proleptic of "a new kind of agonizing transformation"'.

Heaney sees this transformation as characterised by Hughes as a 'shift in the plane of understanding from the tragic to the transcendental', and writes that he has always tended to read 'Littleblood' as an instance of just that kind of transition. He suggests that, at the last moment, 'grace has entered into the crow-cursed universe and a voice that had hitherto been as obsessive and self-flagellating as the Ancient Mariner's suddenly finds that it can pray'. Littleblood is granted a 'little moment of epiphany, sitting on the poet's finger, singing in his ear, singing the song of both omen and amen'.[22]

GAUDETE AND AFTER: NON-REALIST MODES: TERRY EAGLETON AND KEITH SAGAR

G is mentioned in a number of later full-length studies of Hughes's work discussed in this chapter, usually as exemplifying the evolution of a philosophical or spiritual underpinning to Hughes's writing, following that of *C*, and Hughes's definitive break with realist modes. In 1977, however, in a review of new poetry for *Stand*, Terry Eagleton doubts that this break has been made. Whilst not diminishing the ambitiousness of *G* as an experiment with 'open forms'; an experiment with undoubted, if sporadic power, Eagleton finds that the poem's language fails in self-reflexivity.[23] Failing to 'take the measure of its own limits and capabilities', the language is locked into the 'bursting fullness of its presence', and a sometimes 'tyrannically controlling' mode of speech is in authority, which makes G closer to conventional realism than to non-realist modes. Eagleton quotes from 'A stag' to 'spray and limbs', and notes that though these are not the most distinguished of G's lines, they are symptomatic. He finds that the complex articulations of language have been sacrificed to the 'discrete immediacies' of visually organised images which are 'marooned in their own space'.

For Eagleton, the breakdown of conventional linear causality is not progressive if the result is nothing more than a 'staccato set of "suggestive" juxtapositions'. Although Hughes's subject is non-realist, the stance of the writing and the lack of any doubling or real 'interplay of writing forms' means that the poem remains in the 'realist problematic'. Eagleton asserts that the language of G fails to assume an attitude towards but is positioned laconically outside the events it describes, 'mirroring rather than constructing'. In spite of his experimentation, therefore, Hughes is 'one of the most characteristically English of poets'.

Sagar finds that many of the best poems in RE celebrate the recognition, an exhilarating one, that out of the uncompromising materials of the post-industrial landscapes of the Calder Valley described in the poems: 'this graveyard, this vacancy of scruffy hills and stagnant pools and bone-chilling winds', the place 'continually renews life and makes miracles'.[24] At the end of the same essay, Sagar seems to suggest that Hughes's depiction of the reclaiming of the landscape, cleansed of the works of humankind, by nature, is not a prelude to the triumph of nature and eradication of humanity, but to the return of humanity, properly humbled and redirected, to an interaction with nature.[25]

This vision, for Sagar, fulfils the business of a poet, which is to effect subtle changes in the consciousness of his readers, or at least the most responsive readers, not necessarily instantly, but 'poem by poem, book by book'. Those changes will be towards 'a more whole and balanced sense of themselves and of their dependence on and obligation towards all that is not themselves'. The great poet has to do yet more: 'He will have to save himself, cure himself, in the role of Everyman', and his imagining and poetry are themselves part of the process, not merely a record of it. 'The right metaphors are simply those which work, which actually do carry out the operation, or the required stage of it.'[26] Though insisting that the poet 'must recognise that he is not in the business of initiating a revolution or peddling propaganda', Sagar squarely locates the poet's function within that of the priest and visionary, or healer.

The introduction to the essays collected in *The Challenge of Ted Hughes* (1994), developing the point raised by Scigaj,[27] describes the different ways in which Hughes's work challenges the reader; positively, in containing great, though deeply embedded, gifts; problematically in that it is difficult. Sagar also stresses the importance of reading the whole of Hughes's *oeuvre*, not only the shorter poems. For Sagar, a problem for readers is that when Hughes's imagination 'is at full stretch' he 'tends towards works on an almost epic scale'.[28] These works 'are rarely completed according to the original conception, but end up concentrated into sequences of poems which relate closely to each other, clarify, support and enrich each other, develop out of each other, or fight each other to the death'. Often, the published form of the work is 'merely the tip of an iceberg', which means that the reader must infer the 'narrative or dramatic or thematic context', and 'each sequence is in turn part of a dramatically developing oeuvre, a poetic quest'. This in turn means that 'though the anthology poems reveal a gifted and powerful poet, only the reader who has read the complete works is really in a position to recognise the magnitude of the achievement'.[29] This become crucial to Sagar's analysis of the sequences in his later work. (See below, pp. 80–7.)

Like Scigaj, Sagar suggests that standard critical equipment is insufficient for readings of Hughes's work. The linguistic simplicity does not repay anatomisation in the style of the New Critics by verbal texture rich in literary tropes or 'those other tricks the critic is trained to put his finger on'. Hughes cannot be judged by the usual criteria. 'Even the coordinates provided by an enlightened literary education are inadequate, and may be even worse, since they pretend to be on the same scale. Hence the failure of so many of our most respected Establishment critics to respond adequately to Hughes.' For Sagar, the poems are 'sources of great psychic or spiritual power if we can tap them', but in order to do so, we need to grapple with a redefinition of the poetry and of art.

HUGHES'S REIMAGINED MYTHS: GRAHAM BRADSHAW

Graham Bradshaw, in an important essay on 'Creative Mythology in *Cave Birds*' in Sagar's *Achievement of Ted Hughes*, analyses at length the importance in Hughes's work of myth both recorded and newly re/imagined. Bradshaw asks: if we were to accept that a figure analogous to the Great Goddess, or Robert Graves's White Goddess, figures in most mythologies, what questions would it answer or tell us about Hughes's work, and 'supposing that the Goddess is some kind of figuring forth of deep inner needs, what needs are satisfied by reading or writing a poem about her?'[30]

Taking for his example the falcon in 'The Risen' from *CB*, Bradshaw acknowledges that there is clearly some connection between the falcon and the Egyptian gods Horus and Osiris, but points out that it would be 'critically evasive' to identify the connection without specifying its significance. The special significance of the vulture and falcon to ancient Egyptians was in part the product of the Egyptian landscape, with its stark contrast between the lands of the Upper and the Lower Nile. The birds' significance as symbols is likely to be different for twentieth-century Westerners. Bradshaw posits the question of how far the Celtic raven or crow could be available for us, today, as an 'autochthonous Totem' (indigenous or primitive, from the Greek *autochthon*, sprung from the soil). He adds that readers who assume that some 'ready access to the Goddess is, happily and mysteriously, plumbed into the psyche' will find it more rather than less difficult to understand why Hughes's *G* moves to a 'painful crisis and conclusion'.[31]

Bradshaw affirms that the power and imaginative reality of Hughes's greatest poems depend on an 'achieved miracle of language within a rich cultural and literary tradition (which his work is also extending)' rather than on 'obscure mechanisms and psychic imprints, like the so-called innate releasing mechanism that tells birds what to eat or hide from, and where to fly when they migrate'. In making this assertion he does not denigrate the concept of the archetype, but points out that archetypes, for critical purposes, are elusive entities.[32]

Bradshaw admits that in practice a critic will want to mention the Goddess, for example, in tracing continuities within Hughes's work, as well as in indicating the range and human relevance of the work, and in understanding how the poetry reflects the poet's interest in mythology and folklore. He finds that Jungian exegesis of the work, however, encouraged by Hughes's emphasis on the shamanic role, tends to dissolve the distinction between archetypes and the achieved miracle of language to which he refers. He points out that the power and efficacy of the utterances of an Australian or Siberian shaman are not dependent on their literary qualities, whereas conversely the shamanic character that Hughes finds in T.S. Eliot's *Ash Wednesday* (1930) or Shakespeare's *Venus and Adonis* (1593) is thus dependent. Bradshaw further argues that since the role of the shaman is defined in relation to a specific body of communal beliefs, any analogy with what we regard as the Romantic poetic temperament will seem loosely metaphorical unless it is tied to Jungian assumptions. He asserts that *CB* could be interpreted in terms of a shamanic magic flight, dismemberment and reconstitution, but that reading would 'offer assumptions as explanations, shackle [the] poem to a tendentious, or at least controversial, analogy, and alienate at least as many readers as it excited'.[33]

Literary critics, Bradshaw argues, have certain responsibilities, which include not passively to accept the shaman as a symbol of a psychic integration lost to the industrialised West. Critics should ask practical questions, such as: 'Do we believe that shamans fly, or that their intestines turn to opal after death? What do we actually know about the incidence of neurosis and schizophrenia in primitive societies?' Bradshaw's own 'shorthand way' of making the point that Hughes's mythology is imaginative creation is to say that 'Crow's Undersong' (*C*, *CP*, p. 237) is not a functional invocation of a shaman, but 'a poetic evocation', therefore an imaginative creation which differs in both form and function from 'myths that are rooted in communal beliefs and in rituals on which the life of the community is thought to depend'. He finds the term 'creative mythology' ungainly but useful in implying important distinctions, giving the example of works such as Joyce's *Ulysses* (1922), Eliot's *The Waste Land* and Mann's *Joseph und seine Brüder* (1933–43), which themselves cannot be defined as myths but which treat mythic themes and mythic material. Bradshaw makes a further distinction between, for example, Classical Greek dramatists' treatments of Greek myth and versions of *Tristan* by Béroul, Thomas, Gottfried and Wagner. Though each one is an individual creation, the Greek myths were also 'communal and rooted in ritual'. In order for criticism to do justice to Hughes's achievement, Bradshaw argues, distinctions such as these must be pressed, since creative mythology is itself critical, and Hughes's creative mythology embodies a 'profoundly serious critique of Western culture and modern civilization'. Examples he offers are the 'ironically diagnostic opposition', in *C* and *G*, between the 'suppressed Goddess and the usurping God, or Logos' and the similarly critical contrast in *CB* between pre-Christian and post-Christian, and pre-Socratic and post-Socratic, modes of thought and feeling.[34] Hughes's criticism is more 'analytically diagnostic' and less dependent on inspiration than the analogy between poet and shaman would suggest. Bradshaw argues that it could be said that an important function of Hughes's creative mythology is 'to dramatize the lack of a sustaining communal myth'.

Bradshaw suggests that, like the cultural anthropologist Joseph Campbell, Hughes sees in the various world mythologies 'profoundly suggestive similarities' which together comprise a huge body of 'elemental lore' dating back to the earliest period of our recorded history. He traces the development of the quest for a common interpretative principle or Key to All Mythologies, and notes that there has been disagreement about whether agreed resemblances are the result of independent evolution or culture-spread. One might concede that there are similarities between myths from different cultures, but none-theless interpret the significance of those similarities in different ways, as would Freud, Jung or Lévi-Strauss. Having lost contact with the old myths, we have not found 'generally acceptable new myths' that can perform similar functions. Bradshaw sees Hughes, like Campbell, as attempting to diagnose something that is, in the view of both, an unprecedented crisis, a crisis 'manifested as a failure to render modern life spiritually significant'.[35]

Bradshaw notes the continuity between the central myth of *Orghast* and *CB*, but argues that simply reading *CB* through that myth would obscure or distort the significant developments in technique and subject matter that Hughes demonstrates in the later work. He finds that creative myth 'distinctly Blakean', pointing out that the 'mental tyrant' Holdfast sounds very like Blake's Urizen, a symbol of oppressive authority, just as the ineffectual but presumptuous and dangerous 'God' of *W* and *C* recalls Nobodaddy, Blake's version of the patriarchal God of Christianity. Bradshaw finds a more pertinent literary analogy, however, provided by D.H. Lawrence, at least in a diagnosis of Western civilisation and its discontents which is similar to that of Hughes.[36] In this view, Hughes's development can be characterised by seeing Lawrence's 'The Fox' (1922)[37] as prefiguring the early Hughes, and Hughes's later, mythologising, writing, as steadily reworking Lawrence's 'The Man Who Died' (1929).[38] Bradshaw explains that in Lawrence's late story, Christ survives crucifixion, realises the error and disabling effect of Christian attitudes to Nature and sexuality, and turns to the worship of the Mother Goddess. *CB* has 'a parallel return to Egypt and the mythological motifs of the pre-Christian, pre-Socratic "cultural cradle" of the Near East'.[39]

Bradshaw agrees with others that behind *C*, *Orghast* and *CB* is the history of a cultural crisis, a Fall entailing the suppression of the natural and animal world in humankind and the inception of Socratic and Christian philosophical abstraction and Manichaean binarisms. *Orghast*'s deposition of the Creatress by the Violator parallels the replacement of Anath, a mother-goddess, by Jehovah. Egyptian mythology includes the reuniting in a sacred marriage of the part of the self that can be reborn after death and the part that corresponds to the source of all life. 'The living Pharaoh is Horus the Falcon, son of Isis and Osiris, while the dead Pharaoh is Osiris, who fuses with the sun-god Re.' In *CB*, Bradshaw notes, that which survives of the protagonist returns to the source, which is the sun, and, after an alchemical Sacred Marriage, 'is reincarnated as Horus the Falcon, "The risen"'.[40]

Echoing Graves, Bradshaw writes of the disaster of the religions of the Near East (Sumer, Mesopotamia and Egypt) gradually becoming subject to the suppression of the Mother Goddess, with concomitant suppression of Nature and sexuality, and radical alteration of our apprehension of the world and our place in the world. This, he writes, was followed by the convergence of attempts, Socratic and Christian, to 'isolate dualistic, abstract conceptual principles of Good and Evil'. *C*, *Shakespeare and the Goddess of Complete Being*, and later poems about Shakespeare and England, show that Hughes represents these disasters as entering a new, 'peculiarly demented' stage during the Reformation and Counter-Reformation. Bradshaw notes that the effect of Socratic idealism is barely treated in Hughes's writing before *CB*. Hughes's attacks on 'hubristic and dualistic rationality', however, prepare the reader for the 'pointed allusions to Socrates in the poems concerned with the strutting cockerel ego'. He asserts that this relationship is clearly indicated by Baskin's title for the drawing that accompanies Hughes's poem 'The Accused', 'A Tumbled Socratic Cock' (*CB*, *CP*, p. 425).[41]

For Bradshaw, Hughes's diagnosis of the effects of Christian dualism is either implicit or explicit in all of his work, even in some of his writing for children. This includes *The Iron Man* and 'Gog', which, Bradshaw points out, 'correct' the legend of St. George, a legend that, as Hughes remarks in 'Myth and Education', is 'deeply suspect since it advocates "the complete suppression of the terror": "It is the symbolic story of Christianity. Christianity in suppressing the devil, in fact suppresses imagination and suppresses vital natural life."[42] Bradshaw finds a parallel between the error of St George and that of Crow in 'A Horrible Religious Error' (*C*, *CP*, p. 231). Both strike out at 'the womb-wall', 'the root-blood of the origins', 'the rocking sinking cradle' of the presumed dragon 'whose coil is under his ribs'.

For Bradshaw, the emergence of the 'creative myth' in *W* can suggest why *CB* has so many 'counter-images that evoke a pre-Christian, pre-Socratic era'. Idealistic isolation of abstract conceptual principles involved identifying Good with God as *Logos*. Bradshaw illustrates this representation of the binary in 'You Drive in a Circle', (*W*, *CP*, p. 177) and adds that necessarily, 'whatever is not God is the world, Evil, Satan, the serpent'. He notes that 'Logos' ends: 'God is a good fellow, but his mother's against Him' (*W*, *CP*, pp. 155–6) and that at the end of 'Reveille' (*W*, *CP*, p. 156) dispossessed Nature becomes the serpent that spreads over Creation.[43]

In 'Gog', Bradshaw finds, the arrogant and presumptuous cry of God: "I am Alpha and Omega", rouses nature to malevolent anger and creates and releases the problem of Evil (with, Bradshaw notes, the abstracting capital) that confronts Christians, since Christians are committed to the belief that God is both benevolent and omnipotent. Bradshaw argues that the pain and abundant horror filling creation must be seen as a privation, a withdrawal of God from material Nature, 'a tenuously metaphysical absence that actually corresponds to everything that is'. He concludes that one effect of the 'perversion of reality' is the isolation of humanity from the rest of creation, so that humanity becomes 'hybrid, straining to be released from the body of this death'.[44]

Ancient Egyptian religion, with its pantheon of half-animal, half-human gods, is thus representative of a prelapsarian state in which humanity was not divided from the rest of creation. Bradshaw notes that the motif of a man with the head of a bird is older even than the great civilisations of Egypt, and appears in the Lascaux cave art. In the innermost cave there is a picture of a man apparently wounded by the bison he has killed. The man has the head of a bird resembling the sacred Egyptian ibis, and has dropped something, which might be a shaman's stick, with a bird-head handle. Bradshaw observes that the figure has four digits on each hand, and notes that in other cave paintings are found pictures of hands with missing digits, perhaps indicative of an accepted sign of grief and bereavement. Baskin's illustration of 'After the First Fright' (*CB*, *CP*, p. 420) shows a hybrid bird-man. Bradshaw quotes from 'The disputation' to 'cross-shaped cut', and notes that to our civilisation cutting off one's fingers would not seem civilised or sane, and the Japanese ritual suicide of *hara-kiri* seems 'unspeakably alien' to Westerners, but that ritual comes from a culture that is far from primitive, and that we can understand the need to give inner anguish a concrete, physical reality.[45]

Going back to his question about the significance and usefulness of the Goddess myth in interpreting Hughes's poetry, Bradshaw cites 'After the First Fright' as illustrating 'the relativity of different cultural responses to the facts of existence'. For Hughes, as for Nietzsche, he adds, the question to put to mythology or religion is, 'how well does this help us to manage our lives – and, in this poem, to cope with that "stopping and starting Catherine wheel in my belly"?' He answers for Hughes that post-Socratic and post-Christian civilisation, rather than helping us, has suppressed the 'archaic sense of a morally ambivalent nature in which men could feel more truly at home'. *CB* explores the concomitant sense of displacement, in an original moving way which might direct the reader back to earlier poems with increased understanding.[46]

HUGHES AND BEING

Another view of Hughes's Goddess myth and his quest for unity, as well as a proposed insight into his sense of his function as a poet, are provided by Craig Robinson's readings of Hughes's poetry through Heidegger's *Poetry, Language, Thought* (1959/1971). Robinson aligns the work of Hughes with that of Heidegger, based on their shared high valuation of thought and language and thus of the poet.[47] For both Heidegger and Hughes, Robinson argues, language is not the linguist's closed system of interrelated but arbitrary signs, but 'an ever-closing, but openable path to Being, the reality of what is'. Language is 'ever-closing', in this view, as it falls from the true and original (poetic) into the representational, cliché-ridden chatter of those who 'have turned our backs on the call of Being'. *Poetry, Language, Thought* declares that 'everyday language is a forgotten and therefore used-up poem, from which there hardly resounds a call any more'.[48]

For Robinson, Hughes, like Heidegger himself, 'reconnects words with their roots, and with Being'. Sometimes he is 'simply reinvesting clichés with new feeling and conviction, sometimes taking an abstract word back to its physical basis (as he does with the word "abstract" itself in "A Disaster" (*C, CP*, pp. 226–7) and, more often ... through his music'. Hughes, Robinson notes, also harnesses the power of metaphor 'to make vital reconnections'; he 'argues for world unity by generating a sense of sameness within difference'.[49]

If Hughes shares Heidegger's important but elusive concept of Being, and the proposition that language is the precinct or house of Being, then for him, the poet has a vital function, as 'shepherd of Being'. Robinson quotes from Heidegger:

> ■ It is because language is the house of Being, that we reach what is by constantly going through this house ... all beings ... each in its own way, are *qua* beings in the precinct of language. This is why the return from the realm of objects and their representation into the innermost region of the heart's space can be accomplished, if anywhere, only in this precinct.[50] □

For Robinson, the poet who discharges this responsibility fulfils the most important task of the human, 'to achieve his essence, which is, as *The Question Concerning Technology* has it, "to be the one who waits, the one who attends upon the coming to, as the presence of Being in that in thinking he guards it"'. 'For Heidegger, the real poet is exceedingly rare; for Hughes, he is the better part of each of us.'[51]

Robinson reminds us that Being is Heidegger's most important and elusive concept, and though Heidegger strenuously defended this concept against assimilation with others, especially those of biology and psychology, it has 'noteworthy', but wider similarities to Hughes's goddesses. There are differences: Robinson sees the Goddess as 'coextensive with life', so that the 'inanimate is bereft of her', whereas Heidegger's Being encompasses all that is, both animate and inanimate. Further, though the divine is important to Heidegger, the feminine is less so. That he does call our attention to a goddess in Parmenides' 'On Nature' is, for Robinson, significant. Robinson notes that the pre-Socratics are important for Heidegger, 'for evincing a true openness to Being lost in post-Socratic thought', and argues that Hughes 'discovers something like this other, non-Classical Greece in Seneca's *Oedipus,* and offers a parallel valuation of the pre-Socratics in "Myth and Education"'. The goddess to which Robinson refers is Aletheia, Truth, which, he says, is the unconcealedness of Being. Being is present in beings only, but 'is not the same as any one or any group of them; when we apprehend a being we therefore do and do not apprehend Being, which remains hidden even in its unconcealedness'.[52] This is true of Hughes's goddess, who is present only in her creatures, but is not any single one or any group of them.

Robinson points out correspondences between the terms employed by Heidegger and Hughes in the representation of the path 'along which Being grows nearer'. That path is partly that of feeling and emotion, Heidegger's *Angst,* or in Hughes's word, 'pain', which breaks the characteristic mood of our usual divorce from Being. We are usually, in Heidegger's word, 'tranquillised', in Hughes's word, 'numb'.[53]

By feeling or emotion, Robinson explains, is meant not just fluctuations of temper, but 'the spectrum of deep persistent moods or dispositions each of which accompanies and underpins an understanding of the world'. Heidegger sees that the base mood underpinning the 'narrowly rational understanding', though only one of many possibilities, has become dominant for humanity because it is 'buttressed by systems of logic which claim probative force precisely by avoiding the questioning of their existential assumptions'. Hughes's career, Robinson argues, presents such a broad spectrum of moods and understandings; he re-licenses feelings and intuitions 'banned by the unwritten codes which dictate successful behaviour in the modern technological world' in order to give a 'renewed and broadened access to reality'.

Robinson describes his work as calling on Heidegger to help to define and place Hughes's 'creative attack on debased reason' or 'narrow rationalism'. He adds that the path of 'thought-with-feeling which runs through the poet's precinct of language towards Being' also runs via the 'unsettling confrontation with one's own death', and it is this which 'calls us from inauthenticity to authenticity, from exile from Being to its nearness'. Connecting the attack on narrow rationalism to the 'Jungian paradigm, with its ego-death', Robinson suggests that this needs to be set alongside *CB*, as the chief amongst many of Hughes's poems for which this confrontation is key.[54]

For Heidegger, 'the endlessly remade confrontation with death establishes the primacy of Being over ideas and theory, and reminds the individual that he is a Being-in-the-world, with responsibilities to that world, and not a separate unshatterable atom cut off by a defensive wall of opinion'. To make this apparent is to reverse the general trend of the modern world, with its 'fall from unity of man-and-world into the Socratic-Cartesian dualism of subject and object, man-set-over-against-world'. Robinson argues that Heidegger's concept of 'Enframing', the process of objectification and rationalism by which the world is reduced to a picture or representation in ideas, is central to Hughes's work because it is through our 'devotion to ideas that the world dwindles to a technologically exploitable resource and to what Heidegger calls the "standing reserve".'

> ■ As soon as what is unconcealed no longer concerns man even as object, but does so, rather, exclusively as standing reserve, and man in the midst of objectlessness is nothing but the orderer of the standing-reserve, then he comes to the very brink of a precipitous fall; that is, he comes to the point where he himself will have to be taken as standing-reserve. Meanwhile man, precisely as the one so threatened, exalts himself to the posture of lord of the earth.[55] □

This leads to the solipsistic illusion that all we encounter is our construct, which in turn leads to the delusion that man 'everywhere and always' encounters only himself, though in reality, man no longer encounters himself, that is, his essence.

In Robinson's interpretation of Heidegger, humankind has stepped out of the world '(leaving himself behind) so that he can turn back and look at it like a framed picture'. He cites Hughes's story in a talk on 'Myth and Education', of a photographer who photographed a tiger in the process of killing a woman. Robinson finds the photographer to be, for Hughes, the quintessence of Heidegger's Enframing rationalism; a monster detached from the human life inside him that would have felt empathy with and compassion for the woman.[56]

Robinson identifies the use of lensed optical equipment; binoculars, telescope and camera in *G*; as in the same interpretative context as this

Enframing, and that concept helps also to explain the barriers in early poems of Hughes's career such as the cage in 'Jaguar' and the water surface in 'Pike'. He characterises Hughes's attack on the 'excessively rational mind, on scientific-technological thinking and Cartesian dualism, on earth rape, and on psychological closure' as coming from a single and united body of thought.[57]

Robinson finds Heidegger and Hughes optimistic because both believe that error is the source of salvation, and that Nothing is a positive. Also, Being cannot be defeated by rational-technological thinking because it is the 'ultimate foundation, the deepest layer of reality, it encompasses and underpins even all deviations from itself'. Robinson finds abundant parallels in Hughes's work, including the second of the *Seven Dungeon Songs* (*Earth-Numb*, third section of *M*, *CP*, pp. 559–60) in the 'murderous male figure seen as a deviant part of the all-encompassing female; in the Goddess of *River* who "will wash herself of all deaths"; and in the unkillable female presence in "The Head" who walks, arms outstretched, towards the hunter's firing rifle'.

In addition to these parallels, Robinson finds a further use of Heidegger's work for Hughes's readers in his identification of that which is needed to counter the confident, assertive manner of the excessively rational. He points out that Heidegger speaks of 'a reticence, of the courage of submission, of a willingness to have one's thoughts overturned again and again, of reverence before Being (and the relationship of this to creativity), of a kindness which allows what is a lodging in the heart's space, and above all of questioning, as the piety of thought, the mode by which thinking becomes thanking, our way of repaying the world for existing'. Robinson finds many echoes of these in Hughes's writing, in particular, in a number of the major works, the last poems, as these move towards that questioning as the mode of mature thought.[58]

Hughes is said to open readers to Being through his 'music', that is, his prosody, so that the sound of Hughes's poetry has a healing property. Robinson sees Hughes's poetry driving towards simplification and a line which reveals 'the deepest music already latent in words' rather than adding poetic melody to the surface of those words. Robinson suggests that Hughes's aim can be seen in his discussion of the work of Emily Dickinson and John Crowe Ransom. Hughes identifies Dickinson's 'slow, small metre' which brings into close-up every syllable, whose resonances it liberates. He also identifies the way in which every word of John Crowe Ransom's line is physically connected to the way in which it is spoken, so that there is a solid total range of sensation in each word's pitch. Robinson finds those qualities in Hughes's readings of his own work, which in liberating the deepest resonances of a syllable do not take it back from meaning into pure sound, but do take it away from 'abstract, disembodied meaning to its roots in a visceral and gestural meaning'. Robinson attributes Hughes's favouring of heavy stress, monosyllables that make the reader pause, and large vowel sounds, to a desire to make every word 'bear its full weight of world'. Hughes's loosening and simplification of syntax, Robinson asserts, are Hughes's invitation to take to heart each element of a scene or action. Hughes's verbal music has its 'righting effect', through the forming of the sounds in our minds and bodies.[59]

HUGHES'S JOURNEY FROM 'WORLD OF BLOOD' TO 'WORLD OF LIGHT': KEITH SAGAR

Keith Sagar's thoughtful and thought-provoking discussion of Hughes's sequences in 'From World of Blood to World of Light' requires, but justifies, reading of his discussion of the subjects and themes in Hughes's earlier work. Sagar argues that though Hughes's work has a complex bibliographical history and passes through many different phases of subject, style and form, it is consistent and homogeneous in its aim and its broader theme, which Sagar sees as a journey from the 'world of blood' to the 'world of light'. Thus the whole of Hughes's *oeuvre* is in a sense a mythology and each poem is a chapter in a mythology whose plot, the mythic quest, seen retrospectively, is clear.[60] Sagar condensed Chapter Four of his *The Laughter of Foxes* (2000) into an essay for a collection of pieces, *Lire Ted Hughes: New Selected Poems 1957–1994*, edited by a leading French authority on Hughes's work, Joanny Moulin. The chapter is central to *The Laughter of Foxes* (Sagar's sixth book about Hughes) in that it sets out Sagar's thesis, and it offers an invaluable survey of Hughes's poetic career.

For Sagar, almost all of Hughes's poems from *THITR* to *R* are stages on a journey, both spiritual and poetic, which has had many setbacks and dead ends, and which eventually brought Hughes to the same world from which he started, but a world which no longer seems made of blood. As a result of that journey, 'with all its transfiguring pain' the world can be seen as made of light.[61]

In order to follow the mythic plot of Hughes's work in all its complexity, Sagar argues, it would be necessary to read all of the poems in the order in which they were written. Hughes's imagination, he asserts, needed a larger canvas than is usually afforded by lyric poetry, which is why he tended to arrange his poems in sequences, whether narrative or dramatic, as in *C*, *Prometheus on his Crag*, *CB*, *G* and *Adam and the Sacred Nine*. Even collections such as *M*, *RE* and *R*, which do not have an obvious narrative or dramatic organisation, 'add up to much more than the sum of their parts'. This is why, for Sagar, Hughes is not well served by selections or anthologising.[62]

Sagar suggests that Hughes inherited from T.S. Eliot and Dylan Thomas, two dominant and often opposed figures in the poetic canon when he was growing up, the belief that the poet was a deeply important, priestlike figure, and poetry a profoundly significant language with a spiritual function. He notes, however, that before Hughes had published his first work, Dylan Thomas had died (in 1953) and T.S. Eliot had ceased to write poetry, and that there was a strong reaction against both. Like many writers about Hughes's work, Sagar observes that Hughes was initially writing in an austere post-war climate when poetry could seem pretentious, and there were calls for it to be accessible to and about ordinary people. He quotes Kingsley Amis's 'Here is Where' as characteristic of the mockery levelled at the romantic–nature–poetry tradition 'from a rational-humanist perspective':

■ Why drag in
All that water and stone?
Scream the place down *here*,
There's nobody *there*. □

Sagar remarks that by 'here', the next stanza makes clear, Amis means 'in a room with his back to the closed window, engaging in a human relationship'.[63]

In a riposte to the attitude he finds in Amis and his contemporaries, Sagar quotes from a 1970 interview in which Hughes describes the *New Lines* poets as seeking domesticity while he 'was all for opening negotiations with whatever happened to be out there' (see above, p. 18). He continues by asserting that Hughes does look 'out there', and that by 'out there' Hughes means both the '"Great Outer Darkness" of the non-human world, and the deep inner darkness, the unknown within the human psyche, which [Hughes] calls "the mind's wandering elementals"'. This, Sagar argues, is very different from what is beyond Amis's pretty window-box. Sagar notes that in Hughes's 'Wind' (*THITR*, *CP*, pp. 36–7) the window is fragile, trembling to come in under intolerable pressure 'from a wind which would sweep away books, thoughts, normal human relationships, all sense of the security and centrality of selfhood; shatter the house itself, the carefully built structure of civilization with which we try to insulate ourselves against the energies without and within'. In this poem, he finds that Hughes 'brilliantly mimes the distorting and levelling power of a gale, seeking to find words, like those of the Border ballads, "that live in the same dimension as life at its most severe, words that cannot be outflanked by experience"'.[64]

Like Robinson, Sagar sees Hughes as having taken on the role of poet as quest-hero, who undergoes an ego-death on behalf of the race, who enters the unknown pitch dark 'where the animal runs', and who goes, at great risk and personal cost, to negotiate with what is 'out there'. His assessment of the implication of this role for the language and form of poetry differs from that of Robinson, though both suggest that the phonemes of Hughes's writing are themselves a signifying system. Sagar emphasises that Hughes's words do not distance or defuse, nor are they 'outflanked by' experience, but are inseparable from it. Hughes's words 'exist in the same dimension as water and stone, blood and death (a kind of language he found in the Border ballads)'. Sagar sees Hughes as struggling to be free from 'the maternal octopus of the English poetic tradition', and doing so by plundering Anglo-Saxon and dialect for words and rhythms. In this view, Hughes sets the alliterative tradition of Old English poetry against the 'Latinate politeness' of artificial society, and even transforms Latinate words, dragging them into the 'unruly, self-ruling world' of alliterative verse so that they seem to sound northern and Germanic.

For Sagar, the effects of Hughes's rhythms are visceral as well as onomatopoeic. Trochees are 'pummelling' and 'lead-weighted', spondees are 'bludgeoning'. The effect is 'mesmeric', it beats and roots out of us 'those once apparently safe underlying rhythms of rhetorical and philosophical discourse, mental scene-painting and nostalgic or evocative reflection, with which the iambic pentameter is so closely associated'. By asserting 'the naked, deeper rhythms' of the Germanic heritage of English, Hughes is taking the language 'back to its roots'.

Returning to 'Wind', Sagar notes that it is the very control of language that reinforces the 'world of order and ordinary' and keeps the wind out in this early poem. The verbal music is deployed to resolve the 'chaos and uproar of nature'. Conflating the 'I' of 'Wind' and the poet himself, Sagar asserts that this man 'who "cannot entertain book, thought,/Or each other", can still write a splendid poem' with finely crafted lines. Later poems, such as 'The Guide', however, no longer contain such 'verbal barricades'.[65] Taking *L* as his example, Sagar suggests that Hughes there 'strips away from the face of Nature the accumulated layers of cosiness and gentility and piety of the English tradition of nature writing, the preoccupation with beauty, the domestication of nature'. He finds that when the comfortable layers have been stripped away, Nature becomes terrifying. Hughes's 'painterly appreciation' of the colour and form of a water lily is 'undermined by an awareness of the horrors that nudge its root'; in describing a hawk, Hughes 'finds that he has conjured something indistinguishable from "Hitler's familiar spirit"'. If Nature is sought as a refuge from the turmoil of human history, the poet finds in Nature the same turmoil, but on a larger scale. 'Nature is "all one smouldering annihilation", unmaking and remaking, remaking in order to unmake again.' Thus, images of the horrors of world wars fuse with images of nature which will not communicate its meanings to the human observer and is therefore absurd ('Relic', *L*, *CP*, p. 78).[66]

Sagar sees Hughes's poems of the 1960s as overwhelmed by nature; the energies of nature no longer have to be invoked, they are here. Referring to 'Wind', he says that the window of that poem comes in and the wind sweeps away order and ordinary; 'terrible energies are released'. Those energies are too inhuman and overwhelming to be handled; they supplant the normal consciousness of the poet, strip him of defences and take him over. 'The "elemental power-circuit of the universe" jams through him, blowing every fuse.' The face Hughes now sees on 'his god or not-god' is Blake's dragon or serpent, 'the serpent as swallower of everything ("this is the dark intestine"), the dragon waiting with open mouth for the woman to deliver her child'. Sagar asks how such a god could be worshipped; how fragile creatures of flesh and blood could cope with such a world. The answer he gives is that negotiation was very one-sided.[67]

Hughes's negotiation with the elemental powers of nature required the abandonment of everything, 'of arrogance (the assumption of human centrality), complacency, rhetoric'. The early 1960s, in Sagar's view, were for Hughes 'a period of intense experimentation in search of a poetry able to find its way back beyond all preconceptions, to generate itself again as it were from a single cell, then to grope its way through that darkness without the map-grid of imposed form or the flash-light of rationality which would have scared away all its creatures'. In this experimentation, 'Wodwo' was a significant breakthrough, a departure from the bludgeoning of the earlier poems. This came partly from the choice of the persona of the poem, a 'little larval being' exposed and tentative but with 'human intelligence and curiosity', and the human temptation simply to appropriate whatever it encounters, but mainly from Hughes's having found the voice of this creature. 'Wodwo' has been stripped of 'poetic effects': rhetoric, rhymes, stanzas, grammar, punctuation. With them, Sagar asserts, has gone 'the imposition of personality which those techniques had largely served', so that what remains is 'a very free verse, close to collo-quial prose, flexible, responsive at every moment to the demands of the sense and to nothing else'. Language is distilled to a functional mini-mum 'from which, like the wodwo itself, it is now free to move out into new, less manipulative forms of expression'. Sagar quotes Hughes: 'The nearest we can come to rational thinking is to stand respectfully, hat in hand, before this Creation, exceedingly alert for a new word', and cites as a product of this new freedom the poem 'Full Moon and Little Frieda' (*W, CP*, pp. 182–3).[68]

Hughes's further development in the direction of light was arrested, however, Sagar writes, by events which plunged him back into dark-ness, and poems such as 'The Howling of Wolves' (*W, CP*, p. 180) and 'Song of a Rat' record a vision more bleak than ever, compounded with a 'more personal agony'. Nature, celebrated in later poems as 'an illim-itable abundance of life and plenitude of spirit', is in poems such as 'Stations' (*W, CP*, pp. 158–9), a repetition of suffering and loss, 'one "doomed bid" after another, within a total absence, without mean-ing or purpose'. Significantly, however, Hughes did not give up. Sagar quotes from a 1996 interview in which Hughes stated that every work of art stems from a wound in the artist's soul, and compared art to the self-healing process of the immune system. As the psychological component of the auto-immune system that 'gives expression to the healing process, the work of art makes us feel good'. '"There are artists who concentrate on expressing the damage, the blood, the mangled bones, the explosion of pain, in order to rouse and shock the reader. And there are those who hardly mention the circumstances of the wound, they are concerned with the cure."'[69] Sagar reads the Crow poems as an attempt to do both at once.

The process of turning pain into cure, for Sagar, involves a recogni-tion that many of the appalling horrors we see in nature are projec-tions from 'our own distorted, corrupted psyches'. He notes that *C* as published is the equivalent of the first three acts of a five-act play, but that the last two acts of that play were sketched but not completed. Crow's quest, he writes, begins as a search for his creator, becomes a quest for his victim, and then becomes a quest for Crow's own reborn, corrected self. Initially, Crow fights the Blakean serpent/dragon ener-gies before coming into the 'right relation with the female, who is also Nature and his own true demon'. As with other quest narratives, the first two-thirds are composed of 'terrible happenings and "torments of spirit"', the purpose being to demonstrate that this suffering can be the ground of growth. The poems that we have show Crow suffering terribly for his mistakes, his 'mutually destructive encounters with the

Energies, his ego-death, his first glimmerings of conscience, his first tentative steps towards reconstituting himself and reinterpreting the world, with the help of his Eskimo guide'. Sagar writes that his 'errant quest', which constitutes a 'blind fear of the female', and failure 'to locate the Black Beast within himself', was, however, following adventures in which Crow would be 'dismembered and reconstituted', to have culminated in 'a painful reintegration and a shamanic initiation ordeal'. Crow's quest, Sagar asserts, is ultimately the same as that of Hughes, 'to achieve fourfold vision and thereby become fully a man, reborn into a redeemed world of joy'. As before, when Hughes was on this journey upward toward light, Sagar reminds us, he was 'knocked back into the pit' by another personal tragedy, a tragedy which made the 'personal affirmation' of the conclusion of his quest impossible, so that the story of Crow was abandoned.[70]

Sagar asserts that is at this point that myth, initially that of Prometheus (in *Orghast* and *Prometheus on his Crag*), becomes crucial for Hughes's work, releasing him from silence and stasis. His extension of *Five Autumn Songs* (1968) into a set of poems on the seasons served 'to ground his vision once more in the substantial, phenomenal world'. Sagar concludes that while Hughes's eyes had been focused on 'the Needle of Elbruz or the furthest stars', he had neglected 'the mundane miracles under his feet'. This refocusing enabled Hughes, in *Season Songs*, to show readers things that we might see every year, but which we take for granted or miss, unlike Hughes, who writes as though he were the only one of us 'really awake'. Sagar observes that the collection is neither sentimental nor escapist, but shows death as ever-present in nature. 'A fledgling swift suffers "the inevitable balsa death"' ('Swifts', *Season Songs, CP*, p. 315–16); foxes and stags are hunted; a pheasant hangs from a hook with its head in a bag ('The Seven Sorrows', *Season Songs, CP*, p. 330); a cranefly is dying slowly. The poet is a 'watching giant who "knows she cannot be helped in any way"' ('A Cranefly in September', *Season Songs, CP*, p. 332). Nonetheless, in these poems, death evokes compassion but does not cancel vitality.[71]

Sagar sees Hughes's life as a farmer as an attempt, whether conscious or unconscious, to correct the 'psychic imbalance' that had led to suppression of the right side of the brain, which, he says, 'preserves the bonds between nature and human nature', and the concomitant dominance of the left side, favouring 'intellect, analysis and abstraction'. This dominance had produced a feeling akin to that described by Robinson in terms of Heidegger's 'Enframing': 'the feeling of living in a state of Prometheus-like alienation from real things'. In the 'hard disciplines of stewardship and husbandry', Sagar writes, Hughes lost any aloofness from tangible realities.[72] Sagar acquiesces with Robinson's view that Moortown farm became, for Hughes, '"a working laboratory of co-operation between man and nature"'.[73] Sagar judges the poems that came out of this period of Hughes's working life as having a tighter grip on reality than any others known to him.

In Sagar's view, Hughes's renewed daily contact with the natural world revitalised and transformed his entire vision. He finds all of the poems of this period sacramental, and some of them visionary, but asserts that all are rooted in common everyday realities. In these poems details are observed, selected and rendered to reveal not the appearance of things but their inner workings and connections. Sagar finds, after the 'isolation and paralysis' of *Prometheus*, that all is now 'colour and variety, bustle and change, as the earth swings through its cycles on the poles of birth and death'.[74]

The transformation means that blood, rather than connoting pain and death, is associated with birth, through menstrual placental blood, and mud has become a marriage of earth and water. Thus Hughes was able to continue the quest abandoned in *C* through *CB*, this time as far as the planned reconciliation with the female. Sagar reads the poem 'Bride and Groom Lie Hidden for Three Days' (*CB*, *CP*, pp. 437–8) as not only a stage in the resurrection of the Crow/Cockerel/Falcon/Man, but also as the correct answer to a crucial question. In *C*, Crow was to have encountered a female being, an ogress, who was to question him as he carried her over a river. The seventh and last question that she was to have asked Crow was, 'Who gave most, him or her?' In this poem, Sagar sees the coming together of the broken hero and his former victim as 'with fearfulness and astonishment' they begin to reassemble each other.

Sagar finds that rivers are as significant for Crow's creator as for Crow. Just as the river crossed by Crow at the end of his quest is purifying and revitalising, so standing in a river, the 'distillation of sacred life', and hooking a fish releases Hughes's 'real self'. In this view, for Hughes every fishing trip is a kind of mythic quest, a search for the primeval self which reconnects to 'the divine influx'. In the river, Sagar writes, the 'human intruder' loses the sense of centrality and power as a lord of language, and even of identity, as the rivers wash this away. Sagar argues that in his early career, this would have been unthinkable for Hughes; the wind in 'Wind' represents a terrifying force which could loosen our grip on the self and the world; in poems such as 'The Gulkana' (*R*, *CP*, pp. 665–9), he embraces the loosening of that grip. After this experience, Sagar says, Hughes is a 'new and nameless' creature like a wodwo, 'no longer supposing itself to be the exact centre, no longer appropriating the most secret interiors of other creatures'.

Thereafter, to enter water is to be 'reconnected to the source, washed clean of the stain of blood', and 'readmitted to an unfallen world'.[75]

At the end of the mythic quest, the hero returns to the everyday world, and Sagar notes that after *R* Hughes returned to his home, the familiar themes. He writes again of wolf and hawk, but approached with a new poise and gentle unforced strength, and of family history and the First World War, with greater humility and humanity.[76]

Sagar's underlying thesis stays consistent into his 2009 *Ted Hughes and Nature: Terror and Exultation*. He notes that the first words of Hughes's first published book are 'I drown',[77] and that water and fishing in water remain central to the development of his work and his self.[78] Whereas in the early poems, rivers and ponds hide monsters, and the only achievements of the sea are 'the bones of its killers and their victims', by the *R* sequence 'water has become the healing element' and 'the life-blood of poetry'. Those qualities of the natural world 'which had terrified Hughes' in earlier poems, 'such "wandering elementals" as wind and water, such unnegotiable realities as stone and blood, the inevitability of suffering and death, are now seen to constitute not an oppressive and alienating other, out there, but "home"'.[79]

Sagar quotes from Hughes's comments about fishing, both its importance to him and the wider implications of its effects. He concludes that fishing was for Hughes a kind of Holy Communion;[80] for him, hooking a big fish 'felt like plugging in to the power circuit of the world' but equally, the 'fish hooked by the man is simultaneously the man being hooked by the river'.[81] He also quotes from an interview with Thomas Pero in which Hughes said that after fishing alone he would find that he could not speak properly, as though 'I'd been into some part of myself that predates language',[82] and from Nicholas Bishop, who points out that the poem 'Go Fishing' completely omits the personal pronoun.[83]

The flow of water, as well as healing wounds, can wash away words: 'take the misshapen ego back into the womb from which it would issue nameless and faceless and ready for a renewed attempt at living in time and with other people'. Words have to be recaptured, but they will not be the 'monkey chatter of our daily discourse or the "emergency words" of our accidental lives'. Sagar notes that finding the right words is 'a delicate balance'. The power of the words that come out of that balance, Sagar argues, makes the photographs which accompanied *R* redundant, since they 'cannot hope to convey what concerns him most – the flow, the constant change, the power, the voice and music of the river … and the interrelatedness with the weather and the whole ecosystem of which it is the life-blood and generator'.[84]

MYTH AS TECHNIQUE: JOANNY MOULIN

Joanny Moulin is less reverential than Sagar, less focused on the benefit to the individual or humanity of the poet's work, and more focused on myth as technique. Moulin contrasts Hughes's concept of myth with that of T.S. Eliot. For Eliot, Moulin writes, myth was a tool, and the 'mythic' method' was an extension of his objective correlative. Hughes's definition of myth, however, is closer to that of the referent, 'that is to say an extra-linguistic fact, of which a given group of people may have a common experience or mythology'.[85] Hughes's 'mythos' is a 'set of such given referents, which amount to the common "picture language" of a poet and his readers'. These terms, 'mythology' and 'mythos', have, however, reversed their dictionary meanings. Moulin argues that Hughes does not mean mythos as in 'legend', in the sense used by Pindaros of Thebes, who opposed the term to *logos*; on the contrary, for Hughes, myth is truer than *logos*. 'Seeing something as "real" or "sacred" is tantamount to seeing it on what Hughes calls the "mythic plane"'[86] (*Shakespeare and the Goddess of Complete Being*, p. 219).

Hughes's myth, for Moulin, is anti-myth, not 'a random element of some "myth-kitty" as Larkin would have it, out of which the poet might pick and choose, as in a creative writing tool-box, to express whatever ineffable emotions'. On the contrary, myth is emotion, and not a method, but the target, 'the connective side of *logos*'.[87] Moulin finds surface agreement between Hughes and Derrida that '"there is nothing outside of the text"; he makes no difference between "the referent or the transcendental signified" and what would be a transcendental signifier'. Moulin points out that even nature and the Goddess are always already a myth, that is, a text, or tissue. He finds that this 'biological metaphor of myth as living text pervades and sustains the whole of Hughes's poetry'. As early in Hughes's career as *THITR* this is verified by the Thought-Fox, which is a 'literal-cum-animal hybrid'.[88]

OPPOSED EVALUATIONS OF HUGHES'S SEQUENCES: KEVIN HART AND TERRY GIFFORD AND NEIL ROBERTS

Kevin Hart's chapter on Hughes in Neil Corcoran's *Cambridge Companion to Twentieth-Century English Poetry* (2008) compares Hughes's sequences unfavourably to those of Geoffrey Hill. Hart suggests that in trying to efface themselves as poems in order to seem closer to anonymous myth, the initial Crow poems produce a 'thin' 'poetic yield'.[89] The later sequences he finds mostly confined to a 'stripped-down language with little sensuous interest' with a 'narrow range of tones' and 'little regard for the pitch of words and phrases'.[90] For Hart, the finest poem of *CB* is 'The Knight', the only poem of the collection, he states, in which language becomes specific and memorable. Unlike other critics, rather than praising the immediacy and authenticity of *Moortown Diary*, Hart finds in it *'materia poetica* rather than finished poems', and that the 'raw immediacy that is desired is more often than not compromised by slapdash technique'.

Conversely, and perhaps more representative of critical opinion, Gifford and Roberts, in summing up their study, contrast Hughes with the men represented in 'Thrushes', who are victims of their potentialities.[91] They see Hughes's emotional character expressed in the 'practical skill of his craft'. This is an 'individual human image of the wholeness of self and relatedness with material reality' towards which are moving 'the symbolic images of the sequences' of *C, G* and *CB*. The fine poems of these sequences are, in the authors' view, more representative than any others of the difference between *M* and Hughes's earlier work. Hughes had been through a long discipline of imaginative objectivity, bringing him to the point where 'positive connections between man and nature can be expressed, and in directly personal terms'. For Gifford and Roberts, that sense of connection is the criterion by which Hughes's work should be judged. That work, they argue, has not striven towards mystical transcendence or a stance offered as invulnerable. Rather, Hughes has sought 'a position of practical engagement with the world that is utterly honest, stripped of self-deceptions, humble and respectful but at home in the only world, that is our life and death'. The authors find remarkable in Hughes's work not only the few failures but also the 'consistency of focus that runs through the varied forms of the successes'.

The criticism reviewed in this chapter illustrates the diversity of approaches to, polarised evaluations of, and interpretation of Hughes's writing in general and his linked collections and sequences in particular. Chapter 4 offers further examples of diverse approaches, and of approaches that are reverential and quite the opposite, to Hughes's interactions with Sylvia Plath.

CHAPTER FOUR

Hughes and Plath

This chapter looks at discussions and speculations about the working relationship between Ted Hughes and Sylvia Plath, their mutual support and influence, and Hughes's editing of Plath's work. It also touches on reviews of *Birthday Letters* which discuss the relationship, though close critical analyses of the *Birthday Letters* poems appear in Chapter 5. A number of critics have written about Hughes's and Plath's relationship, both personal and literary, and a number of biographies of Sylvia Plath and studies of her poetry also touch on that topic, but this chapter looks at criticism whose primary focus is the work of Hughes or the mutual influence of Hughes and Plath.

READING PLATH AND HUGHES TOGETHER: MARGARET DICKIE UROFF

The first full-length study of the mutual influence of Hughes and Plath was Margaret Dickie Uroff's *Sylvia Plath and Ted Hughes* (1979). Uroff notes that, although the obvious approach to the work of the two poets would seem to be to read them together, Plath is usually bracketed with American and Hughes with English contemporaries, as though both were exemplary of their respective nationalities, even though they lived in both Britain and America, and read and were influenced by both American and British writers.[1] One of the problems with this approach, Uroff writes, is that the poets are then judged by different standards, which gives a distorted reading.

Quoting from a section on Plath's 'Wuthering Heights' (*SPCP*, p. 167) in a review of Plath's poems by an American writer,[2] and an English writer on Hughes's 'Wind',[3] Uroff finds that the self in Plath's poem is said to be weak, submissive and indulging in regressive fantasies, whereas comparable lines in Hughes's poem are seen as representing 'a witness [to elemental power] in control'.[4] Uroff sees behind Oates's reading of 'Wuthering Heights', Ralph Waldo Emerson's 'transparent eyeball, Whitman's more boisterously celebrated inclusive self' and 'Stevens's ordering imagination'. Behind Sagar's reading, however, is the nature poetry of Wordsworth, Blake and Yeats. He therefore locates Hughes in an English tradition by assuming that the natural world really exists apart from the poet's imagination; 'that the powers of the world are in opposition to civilization rather than to self; that the poet's fears are real, not pathological'. Uroff argues that though there are differences between 'Wuthering Heights' and 'Wind', they are 'not best defined as the difference between a desperate statement and a vital awareness'. She suggests that the very intensity of Plath's fears may come from a 'heightened sense of the continuum of outside human life', whilst the 'gripped heart' of Hughes's poem could be considered 'a fairly desperate response'.[5]

In a penetrating discussion of Plath's and Hughes's respective contributions to a collection of essays for a BBC production, *Writers on Themselves*,[6] Uroff looks at the superficially very different accounts given by the poets of the origins of their creativity, and finds striking similarities in the persistent importance of early-established images and symbols. Both writers recall significant defining moments and places of their childhood; Hughes the contrast between the oppressive and confining presence of Scout Rock and the exhilaration and freedom of being on the moors; Plath the changeable movement, lights and 'breath' of the Atlantic.[7] Uroff notes that the two sets of memories focus on natural land- and seascapes from early childhood, even though Hughes's family moved to the industrial town of Mexborough and Plath's, after the death of her father, to surburban Wellesley. Both skate over the long years of study, reading, imitation and apprenticeship. Uroff states that while poets have the right to offer their own myths of origin, 'such a myth may be best understood by attempting to discover how it served its purpose'.[8]

Hughes's myth of origin identifies him as formed by the elemental forces of West Yorkshire, and in the line of Wordsworth, Yeats, Lawrence, Thomas and Graves. 'Man face to face with the elements may experience a primordial thrill and fear, that, Hughes feels, is the basis of poetry';[9] the 'condition of creativity' for Hughes, as for Wordsworth, is 'a prepared receptivity'.[10] This, the idea of poetry as a raid on the inner life, is hardly new, but Hughes had refashioned the insights of his predecessors to suit his own purposes. He offers himself as having become a poet when fishing, but whilst this is a more homely figure than Eliot, 'who became a poet through the extinction of personality or [Yeats] who masked himself as a beggar, an aristocrat, a stylised character', the fisher-poet is 'as much a literary pose as the impersonal artist'. The young Hughes had to study anthropology and English literature before he could 'identify a world that could sustain him and to make the connections between that mythic world and his own native landscape'.[11]

Plath's piece for the same collection, 'Ocean 1212-W', was written, Uroff suggests, for an English audience, to indicate that the American writer, like the British, has a 'home territory' that can inspire, though Uroff points out that the Massachusetts coastline does not have the roots in ancient mythology or dialect that West Yorkshire does. What the essay can tell us about Plath is that whilst Hughes's infancy 'oscillated between the evil eye of the rock and the gentle female line of the moors', Plath's 'clear vision was informed by the "motherly pulse of the sea" with its own dual aspect: its miracles and violence'.[12] Where Hughes locates the forbidding, repressive character which he attributes to English Puritanism in the rock, and the release of that repression in the moors, Plath projects on to the sea 'the psychic divisions between the forces that nourished and sustained and those that threatened and destroyed'. The sea is a mother-nurturer and threat; as in Plath's poetry, the maternal image is divided into the sweet and good false mother and the violent or 'even evil' true mother. Uroff sees in these ambivalent vistas Plath's identification of her own divisions of self-image.[13]

Uroff finds parallels, continuations, developments and influences between a number of poems by Hughes and Plath, ending with C. In this work she finds a number of lessons learned 'with and from' Plath.[14] These include the breaking of the four-stressed poetic line into two, or into single words, or the expanding of it to 'Whitmanesque lengths', and the abandonment of rigidity for an organisation based on 'incremental repetitions, catalogues, refrains'. Hughes has come to share with Plath a colloquialism that is not a relaxation but a stiffening of diction. Techniques new to Hughes such as caricature, parody and hyperbole, Uroff suggests, were employed by Plath from the beginning. Behind these parallels, she finds common thematic obsessions. She sees the achievement of C as testifying to 'the importance of the creative relationship ... and to the energies it unleashed'.[15]

HUGHES'S AND PLATH'S 'SHARED MYTHOLOGY': EKBERT FAAS

Ekbert Faas attempts to read the two poets' works as in a sense a whole, 'chapters of a shared mythology'[16] of which Hughes's poems form a sequel to Plath's, so that 'her mythic journey was not discontinued altogether' on her death.[17] Faas suggests that Plath's fascination with the seductive beauty of death, temporarily diverted during the early, happy days with Hughes, returned, so that more characteristically dark and sinister poems resurfaced.

Faas begins by quoting from the *Letters Home: Correspondence 1950–1963* (1975), which Plath wrote to her mother during the first months of her relationship with Hughes. These refer to Plath's having been, like Lazarus, on the other side of life, and her desire now to make her own being 'one song of affirmation and love all my life long'.[18] For Faas, Plath did, during that period, manage to turn her manifesto into practice. He finds the changes in Plath's content, style and mood remarkable. In the old style is the poem written after her first meeting with Hughes, 'Pursuit' (*SPCP*, p. 22). Faas asserts that Plath felt hypnotised by 'the simple, seductive beauty' of her own words in evoking a 'symbol of the terrible beauty of death'.[19] He adds that it was Hughes who prompted Plath to write 'Pursuit'. Their love and marriage, he notes, inspired Plath to write poems of a different kind, many about Hughes. In 'Ode for Ted' (*SPCP*, p. 29) Hughes has changed from a symbol of death into a fertility god like Osiris, and 'Wreath for a Bridal' (*SPCP*, p. 44), from the same period, 'shows how nature is reborn from the mating of two lovers who "bedded like angels ... burn one in fever"'. Hughes's writing of the same period, however, does not have similar imagery of 'birds and bridegroom, love and rebirth', and that imagery does not persist in Plath's poetry. Whilst Plath 'continued to rave about the creative forces of nature which, prompted by her husband, she would henceforth celebrate in her verses, poems of more sinister note soon made themselves heard again', and even poems from 'the happy years of her marriage do not return to the simple celebration of a life-giving "wedlock wrought within love's proper chapel"'. Faas finds it unsurprising that the 'defiant opening' of 'Wreath for a Bridal' is more convincing than the message of the rest of the poem. However strong her desire for rebirth, he states, Plath's 'sojourn on the other side of sanity and life had left traces not to be erased by a mere new philosophy of life'.[20]

It was that sojourn, that 'season in hell', Faas asserts, which, when Plath did confront it, inspired her greatest writing: the story 'Johnny Panic and the Bible of Dreams', *The Bell Jar*[21] and the poetry which followed 'The Stones' ('Poem for a Birthday' 7: 'The Stones', *SPCP*, p. 136). Even in these, however, he finds little to suggest the rebirth which some critics have sought to find in Plath's work. Plath's poems, then, may well be 'chapters in a mythology where the plot, seen as a whole and in retrospect, is strong and clear', but it would be adding chapters not written by Plath to trace that plot from Plath's descent into disintegration towards a 'rebirth and Transcendence'. Faas argues that the transformation of Lady Lazarus into a vampire who will 'eat men like air' (*SPCP*, pp. 244–6) 'hardly qualifies the poet for a rebirth in mythic terms, and little else in her late work sustains this transformation beyond the occasional yearning in that direction'.[22]

Faas finds in Hughes's work a mythic journey which continues Plath's. The opening scenario of this is 'the city of spare parts ... where men are mended' from 'The Stones'. This poem, written in late 1959 at the writers' colony, Yaddo, describes a rebirth process *à rebours* (that is, against the grain, or backwards). Faas sees the patchwork reconstruction of the 'I' of the poem with the help of technological medicine as ending on a note of grim irony, for which Plath's source, the story 'The City Where Men are Mended' in Paul Radin, *African Folktales and Sculpture* (1952), provides a backdrop.[23] An ugly daughter killed for the purpose of rebirth is resurrected in a far more monstrous form: 'With only one leg, one buttock, one hand'. Faas finds that Plath's poem lacks this fairy-tale directness, but that the speaker's final 'I shall be good as new' points up an equal failure. He asserts that the rebirth achieved here is as cosmetic as a facelift. Not new but good as new.[24]

Faas suggests that Hughes exerted a powerful influence on Plath's poetry by helping her to break her writer's block, setting her a course of reading (including Radin's writing) and daily 'exercises of concentration and observation', as well as undertaking mutual exploration of dreams which helped them discard the conscious use of 'symbols, irony, archetypal images and all that'.[25] Faas conjectures that Hughes played a significant role in freeing Plath's imagination 'and hence unleashing her worst nightmares',[26] and in liberating the biographical impulse behind her poetry, suggesting that an all-absorbing working partnership with Hughes gave Plath the courage 'to enter that secret focus of her anguish'.[27] Hughes describes Plath, after her nervous breakdown, electrotherapy treatment, suicide attempt and further treatment, as 'desecrated' and 'fragmented'; a patchwork person who has been put together and sent back on the road, passed good as new, but indelibly damaged. As criticism in other sections of this guide show, some of Hughes's poems feature a central male protagonist who has an underworld encounter with a 'patchwork woman', a desecrated or fragmented figure who is ambivalently goddess and ogress, and becomes her bridegroom. For Faas, this episode is central to Hughes's mythology.[28]

In Faas's view, Plath, after the estrangement from Hughes, was left to write poems such as 'Purdah' (*SPCP*, pp. 242–4) 'in the presence of her most anguishing memories but without the safeguards that had

made her dare confront them'.[29] This led to a self-demonisation which
enabled Plath to have a 'spurious defence against despair', to metaphorically 'destroy her destroyers'. In 'Purdah', rather than being born
through her bridegroom, the narrator will become a lioness out to kill
him. In Faas's reading, however, poems such as 'Purdah' and 'Lady
Lazarus' admit failure even in their defiance. The attempts to change
roles with the murderous panther become 'mere gesture' which is
'powerful for its self-conscious irony rather than for suggesting fulfilment'. This irony becomes elaborate sarcasm in 'The Applicant' (*SPCP*,
pp. 221–2): 'As a worthy partner of his desecrated bride, the applicant
bridegroom is supposed to share her patchwork personality.'[30]

Faas finds that the continuance of Plath's mythology in Hughes's
work owes little to direct borrowing, though he suggests that Elaine
in Hughes's radio play *The House of Aries* (broadcast on the BBC in
1960) may owe some of her insight into her dilemma to Plath's
'Johnny Panic and the Bible of Dreams', and that 'the sudden emergence of a Lady Lazarus-figure in [his] 1962 radio play *The Wound* is
an instance of "subliminal transference"'.[31] Whereas both *The Wound*
and 'Difficulties of a Bridegroom' are in the dramatic mode, Faas
sees Hughes's poems after 1962 as offshoots of a continuous narrative
increasingly focused on the story of Crow. Faas quotes Hughes: '"It's a
way", Hughes explained to me in 1972, "of getting a big body of ideas
and energy moving on a track. For when this energy connects with a
possibility for a poem, there is a lot more material and pressure in it
than you could ever get into a poem just written out of the air or out
of a special occasion."'[32]

The general framework of this extensive narrative, Faas writes, is the
attempt of God to improve on man. That second creation is nightmarish.
He finds the roots of the central episode of the narrative, however, in
'the Plath mythology', and asserts that this illustrates a continuing concern of Hughes's with the rescue of 'a desecrated female at the hands
of an equally desecrated male'. Faas again cites his private discussions
with Hughes to explain that at a point early in the adventures of Crow,
a woman appears and repeatedly reappears at the episodes' nadirs.[33]
The woman is always in a terrible condition and undergoing terrible
torment, so that in a way the quest of the protagonist becomes to save
her. He fails, saves her, loses her again and pursues her again. This
theme is reiterated in *G*, when the substitute Lumb attempts to resurrect the Great Mother on Earth, and the 'real' Lumb fails to rescue the
dying animal-woman in the underworld. Lumb does, however, suc-
ceed in pulling out of the underworld mud a strange female patchwork
creature, which, embracing him, is reborn through his body. This, Faas

argues, 'makes real what in "Lady Lazarus" and other of Plath's poems remains an ineffectual gesture'.[34]

RIVALRY: SUSAN VAN DYNE AND HEATHER CLARK

Sylvia Plath, interviewed by Owen Leeming for the BBC in January 1961, stated that without her husband's 'understanding and cooperation' she felt that 'I'd never be writing as I am, and as much as I am'.[35] Writing more than three decades later, however, Susan Van Dyne found Plath's idea that the relationship with Hughes was 'a mutually beneficial collaboration' Plath's 'fondest fiction'.[36]

Four years after the BBC interview, in an article published in the *Guardian* in March 1965, Hughes insisted that there had been no rivalry between him and Sylvia Plath, as poets or in any way. He did, however, say that living together led to mutual influence, and writing 'out of one brain'. Nonetheless, Van Dyne asserts that 'Plath's dialogue with Hughes's poems is always competitive and her strategy revisionary.'[37]

Hughes compared his relationship with Sylvia Plath to a pair of feet, each using whatever the other did. It was a working partnership, he wrote, which was all-absorbing, and there was an unspoken unanimity of their criticism and judgements.[38] In spite of statements such as these, critics continued to read not only mutual influence and borrowing, but also rivalry and competitiveness between the poets. Hughes himself warns the author Lucas Myers against writing about Hughes's and Plath's mutual borrowing; even though 'No doubt Sylvia and I plundered each other merrily' there would be 'new theses of accusations' and 'Job-loads of righteous wrath ... our generous readers will multiply by ten'. That wrath would be one-sided, Hughes predicts: it would be no good for him to say that he 'designed prototypes which she put into full Germanic production' even though 'there's truth in it', since he would 'never be believed'. Were Myers to say that Hughes stole from Plath, however, 'that would be an instant religion of verification'.[39]

Heather Clark portrays the relationship between Plath and Hughes as a rivalry covered by a superficial amity. She sees the collections *Ariel* and *Birthday Letters* as attempts to free Plath and Hughes from each other's hold, but attempts which fail.[40] Their rivalry begins, for Clark, in recognition of a different approach to but mutual interest in violence, and a consequent draw to one another as reader. The 'negotiation of violence' thus became 'an important part of the couple's creative dialogue'.[41] Clark argues that each poet feared the other's attempt to impose a remaking on the other: Hughes feared Plath's 'emasculating influence'; Plath Hughes's neutralising and possible Anglicisation of 'her female poetic voice'.[42] Clark sees resistance to these inferred impositions not in person but in poems 'that seem to offer up clichés of masculinity and femininity'. For example, where Plath puts forward an 'optimistic, Emersonian view of the natural world, Hughes counters with a colder, more violent aesthetic'. In addition, 'Plath seems to have self-consciously resisted a violent voice, in order not to appear to mimic Hughes', whereas Hughes was 'determined to counter and even mock Plath's verse when it appeared too neat, too optimistic, and too evocative of Movement decorousness'.[43] Plath, then, was caught in a double bind: seeking to cultivate 'a masculine "hardness"' in order to win the approval of Hughes and contemporaries 'still under the spell of Pound and Eliot', but still needing to 'remain sufficiently feminine so that she would not have to compete with Hughes'.[44]

Clark identifies poems which answer back to others: Plath's 'The Great Carbuncle' (*SPCP*, p. 72) challenged Hughes's representation of nature in 'Wind' with an 'optimistic Emersonian vision' focused on the benign and restorative rather than terrifying effects of nature.[45] Clark notes that whereas the characters in Hughes's poem huddle inside the house, away from nature, in 'The Great Carbuncle' the speaker and companion enjoy walking outside; where Hughes 'concentrates on the destructive force of the wind', the focus of Plath's poem is 'the unmoving, healing quality of the light'. Hughes's wind is 'almost diabolic', but Plath 'invokes the language of transcendentalism' to explain what moves her speaker. In 'Wind' the domestic interior is protective, but in 'The Great Carbuncle' the speaker's 'feelings of transcendence' are destroyed by contact with the material world.[46] These examples are not one-sided; Clark reads Hughes's poem 'Relic' as a response to Plath's 'Mussel Hunter at Rock Harbor' (*SPCP*, pp. 95–7).[47] Clark notes that similarly, Uroff sees Plath's 'Black Rook in Rainy Weather' (*SPCP*, p. 56) as a response to Hughes's 'The Hawk in the Rain'.[48]

BIRTHDAY LETTERS: JAMES FENTON, JANET MALCOLM, GAYLE WURST

The typescript of *BL* was delivered to Matthew Evans, chairman of Faber & Faber, in the summer of 1997, and in November the collection was offered to *The Times* newspaper for serialisation. The extracts were published in *The Times* between 17 January and 22 January 1998, and the book was published by Faber on 29 January. Stephen Moss, writing in the *Guardian,* called the publication the 'literary scoop' of 'the decade, the century, the millennium. Take your pick.' It was 'the kind of publicity money can't buy'.[49] According to the Literary Editor of *The Times,* Erica Wagner, Hughes specified the date, which he had selected as astrologically propitious for collective awareness. He also retained the right to refuse permission for some of the poems to appear out of the context of the collection, and exercised that right over 'Dreamers', 'The Inscription', 'The Laburnum', 'The Cast', 'The Ventriloquist' and 'Life After Death'.[50]

Hughes had not described the *Birthday Letters* poems as messages of self-defence or self-exculpation to either his first wife or his critics, but as evocations of Plath for a personal purpose. Nonetheless, some journalists chose to see them as either posthumous letters or belated diary entries; rewritings of the 'history' recorded in the poems of Sylvia Plath.

In a review of *BL* the poet James Fenton examines some of the critical writing that had denied Ted Hughes either the right to silence or the right of reply in the matter of his relationship with Sylvia Plath, and he reflects on the relationship between such writers and Plath, who herself had undergone something of the process to which Seamus Heaney referred in his memorial address.[51] Fenton writes of the enduring strength of the myth of 'Sylvia Plath', which, he claims, leads to assertions by journalists such as Katherine Viner, whose *Guardian* article suggested, erroneously, that Plath in her own lifetime attained fame in way that few women had done before. Fenton points out that Plath achieved only modest success during her lifetime and a greater fame only posthumously. He also takes issue with Viner's statements that Plath would have been a feminist heroine even had she not been 'abandoned by her husband', and that Hughes was seen as a villain not only because he left Plath 'to look after two children when she could barely look after herself', but because he 'abused' the Plath Estate and remained silent for 35 years about a woman who 'died for her art'. Vehemently refuting Viner's statement that lovers of Plath's work can never forgive Hughes for failing to ensure that 'the blood jet' of her work would continue to flow, Fenton remarks that what they actually cannot forgive is that Hughes was the father of Plath's children, her lover, and the 'Keeper of the Flame', positions which such critics felt they would themselves better have filled. He notes that Viner could hardly improve upon the impertinence and insensitivity of her response to the tenderness she detects in *BL*, which she describes as an indication of the passion Hughes felt for his wife, retrospectively.

Fenton finds Diane Wood Middlebrook's *New York Times* piece in friendly contrast to what he calls Viner's vicious self-righteousness, since Middlebrook compares the public anger at Hughes's refusal to be interviewed on the subject of Plath with the outrage about Queen Elizabeth's silence on the death of Diana, Princess of Wales.[52] For Middlebrook, the *Birthday Letters* poems offer an affirmation of the power of Plath's work, because they record the awakening of Ted Hughes to Plath's inner life, and his acknowledgement of her literary achievement. That Middlebrook suggests that it took decades for Hughes to acknowledge Plath's poetic achievement is, for Fenton, part of the myth, which demands that the man killed the woman or failed her or in some way suppressed the evidence of her talent until he conferred 'the laurel' of 'prestigious understanding'. Hughes's silence, Fenton argues, cannot be attributed to grief and an understandable desire for privacy or to protect his and Plath's children. Because his silence allegedly angers something called 'the female public', it is not considered legitimate but sinister, and he has no right to it. Fenton points out that it was Hughes who arranged for publication of Plath's *Ariel* and subsequent volumes, and he who was the source of the information that he had destroyed a volume of Plath's journals so that their children would not have to read it. Fenton finds himself sympathetic to Hughes's reluctance to publish the rest of Plath's writing in the UK, and to undergo the same kinds of attack as he had already experienced.

Countering the accusation of long silence, Fenton lists the prior publication of poems from *BL*, and the occasions on which Hughes wrote about Plath's work. Of the eighty-eight poems of *BL*, eight were included in Hughes's *New Selected Poems* of 1994, and one, as Fenton points out, dates back to the 1981 *Selected Poems*. Hughes also published an essay on the manuscripts of 'Sheep in Fog' (*SPCP*, p. 262), and an account of the composition of *The Bell Jar* and *Ariel* (1965). In that essay, Fenton recalls, Hughes explains that Plath 'was drawn at first by an ambition to write in a tradition derived from Joyce, Woolf, and James, but how her heart pulled in the opposite direction, that of Lawrence and Dostoevsky'. He adds that Hughes believes that the story 'Johnny Panic and the Bible of Dreams' was 'the divining work that located and opened the blocked spring'.[53]

Fenton's evaluation of *BL* is that most of the poems are straightforward in expression, but combine a Lowell-like plangency with a Lawrentian sense of 'violent nature'.[54] He finds no self-pity in the collection, and, echoing Wurst, argues that in the view of Hughes, it was his lot rather than his misfortune to come between Plath and the father of 'Daddy' (*SPCP*, pp. 222–3). Whilst Fenton acknowledges that a hostile reading of this view could see it as a convenient pushing back of the blame for Plath's unhappiness to her childhood, he asserts that were one to read 'Daddy' as an autobiographical poem (that is, in the kind of reading that has led to vilification of Hughes), then Hughes's view of Plath is not far from Plath's view of herself.

Fenton considers the various representations of Plath in *BL*, from the strangely complimentary view of her body as fishlike to the epiphany revealing that the failure of the marriage stemmed from Hughes's failure to buy a fox cub as a pet ('Epiphany', *BL*, *CP*, pp. 1115–17). Fenton finds the figure of Plath marked as doomed from early in the sequence, and the figure of Hughes as baffled by her, for example in 'Fever' nursing her during an illness but wondering whether she is really as ill as she seems (*BL*, *CP*, pp. 1072–3). Hughes recalls himself thinking that if she does not stop crying wolf, he will not know when things get really bad. Fenton acknowledges that this could seem like carefully placed self-justification, but states that in his view both poem and sequence are perfectly plausible. He adds that self-justification is a legitimate aim and might provide the impulse or impetus for a poem. He quotes Auden: 'Saints will not mind from what angle they are viewed,/Having nothing to hide' ('In Praise of Limestone'), but notes that the rest of us do and should mind. Were we not to mind, he asks, what would such indifference imply?[55]

AMERICAN AND BRITISH RECEPTION: GAYLE WURST

Janet Malcolm, author of *The Silent Woman: Sylvia Plath and Ted Hughes* (1994), suggests that Hughes was far from indifferent, finding his history 'uncommonly bare' of the granting of merciful moments that might 'allow one to undo or redo one's actions and thus feel that life isn't entirely tragic', other than his publication of *BL*, which she sees as giving Hughes such a 'precious second chance in art'.[56] Gayle Wurst, author of *Voice and Vision: The Poetry of Sylvia Plath* (1999), expresses the hope that the avid interest in *BL* in the USA will reconcile American readers of Plath to Hughes, and introduce them to 'his magnificent achievement as a poet', but she suggests that neither English readers of Plath nor American readers of Hughes can fully understand either poet's achievement without an understanding of the 'specifically English social, cultural and literary contexts in which he and Plath both lived and wrote, and to which their writing responded'.[57] She examines the difficulties faced by Hughes as both Executor of the Plath Estate and editor and censor of Sylvia Plath's writing.

Recalling Ian Hamilton's reminder that the memoir by Al Alvarez, *The Savage God*, was probably Hughes's first experience of the kind of publication that was to become a lifetime horror,[58] Wurst points out that 'the Plath biography' would always have to involve at least one chapter of the biography of Hughes, and that anyone wanting to look into Plath's life would feel that they had the right to poke into Hughes's life.[59] Further, as editor, his was the task of making public accusations and insults to which he could make no dignified response, accusations and insults which were inherent in the outpouring of creative energy that came towards the end of Plath's life and which was channelled into creative fury directed at Hughes. Wurst finds Hughes's problem difficult and almost impossible.

Wurst suggests that American advocates of Plath failed to understand not only Hughes's character and very English sense of privacy (she quotes Anne Stevenson's description of him as a very shy man, 'more comfortable with men than with women',[60] and Ian Hamilton's reference to him as 'taciturn', even 'pre-Plath'[61]), but also his poetry, the literary interactions that he had with Plath, and the currents of Plath mythology in Britain. Lack of attempts to gain this understanding has led to condemnation of Hughes's editorial decision as the default position of American criticism, and *de rigueur* in the USA. Part of the problem, Wurst continues, has been that Hughes entered the awareness of American critics and Plath advocates as the 'bastard' so much reviled in Plath's 'Daddy', even though the testaments of friends and others who knew Hughes affirm that his personality was utterly unlike that representation.[62] Wurst argues that since Hughes's sources were in ancient myth and ritual, the animal kingdom and nature, not in the social or domestic spheres, the Plath Estate was an extremely uncomfortable inheritance for him. She again quotes Ian Hamilton, who finds Hughes's poetry, for all its violence, void of personality,[63] and suggests that as such, it was both apolitical and strongly opposed to the confessional and extremist modes 'to which Plath's work was assimilated' in Britain.

For Wurst, the criticism of Alvarez requires particular examination in any discussion of the differences between American and British reception of Plath's work. She argues that few specialists of Plath's work in the USA were aware that Alvarez, a most fervent and influential supporter of Plath, promoted and analysed Plath's work in his *The Savage God* and elsewhere in order to support his call for an 'incendiary' new poetry.[64] Wurst asserts that Hughes's antagonism to Alvarez's appropriation of Plath's poetry and of Plath's suicide became a key element in the hostility of the Plath Estate towards subsequent biographers and critics. This led to years of battles, both literary and legal, fought by Hughes as Executor of the Estate, which, Wurst argues, reinforced Hughes's disinclination to justify his desire for privacy. Nonetheless, Alvarez's writing on Plath led to Hughes assuming a public stance that was to be much criticised.

Wurst suggests that Plath was incited to produce some of her best-known work, including 'Lady Lazarus' and 'Daddy', by finding herself excluded from Alvarez's list of the promising new poets to whom he initially looked for the incendiary writing that was to drag English poetry from its effete cultural doldrums. She also suggests that Alvarez did much to inaugurate the 'myth' of Plath-as-victim, and locates that inauguration in a memorial programme for Plath broadcast by the BBC in September 1963. The programme featured, in addition to record-ings of Plath reading some of her poems, including 'Lady Lazarus' and 'Daddy', evaluation of her work by Alvarez. In his tribute to Plath, Alvarez declared that the poems read as though written posthumously, and referred to Plath's father as both 'pure German' and anti-Semitic. The tribute was published in the *Review* in the UK and the *Tri-Quarterly* in the USA,[65] and thus, Wurst argues, before the poems were avail-able in print, they were made public 'enrobed' in Alvarez's theories of extremist art.[66]

Alvarez described Plath as assuming the suffering of all modern vic-tims and giving herself to the sickness to which she feels prey in the service of the range and intensity of her art.[67] This made her the ideal type of extremist artist and her work ideal for the opposition to the 'genteel poetry' which Alvarez deplored, as well as a rival to the 'con-fessional' poetry of, for example, Robert Lowell and John Berryman. Wurst sees Alvarez's championing of Plath's work and emphasis on his relationship with her as enabling him to argue that he had cleared the ground for such extreme writing. Wurst cites the revised edition to *The New Poetry*, which Alvarez edited, and his much later work, *The Savage God*, in which he refers to the introduction to the anthology, 'Sylvia Plath: A Memoir', published by the *Observer* newspaper in serial form in 1971 as 'Sylvia Plath: The Road to Suicide'. Alvarez asserted that his essay had said something that Plath wanted to hear and that she had spoken of it often, and was disappointed not to have been included.[68] He added that her work was included in later editions, since it, more than anyone else's, vindicated his argument.

Wurst points out that Hughes had in the past regarded Alvarez as a colleague and friend, so it would not be surprising were Hughes to have seen Alvarez's publication on Plath as a personal betrayal.[69] Hughes's measures against Alvarez were both public and personal. He sought to put an end to the publication of the introduction to Alvarez's *The Savage God* by writing in protest to the Editor of the *Observer*, and successfully caused the cancellation of the second extract.[70] He further wrote a piece in the *Times Literary Supplement* which denounced Alvarez's statements as founded on fiction, second-hand scraps, glimpses and half-experiences, recollected after seven years and imaginatively reshaped.[71] Alvarez's alleged facts, he wrote, had to do with the truth of an event which was far more important to the family of Sylvia Plath than it could be to either Alvarez or his readers. His private response, in letters to Alvarez, was less formal and, as Wurst says, more condemnatory, suggesting that Alvarez had no respect for the truth and was 'fouled up' by the egotistical journalist in himself.[72] In this letter, Hughes makes a distinction perhaps fundamental to his own writing between 'sacred' private and personal documents written from the real heart and real imagination, and another self which sells out, whose writing is sucked out into the greedy demands of an 'empty public'. Alvarez, Hughes argued, had made a public spectacle of the most private and humiliating of acts, Plath's ending of her own life, and he accuses Alvarez of feeding wild fantasies about Plath which would henceforth be ten times more confident in their outrageousness.

Even opposition to Alvarez's characterisation of Plath and Alvarez's theory of extremist art, far from supporting Hughes, could cause problems for both Hughes and the Plath Estate, Wurst notes. She discusses the case of David Holbrook, a critic who attacked both Alvarez's claims and Plath's writing. Holbrook wrote of Alvarez encouraging artists to cultivate psychosis, and Plath as both schizoid and insane.[73] Wurst notes that Holbrook frequently wrote letters to newspapers in which he deplored various sicknesses in modern culture, and brackets these with the statements which she refers to as Holbrook's repeated denunciation[74] of Plath's poetry as emblematic of the downfall of English culture.[75]

Holbrook's essay 'R. D. Laing and the Death Circuit', based on the theories of schizophrenia set out in Laing's *The Divided Self* (1960), argued that Plath's poetry exhibits symptoms of mental disorder.[76] A projected book by Holbrook to be called *Dylan Thomas and Sylvia Plath and the Symbolism of Schizoid Suicide* sparked a heated exchange between Holbrook and Olwyn Hughes, Literary Agent to the Plath Estate, in the *Times Literary Supplement* and, Wurst says, gained Holbrook the dubious honour of becoming the first author to be denied permission to cite from the work.[77] Holbrook argued that the Estate felt that the Literary Agent had the right to judge whether or not a critical work was good enough as criticism to be granted permission to quote, and was seeking to suppress debate.

The book on Plath that Holbrook published was *Sylvia Plath: Poetry and Existence* (1976), in which he asserts that the distorted reality and sick logic of the poems must be declared pathological, and that it must be his task to demonstrate that these are psychotic, and to show how Plath 'fell victim to these tendencies'.[78]

Wurst asserts that Holbrook, like Alvarez, set the tone for and defined the issues which marred Hughes's reputation and mired the Estate in disputes and self-justification for years, but that such battles waged in Britain were little known to American readers of Plath, while American interpretations of Plath's life and work seemed foreign to the British context. She sees Plath's reputation in Britain as the extremist artist of the 1960s, and in America, following the development of feminist discoveries, readings and reclamations of women writers, as 'The Woman Writer' of the 1970s. Wurst finds Plath established in the new canon of women writers by Adrienne Rich's essay 'When We Dead Awaken' (1971), which celebrates Plath as having made female anger and furious response to the power over her of men available as subjects of poetry.[79] Rich praises the female energy and dynamic charge of the poetry that, she writes, came from the woman's sense of her embattled and possessed self. This placement in the developing canon was affirmed by *Ms.* magazine, whose second (September 1972) edition featured an article titled 'Sylvia Plath Demystified'. Once *Ariel* and *The Bell Jar* became required reading for many American university courses, Wurst argues, the line between academic criticism and voyeuristic participation in Plath's life grew thinner. Poems in the developing sub-genre of work in homage to and imitation of Plath's poems often restated the poems' rage without the benefit of the poems' art, and openly accused Hughes as a patriarchal oppressor.[80] Wurst concludes that whilst the assessed aesthetic value of Plath's work soared, Hughes's public image plummeted.[81]

Wurst sympathises with the antagonism that she says must have been generated in the Plath Estate by the promotion of Plath as a representative of the woman artist in a society which represses women. This, she says, not only brought explicit attacks on Hughes but also disregarded the actual facts of Plath's literary career, ignoring the role played by many friends, professional acquaintances and critics in promoting Plath's work both before and after her death.[82] Wurst further notes the irony in the coincident rise in Plath's popularity as a proto-feminist author and the publication of Holbrook's criticism which decried her as a 'pseudo-male', and could scarcely find anything in her of femininity at all. Wurst suggests that Holbrook's aggressive attacks on Plath and on the feminist movement did not encourage the Plath Estate to defend feminism against Holbrook's prejudices, but rather to deny any possible connection between Plath and feminism. Wurst finds it unfortunate that this policy ultimately led the Estate to portray Plath in a hostile manner, particularly in terms of Plath's relationships with other women, including Ms Hughes.

Wurst chronicles the meta-life of Plath's work, as interest in the dealings of the Plath Estate with scholars, biographers and journalists itself became the subject of published discussion, and as publication of personal as well as business letters further invaded the privacy of Ted Hughes. She quotes Janet Malcolm's suggestion that the preface to Linda Wagner-Martin's biography of Plath, which refers to 'unhappy dealings' with the Plath Estate, formed the chief interest of the book.[83]

The publication of the authorised biography of Plath, Anne Stevenson's *Bitter Fame*, in 1989[84] brought more controversy and acrimony, including an exchange between Stevenson, Olwyn Hughes and Alvarez which was published in the *New York Review of Books* in September 1989. In his review of *Bitter Fame*, Alvarez referred to Wagner-Martin's preface and commented on what he called her mildly feminist approach in contrast to that of Stevenson, which he described as over 350 pages of 'disparagement'. Wurst observes that Alvarez again took the opportunity of writing about Hughes, this time as a figure 'damned' by his 'recessiveness', and presented himself as the champion of Plath and the nemesis of Hughes.[85] Wurst notes that this is a role in which he continued to cast himself in his review of *BL*,[86] but with the twist that in that piece responsibility for the mythologising of Plath is laid on 'the feminists', for whom Plath was a 'terrible example' of the 'raw deal woman'.[87]

Wurst asserts that it is crucial to note that, although feminists antagonistic to Hughes closely scrutinised every statement that he made about Plath, in America they also unquestioningly accepted Alvarez's version of events and his version of Plath as composing with furious energy at 4 a.m. This acceptance extended to Wagner-Martin's commendation of Alvarez's readings of Plath's work, which, in introducing an extract from *The Savage God* in the *Critical Heritage* volume of criticism of Plath's work (1988), she describes as consistently helpful.[88] *The Savage God*, sold at the same time as the US edition of *The Bell Jar*, became for many readers the first, and assumed authoritative, introduction to Plath's life and work. Wurst also asserts that whilst in his original promotion of Plath as the model of all modern victims Alvarez ignored questions of gender,[89] critics in America ignored Alvarez's argument that Plath was an important link between post-war poets in the UK and USA.[90] Wurst finds that Plath became the archetype of the double bind of women represented in Suzanne Juhasz's lines: 'The woman who wants to be a poet ... is set up to lose, whatever she might do ... . If she is "woman", she must fail as "poet"; "poet", she must fail as "woman".'[91]

Wurst finds it a predictable result of this that Hughes's responses should become increasingly defensive and that he should eventually cease to give interviews or respond to enquiries.[92] She quotes, from a letter to Anne Stevenson of November 1989, Hughes's reference to having been dragged out into a bullring and pricked and goaded into vomiting up details of his life with Plath, and his preference for silence, even though it could seem to confirm every accusation and fantasy.[93] In that letter he refers to protecting Plath from the fierce reactions she had provoked as like protecting a fox from hounds whilst it was biting him. Wurst attributes to what she calls an increasingly poisonous atmosphere Hughes's decision to remove from *Ariel* before publication a number of poems written in the autumn of 1962. In his introduction to Plath's *Collected Poems* of 1981, Hughes explained that he had removed pieces which he considered 'personally aggressive' expressions of 'violent contradictory feelings'.[94] Some of those poems had, however, already been printed and were, like the myth of Sylvia Plath, already ingrained in the public consciousness.

For Wurst, the editorial decisions about the edition of *Ariel* backfired in that when the poems were published in full the sequence was given heightened significance. The apparent sequence of poems encouraged autobiographical interpretations, and the very extremist readings which Hughes had tried to avoid. Wurst quotes Marjorie Perloff, who wrote that reviewers came to see the 'motif of inevitability larger than it really was'.[95] An example given is an article co-authored by M.L. Rosenthal, the originator of the term 'confessional poetry'. The article assumed that the order of the remaining poems was the order of a poem sequence, a sequence which represented a 'pattern of death-consciousness and strangeness ... written in extremis'.[96] Hughes was then caught in a bind, blamed for suppressing material because he was accused, and accused because he suppressed material.[97] Wurst argues that it is likely that rather than protecting poetic sensibilities, Hughes toned down the *Ariel* manuscript in order to calm 'the heady response' and the 'reckless speculation' that poems such as 'Daddy' had brought about.[98]

Hughes wrote that, after initially taking seriously scholars' apparently serious concern for the 'truth' about Plath, he learned his lesson, because when his correction of errors was accepted, 'it rarely displaced a fantasy' but often 'was added to the repertoire as a variant hypothesis'. Needed more than the facts, it could be concluded, is what Hughes called the 'Fantasia about Sylvia Plath'.[99] Ian Hamilton remarks that if Hughes 'were to burn his own diaries in a fit of privacy, he would surely be accused of interfering with Plath studies'.[100]

Wurst suggests that Hughes's edited *Ariel* reflects Hughes's belief that Plath at the end of her life attained a state of 'mystical insight' which permitted her to 'transcend' the violent oppositions and contradictory feelings seen in her original manuscript.[101] She quotes Hughes's 1966 judgement that the world of Plath's poetry is '"one of emblematic visionary events, mathematical symmetries, clairvoyance, metamorphoses, and something resembling total biological and racial recall ... under the transfiguring eye of the great white timeless light"' and escaping analysis in the same way as clairvoyance and mediumship.[102] She suggests that anyone familiar with Hughes's own writing and his statements about poetry would recognise this as high praise, but that this praise of Plath as a poetic 'shaman', like his editing of *Ariel*, 'reinforced the dimensions of mythic sacrifice her work had already acquired'. Referring to Jacqueline Rose's statements about Plath, Wurst writes that Plath was seen as exemplary; 'either beneath or above culture: "beneath" as in "hidden beneath" or "accountable for", "beneath" as in "low"; "above" as "superiority" or "higher forms", "above" as "transcendence"'.[103] The result, for Wurst, was that the truth offered by Hughes to enquiring scholars could seem as much a projection as the 'Fantasia'.

Quoting Janet Malcolm, Wurst observes that Hughes's history seems 'bare of the moments of mercy that allow one to undo or redo one's actions and thus feel that life isn't entirely tragic'.[104] She adds that the publication of *BL*, however, did give Hughes 'that precious second chance in art'. She expresses the hope that the accolades received by *BL* in the USA will open readers of Plath's work to a fuller understanding, which will include the inner life of Ted Hughes, but that interest in the volume would go beyond Plath and Hughes's personal relationship. 'It is high time to thoroughly reevaluate Hughes's role as editor and interpreter of Plath's writing, an endeavor which must also comprehend the specifically English social, cultural and literary contexts in which he and Plath both lived and wrote, and to which their writing responded.'[105]

MUTUAL INFLUENCE: DIANE WOOD MIDDLEBROOK

Both in her full-length study, *Her Husband: Hughes and Plath, A Marriage* (2004)[106] and in her article in the *Cambridge Companion to Sylvia Plath*

(2006), Diane Middlebrook focuses on the relationship between Hughes and Plath as documented rather than as speculated, and in particular on the relationship between the poets' writing. Middlebrook states that Hughes and Plath, working 'side by side', developed a 'dynamic of mutual influence that produced the poems we read today'.[107] She sees this as evident early in the relationship, finding, in Plath's poem 'Pursuit', forms of influence 'that would typify Plath's creative relationship to Hughes's poetry: his words activate her own distinctive poetic method'. Once the relationship began, Plath, hitherto a strict formalist, began to experiment with the form of her verse, taking on 'a mode of archaic diction and extreme terseness' that typified the style of Hughes at that time. Middlebrook quotes from Hughes's poem 'Bawdry Embraced': 'Great farmy whores', 'buttocks like/Two white sows' and 'no dunghills for Bawdry's cock' ('Early Poems and Juvenilia', *CP*, pp. 13–15). She finds that Plath's 1956 poem 'Bucolics' includes 'Hughesianly clotted sound-effects' in, for example, 'Mayday: two came to field in such wise:/"A daisied mead", each said to each,/ So were they one; so sought they couch' (*SPCP*, p. 23).

In addition to influencing Plath's style directly by his own, Hughes, Middlebrook argues, introduced Plath to other stylistic influences, including Dylan Thomas, Gerard Manley Hopkins and W.B. Yeats. 'Hughes read his favourite poems aloud to Plath; she ventriloquized them back in poems that she bragged were "drunker than Dylan, harder than Hopkins, younger than Yeats".'[108] These influences are most evident in 'Ode for Ted', 'Faun' (*SPCP*, p. 35) and 'Wreath for a Bridal' (Dylan Thomas); 'Firesong' (*SPCP*, p. 30) (Gerard Manley Hopkins); and 'Strumpet Song' (*SPCP*, p. 33), 'Tinker Jack and the Tidy Wives' (*SPCP*, p. 34), 'Street Song' (*SPCP*, p. 35) and 'Recantation' (*SPCP*, p. 41) (W.B. Yeats).[109]

Middlebrook suggests that, after the birth of their first child, the fascination that Hughes and Plath felt towards their baby 'issued in a flow of calls and responses'. She tracks these from Plath's poems about pregnancy, 'Metaphors' (*SPCP*, p. 116) and 'You're' (*SPCP*, p. 141), to Hughes's celebration of their daughter's arrival, 'Lines to a Newborn Baby' (*CP*, pp. 96–7), to Plath's poem about breastfeeding, 'Morning Song' (*SPCP*, p. 156), and on to Hughes's 'Full Moon and Little Frieda'. Middlebrook sees the 'initiating calls' as coming from 'Metaphors' of March 1959 and 'You're' of January/February 1960. She notes that, in 'Metaphors', 'the speaker likens herself to "a means, a stage, a cow in calf"', and 'You're' 'depicts a "traveled prawn", a "sprat in a pickle jug./A creel of eels"'. Middlebrook sees Hughes's 'Lines to a Newborn Baby', drafted on the back of a typescript of 'Metaphors', as picking up on Plath's animal metaphors, 'using images of "limpets" and "snails" to characterize the instinctual life of an infant, or "an instant/Coiled caul shell of comprehension"'.[110]

Among other examples of these calls and responses, Middlebrook discusses 'Morning Song', 'whose opening lines express feelings of anxious alienation from the infant', through the rewriting of images from Hughes's 'Lines to a Newborn Baby' and 'To F. R. at Six Months' (Uncollected, *CP*, pp. 97–8). In the latter, Middlebrook notes, Hughes's simile for the parents is two 'masks hung up unlit' after a performance (*CP*, p. 98). In Plath's poem, they 'stand round blankly as walls'. 'Lines' includes a metaphor of 'some cloud touching a pond with reflection' (*CP*, p. 96), whereas the speaker in Plath's poem says, 'I'm no more your mother/Than the cloud that distills a mirror to reflect its own slow/Effacement at the wind's hand.'[111]

One of Plath's last poems before her suicide, 'Edge' (*SPCP*, p. 272), depicts the corpses of a mother and two children laid out in a moon-lit garden. Middlebrook suggests that the poem's image of breasts as empty pitchers of milk may have been a response to the image of a full bucket of milk in 'Full Moon and Little Frieda'. Referring to sleepless nights that Hughes spent in the London flat where Plath had died, listening to the howls of wolves from London Zoo in nearby Regent's Park, Middlebrook conjectures that the sounds gave Hughes an image in 'Life After Death' (*BL*, *CP*, p. 1160–1). This image, of wolves lamenting two orphans beside the corpse of their mother, 'beautifully integrates', Middlebrook writes, the legend of Romulus and Remus, children of Rhea Silvia, who were abandoned in the woods but suckled by a she-wolf, 'with the iconography of "Edge", where the children lie dead next to the mother's body alongside her breasts, "pitcher[s] of milk, now empty"'.[112] She adds that in Hughes's poem, 'the singing wolves forecast the children's rescue by a lupine caretaker, himself'.

BIRTHDAY LETTERS AND *ARIEL*: ERICA WAGNER

Erica Wagner examines the biographical context of the *BL* poems and assesses the relationship between the collection and Plath's *Ariel*. Writing of Plath's desire for Hughes, newly back in Cambridge after the couple's initial meeting, Wagner asserts that Plath was not simply hungry for Hughes but for an imagined predestined lover, and that Hughes presents himself as a helpless puppet in her drama, comparing himself to a frog's legs connected to electrodes.[113]

Discussing the poem 'Visit' (*BL*, pp. 1047–9), Wagner quotes Hughes's lines about finding on a page of Plath's journal her joy, but also his reference to her violent swings of emotion, from that joy to despair and agony. She points, however, to the redemption suggested at the end of the poem, the birth of a daughter who is their future incarnate.[114] Wagner sees Hughes's representation of a future whose existence is separate from either himself or Plath, a future inside the earth, waiting to happen. She also discusses the ways in which the *BL* poems write back to poems of Plath's; Hughes's 'Trophies' (*BL*, p. 1054) recasts the black marauder of 'Pursuit' as not himself but as an earlier boyfriend of Plath's, or rather, the pain and rage that poured out of Plath, which she tried to convert to words, the whiff of which, forty years later, comes out of the page to lift the hairs on Hughes's hands. Wagner-Martin's readings suggest that Hughes represents himself less as predator than prey, and the couple caught in an inescapable force. A poem which imagines the events described in Plath's 'Whiteness I Remember' (*CPSP*, p. 102) envisages an occasion on which the horse Plath was riding ran away with her ('Sam', *BL*, CP, pp. 1049–50). For Wagner, the runaway horse embodies Hughes's contention that he and Plath were subject to a controlling agency, a fate that demanded a kind of worship. She suggests that Plath's work is represented as the product of an almost separate self, with its agency, and which saved itself at the expense of its writer's life.[115]

HUGHES'S ORACULAR UTTERANCES: CAROL BERE

Carol Bere's essay '*Birthday Letters*: Ted Hughes's Sibylline Leaves', like Wurst's piece, is collected in Moulin's *Lire Ted Hughes*. Bere borrows the analogy made by Coleridge between his collection of both political public and intimate personal poems of 1817 and the randomly scattered messages of the Cumaean Sybil, who (in Virgil's *Aeneid*) wrote her oracular utterances on leaves which were taken by the wind.[116] For Bere, the 'Letters', written over a period of several decades, published only in fragments, and now impossible to order by date of composition, are Hughes's 'Sibylline leaves', but in spite of their randomised ordering, she finds much that is significant in the architecture of the collection, and the publishing history of its constituent poems; tracing the shifts in meaning and nuance generated by the different contexts in which poems appeared. It is not quite clear whether Bere is suggesting that Hughes is making a direct association between the characters of the *Aeneid* and the two poets, or that the allusions work on a more general level. She does not comment on the choice of myth, which could be seen as inviting further parallels with Aeneas' encounter with Dido, Queen of Carthage.

In a section that is particularly illuminating of the *BL* poem 'You Hated Spain' (*BL*, *CP*, p. 1068), Bere assumes that when Hughes structured the *BL* sequence, he created 'a frame, a holding line around the material', which implies that 'this was not only the way in which he wanted this basically autobiographical material to be read, but possibly that these were the poems that he was able to publish in 1998, either emotionally or psychologically'.[117] Bere also assumes that location and juxtaposition can alter the meaning of poems. Reading poems such as 'You Hated Spain', 'The Earthenware Head' (*BL*, *CP*, pp. 1079–80) and 'Being Christlike' (*BL*, *CP*, p. 1142) in the later context of the *New Selected Poems* of 1995 (since succeeded by *CP*), suggests, she finds, 'subtle shifts in meaning and impact', and the place of a poem in a sequence will generally determine its meaning within the frame of that sequence. This means a shift in emphasis and perhaps in interpretation of the eight 'Plath' poems that were included in *New Selected Poems* when they are reordered in *BL*. Finally, she argues that 'while Hughes attempts to attribute significance to the poems through the frame of *BL*, the publication history, the contextualizations of a few of the poems, most notably "You Hated Spain", tell a different story'.[118]

Bere identifies 'You Hated Spain' as a break from Hughes's 'determined distance from overt disclosures of the self', an uncharacteristic excursion into 'the first-person autobiographical, even confessional, mode', which became central to Hughes's 'unblocking, restorative process'.[119] One of the earliest poems written by Hughes about his life with Plath, its completion, Bere writes, had a powerful effect on him, releasing a 'bizarre dream life' and much that had been 'locked up inside' Hughes.

Like other critics, Bere sees in *BL* not only Hughes's recounting of the story of a relationship which culminated in tragedy, but also the story of Plath's forging of her own poetic voice, and Hughes's part in that process. For Bere, 'You Hated Spain' anticipates the themes that are fully developed in *BL*. The respective poets' response to Spain; Hughes's feeling at home, Plath's discomfort and sense of dislocation; mark their differences in 'background, sensibility, and/or psychology'.[120]

Bere quotes from 'Spain was what you tried' to 'waiting to be found', noting that the reference to a 'soul waiting for a ferry' suggests another parallel with the *Aeneid*.[121] She adds that in a sense Aeneas, returning from Dis, was reborn. In contrast, Hughes's phrase 'new soul' suggests 'regeneration, that Plath is waiting for the ferry back', but in this reading the transformation is not completed.[122] Bere notes that Hughes has stated more than once that Plath's talent 'lay in a "deep and inconclusive inner crisis", a "wound"', and that the major symbols of this crisis and wound were the death of her father, her suicide attempt and the electroshock therapy she underwent.[123] Whilst Plath achieved a rebirth of sorts in 'The Stones', the final part of 'Poem for a Birthday', and experienced a major breakthrough in the second half of 1962, Bere finds that 'the transformation is incomplete because she was unable to fully free herself from her wound', which is where she is represented by Hughes at the end of 'You Hated Spain'.[124]

'You Hated Spain' appears in Hughes's *New Selected Poems* after the poems of the Crow sequence such as 'Lovesong', 'The Lovepet' and 'Littleblood', which it immediately follows. (These are rearranged in *CP*.) Bere finds this justified, since the poem 'suggests the early stages of *Crow*'s rough shamanic framework – initiation, apprenticeship, attempts at loss of self-consciousness, and movement toward insight or vision – which is developed more fully in *Birthday Letters*'.[125] Just as Crow never attains transformation, Bere argues, so Plath's transformation is incomplete.

WRITING BACK TO PLATH: IAN SANSOM

A fresh approach to *BL* is provided by Ian Sansom in a review that cuts through much of the mystique, reverence and calumny in which the publication was wrapped. Sansom's prose is as readable as it is witty, but his conversational turns of phrase contain needle-sharp observations. Sansom examines Hughes's version of his relationship with Plath as a literary construction. Critical of the enterprise and its execution, but not prejudiced, he traces it without prurient speculation or pre-judgement. Sansom finds that the publication of *BL* made the same kind of 'bang-smash, explosive effect' as Plath reported of the poets' first meeting, and as she saw in some of Hughes's '"virile, deep banging poems"'.[126] He notes that though the roar of the publicity surrounding the book will subside, the shock waves generated by the poems will continue to be felt.

Sansom suggests that the birthday of the collection's title alludes to poems by Plath: 'Morning Song', 'Stillborn' (*SPCP*, p. 142), 'A Birthday Present' (*SPCP*, pp. 206–7), 'Three Women: A Poem for Three Voices' (*SPCP*, pp. 176–87) and the seven-part 'Poem for a Birthday' (*SPCP*, pp. 133–7) in which birth is 'a metaphor for artistic creation and the birthday as a reminder and sign of self-renewal'. In particular, 'Poem for a Birthday' is said to be crucial to Hughes's schematic interpretation of Plath's work. Hughes wrote of the poem as a metaphorical record of the first true breakthrough in Plath's writing, and *BL* could be seen as a long poem in separate sections, recording, like 'Poem for a Birthday', a 'never-ending adventure' and a dwelling on 'madhouse, nature, tunnels, rebirth, despair and old (dead) women', all elements of the poem recorded in Plath's journal. 'Suttee' (*CP*, pp. 1138–40), Sansom suggests, is Hughes's record of that terrible rebirth of Sylvia Plath as a poet, and the most disturbing of the *BL* poems. He observes that it is a rewriting of Robert Southwell's Christmas Day poem 'The Burning Babe' (1595) in which Plath is substituted for the fiery Christ Child, and Hughes is a Frankensteinian midwife who delivers an 'explosion/ Of screams' before being engulfed in a flood of 'new myth'. Quoting from 'Both of us' to 'out of both of us' (*CP*, p. 1140), Sansom sees the poem as representing a 'flaming newborn Plath who, crying for help, will feed on tears, rage, and love'.

Sansom writes that whilst it has always been possible to read the work of Hughes and Plath looking for telltale marks of one or the other, *BL* provides new opportunities for 'rereading, counter-reading and misreading of an entirely different order'. Whereas in the past, readers have peered over Hughes's shoulder, reading between the lines of his poems whilst 'squinting at Plath's private journals and letters', Hughes in this volume faces and addresses his own and Plath's readers directly and unashamedly, indignant and accusatory; presenting his side of the story. There is, Sansom writes, 'no mystification or flim-flam'; it is clear who the poems are about and what Hughes is writing about.

Sansom finds the tone of these public replies to be public rebuke of Plath as well as her readers. A number of *BL* poems, he suggests, attempt an unveiling of the real other self of Plath, a self which, in his Foreword to Plath's *Journals*, Hughes claimed was concealed. Quoting 'You ransacked' to 'rhyming yourself into safety' ('The Earthenware Head'), Sansom suggests that this 'coolly deflates' Plath's 'The Lady and the Earthenware Head' (*SPCP*, p. 69), by representing her compositional methods as 'strategies of evasion'.[127]

In this reading, 'Trophies' is a refining and refutation of Plath's 'Pursuit' which claims that Hughes also was pursued; 'The Owl' (*BL*, *CP*, pp. 1063–4) offers the story behind Plath's 'Owl' (*SPCP*, pp. 101–2); 'Wuthering Heights' (*BL*, *CP*, pp. 1080–2) supplements Plath's 'Wuthering Heights', and 'The Rabbit Catcher' (*BL*, *CP*, pp. 1136–8) comments on 'The Rabbit Catcher' (*SPCP*, p. 193). Quoting from 'Remission' (*BL*, *CP*, pp. 1113–14), Sansom notes that the poem's last line might stand as epigraph to the book. This critical engagement with Plath's poems means that there is nothing simply sentimental or nostalgic about this collection; on the contrary, much of it is fairly unpleasant. Sansom acknowledges, however, that one of Hughes's great strengths is that he 'does not sweeten', but 'often makes his readers gulp'.

None of the new poems of *BL* is 'sugared with affection', indeed, for Sansom, Hughes gives a good rendering of what Janet Malcolm has called Plath's 'not-niceness'. In 'Fulbright Scholars' (*BL, CP*, p. 1045), the first poem in the collection, Hughes recalls Plath's photograph, with its strained grin. Sansom sees in this the establishment of a set of distances: between Hughes and Plath, Plath and her 'true' self, and Plath and her public. He argues that the apparently unimportant question in the first line, 'Where was it, in the Strand?', establishes another crucial distance, between Hughes and memories. This, Sansom continues, allows Hughes the scope to view Plath with distance, as a 'Baby monkey' ('Sam'), with 'monkey-elegant fingers', her face 'a tight ball of joy', at best like a Cabbage-Patch doll, eyes 'Squeezed in your face' ('St Botolph's', *BL*, CP, pp. 1051–2), at worst completely formless. 'A spirit mask transfigured every moment/In its own séance', a face 'molten', unreal, 'never a face in itself', a 'stage' ('18 Rugby Street', *BL, CP*, pp. 1055–8).

Sansom finds that many of the *Birthday Letters* poems describe Hughes as stunned, trapped and manipulated by Plath as puppet-master. In 'St Botolph's', however, Sansom finds Plath meaning to knock out Hughes, and branding him with a vampiric kiss/bite; in 'The Shot' (*BL, CP*, pp. 1052–3) Plath is a bullet, which hits Hughes, and in 'The Machine' (*BL, CP*, p. 1058–9) Hughes is 'yawned' into Plath's dark 'other-world interior'. Sansom finds a disturbing similarity between the voice of some of the *BL* poems and that of the hungry deity of Stevie Smith's 'God the Eater', 'consuming "Everything I have been and have not been. Eating my life all up."' He suggests, however, that the charge of rapaciousness is the occupational hazard of the elegist. Like other critics, he finds a more serious objection in Hughes's alleged suggestion that fate or exterior, supernatural forces determined the course of the relationship, and impelled Plath towards her death.[128]

Sansom regards *BL* as from the beginning setting up the relationship as of mythic and epic proportions and impelled towards tragedy. This is sustained as the collection takes the couple falling through the poems, in the darkness of labyrinths, catacombs and temple crypts, in which, Sansom says, Hughes is often mistaken for Plath's father. The symbolism of the poems is riddled with fairy-tale and monstrous characters: ogres, genies, demons; Plath as priestess, dybbuk, Cinderella and Rumpelstiltskin; Plath's mother as kraken, and a 'Lilith of abortions'; Hughes as 'Not quite the Frog-Prince. Maybe the Swineherd'. In 'Fidelity', two would-be lovers are sacrificed 'Under the threshold of our unlikely future' (*BL*, *CP*, pp. 1060–2). The wedding ('A Pink Wool Knitted Dress', *BL*, *CP*, pp. 1064–5) is like 'a cross between the Transfiguration and a painting by Chagall: Plath brims with god, seeing the heavens open, while Hughes levitates at her side'.

Sansom praises Hughes's great spiritual imagination, asserting that he is a visionary and a modern primitive, but quotes Marianne Moore: '"one cannot discern forces by which one is not oneself unconsciously animated"', noting that it can be difficult for the sceptic or orthodox in belief to accept that Hughes is sincere in this confusing talk of omens and spirits.[129] Although, as Sansom has shown, *Birthday Letters* does not produce sentimental moralising, it does open itself up to 'a kind of sentimental mysticism', which Sansom finds just as bad.

Readers are cautioned not to be fooled into thinking that the detailed and intense rendering of an extraordinary relationship in *BL* will actually tell them much more about that relationship than they already know. Sansom suggests that perhaps Hughes's 'big bang' is a distraction, and that perhaps Hughes, like Robert Frost, wrote 'to keep the over-curious out of the secret places of my mind both in my verse and in my letters'.[130]

The next section of this study, Chapter 5, looks at the changing reputation of Ted Hughes and the reception of Hughes's writing in the later decades of his life. The chapter covers the critical response to the poems written by Hughes as Poet Laureate, both at the time the poems were published in periodicals and in reviews of the collection *Rain-Charm for the Duchy and other Laureate Poems* (1992). It also covers the reception of Hughes's acclaimed final collections, *Tales from Ovid* (1997) and *BL*, and, in the case of *BL*, looks at criticism which offers close critical analysis rather than readings of the poems through the work of Sylvia Plath.

CHAPTER FIVE

Later Work

Simon Armitage, writing in the *Guardian* in 2006, suggested that at Hughes's death eight years earlier, his reputation had been as high as at any time during his life. Armitage contrasted the 'resounding acclaim' for Hughes's final collections, *TfO* and *BL*, with the reaction to public support for either the poetry or the poet, during the 1970s and 1980s, when the former was seen as 'stubborn and entrenched' and the latter as ideologically unfashionable.[1]

Poet Laureate is a title given to a poet chosen to become a member of the Royal Household who would once have been required to write poems commemorating events of royal or national significance such as the birth of an heir to the throne. The Poets Laureate in the modern sense have been John Dryden (1668) (though Ben Jonson and William D'Avenant were unofficial Laureates); Thomas Shadwell (1689); Nahum Tate (1692); Nicolas Rowe (1715); Laurence Eusden (1718); Colley Cibber (1730); William Whitehead (1757); Thomas Warton (1785); Henry Pye (1790); Robert Southey (1813); William Wordsworth (1843); Alfred, Lord Tennyson (1850); Alfred Austin (1896); Robert Bridges (1913); John Masefield (1930); Cecil Day-Lewis (1968); John Betjeman (1972); Ted Hughes (1984); Andrew Motion (1999) and Carol Ann Duffy (2009). Although supposedly selected on the basis of artistic merit, many Poets Laureate have been poor poets, and the subject of critical lambast and poetic satire.[2] Hughes, like all modern Laureates, was elected by a committee that met in secret. It is likely that the then Prime Minister, Margaret Thatcher, would have been advised by her culture ministers, though the final decision would have been hers, subject to approval by the monarch.

RESPONSES TO THE LAUREATESHIP

Not everyone saw Hughes as the obvious choice for the post of Laureate. Neil Corcoran, discussing *CB*, remarks that it is 'one of the crucial poems

of the period', but suggests that the work makes its author's acceptance of the Laureateship 'seem in some ways astounding'.[3] Corcoran
finds that some of Hughes's Laureate poems 'weirdly' divert Christian
implications into, for example, a view of monarchy and nationhood
as quasi-religious entities which are susceptible to a mythologising
which keeps 'one combative eye on the more quotidian views of the
tabloid press'.[4] Whilst Hughes's admirers might be impressed by the
way in which these later poems employ regal metaphors available in
'the concept of "the animal kingdom"', examples of Hughes's patriotism might leave more sceptical or republican readers stonyhearted.
Corcoran find the lines 'your *I do* has struck a root/Down through the
abbey floors' ('The Song of the Honey Bee: For the Marriage of His
Royal Highness Prince Andrew and Miss Sarah Ferguson', *RCD*, *CP*,
pp. 818–19, p. 818), baffling, in that the Anglican Marriage Service
requires the response 'I will', and wonders whether this is an echo of
another 'I do' in Plath's 'Daddy'.[5]

Going further than Corcoran, in an otherwise positive tribute to
Hughes and his work published immediately following the announcement of Hughes's death, Boyd Tonkin wrote that when Hughes's
Laureate poems 'tried to weave the kitsch of British royalty into his
image-world, in works such as *RCD*, the results could be as embarrass-
ing as state-sponsored verse usually is'.[6]

That Hughes collected poems such as 'Song of the Honey Bee' in a
self-contained volume of 'Laureate Poems', and excluded all but one
from his *New Selected Poems*, could seem to indicate that these were
bracketed together as court or occasional or duty poems sidelined from
the mainstream of his work, but the poems are included in his *CP*. An
interview for the BBC radio 'Poet of the Month' programme, however, provided Hughes with an opportunity to explain his motives for
accepting the job. The interviewer was Clive Wilmer. Wilmer noted
that some readers might be surprised by Hughes's acceptance of a
public post which required the composition of occasional poems, but
suggested that those readers had found 'Rain-Charm for the Duchy'
surprisingly effective. Hughes responded by defining the figures of
kings and queens in anthropological, biological and psychological
terms. He stated that he had always believed in the symbol of royalty
as an expression of psychological unity and wholeness. The deepest
centre of our make-up is something to which we give divine names,
and where those divine qualities become human qualities there is an
intermediary figure, a king or queen. Hughes asserts that these figures
did not impose themselves, they were invented. To remove the concept
of divinity or monarchy would be to destroy the essential centre of a

community, and to 'pull out the root that draws up the energies into your ordinary personality from whatever is beneath your ordinary personality'. This, as Wilmer observed, suggests that Hughes's Laureate poems are far more than occasional.[7]

Mythographers have described an ancient belief that the king and the land were one: the fertility and vigour of the land depended on the fertility and vigour of the king, who would be prepared to die for the continuance of the land and its dependent people. If the bard is linked to the king, with the great responsibility of articulating the oneness of monarch, land and people, then he too has a sacred function, and is touched by divinity. Seamus Heaney alluded to Hughes's feelings about the almost mystical significance of the post and its special relationship to England and its monarchy in his eulogy for Hughes. He refers to Hughes's instinct for wholeness and harmony, and for 'the necessary consonance between the good of the land and the good standing of its bard'.[8]

Heaney's earlier response to the appointment of Hughes as Laureate had suggested gratified surprise. He found it remarkable that Britain, obsessed by class war and industrial crises, whose official church was almost embarrassed by the mention of God, and whose universities were faltering in their belief in humanist disciplines, should appoint a laureate with 'an essential religious vision' and nothing to say about contemporary politics, but with a strong trust in the realities of the pre-industrial natural world. In Heaney's view, the state of Britain is indeed a demonstration of the truth of the message of Hughes's poetry, that humanity's instinctual and intuitive side has been 'starved and occluded, and is in need of refreshment'.[9]

For Heaney, the title poem 'Rain-Charm for the Duchy' enacts an ancient Indo-European rite of kinship, the betrothal of the king to the land. He writes that by dedicating the poem to Prince Harry, and 'by drenching the royal domain, the Duchy of Cornwall, in a shower of benediction', Hughes both made a graceful gesture and 'reaffirmed an ancient tradition and re-established, without sanctimoniousness, a sacerdotal function for the poet in the realm'.

Neil Roberts notes the surprise of the literary world that the Laureateship did not go to a poet who had declared that he no longer wrote (Philip Larkin), and that it went instead to the prolific Hughes, the celebrator of all in nature that threatens to disrupt our decorous arrangements, someone 'pagan in the strongest possible sense … who thinks the legend of our national saint represents a vicious relationship with the forces of nature … who … is not merely a non-believer but is positively committed to a rival religion which, in his opinion,

Christianity has done its best to stamp out but which will triumph either with our co-operation or at our expense'.[10] Having read Hughes's first official Laureate poem, Roberts found his sense of the incongruity was clarified, but he no longer felt that the appointment was absurd; 'a clear understanding of how outrageous Hughes's Laureateship is brings with it, on the contrary, a strong sense of challenge and excitement'. The water and river imagery of 'Rain Charm for the Duchy', Roberts argues, would not be out of place in collections such as *Season Songs* or *River*. It conveys a warm and hearty blessing on the christened child, 'exploiting the fertility symbol that pervades Christianity in disguise', but also has a 'lurking, goblin-like amusement at the disproportion between' the natural downpour and the sprinkling of water that took place in the cathedral.[11]

Like other critics, Sean O'Brien notes the seriousness with which Hughes approached the role of Laureate, and that he wrote 'more directly, neither left-handed nor piecemeal, in honour of the institution of monarchy than might now be supposed possible'.[12] O'Brien finds Hughes's Laureate poems surprisingly (almost) politicised, in a body of writing which, like Heaney, he characterises as largely silent on political topics. For O'Brien, Hughes's imaginative vigour is such that even in 'bowing to convention', *RCD*, 'though poetically unsuccessful, is not a simply interesting oddity but an important tool in the understanding of his work'. The importance of the collection is that, with some pathos, it illustrates the 'virtual absence of the public realm from his poetic imagination, while giving hints about why this is so'.

O'Brien locates the source of Hughes's royalism in the late Queen Mother, like Hughes, a keen fisherman, in support of which he quotes from the notes on 'A Masque for the Three Voices' which represent the Queen Mother as the centre of a defining drama of the twentieth century, two world wars. O'Brien finds that the notes amount to 'a short essay on identity and patriotism, which is actually more interesting than the verse'. The poem itself, in O'Brien's view, tries to strike a public note. Quoting from 'Tragic drama' to 'That majesty is me.' ('A Masque for Three Voices', *RCD*, *CP*, pp. 82131, p. 821), O'Brien asserts that the stage on which the tragic royal roles are enacted is not simply a 'convenient Elizabethan or Shakespearean figure, but a sign of one of Hughes's imaginative homes'. That home is the 'else-where of imagined history, in the Renaissance and before, in which action and meaning are seen to be unified, and where, insofar as the poet gives his mind to such things, the social order is justified by the fact of its existence'. Just as T.S. Eliot, also a royalist, saw 'a dissociation of sensibility' set in during the seventeenth century,[13] so the First World

War is the 'graveyard of Hughes's unitary myth'. The central, and in O'Brien's view impossible, task is to resurrect that unity 'through a myth of consolation'.[14]

For O'Brien, the *RCD* poems are most interesting when they are most close to home. Quoting from 'I died those' to 'my Shibboleth' in 'A Masque for Three Voices' (*CP*, p. 825), he finds the poem's third voice 'at once representative and personal. It draws both on family history and the amplified speech of the common man who is heard in discussion with the King in *Henry V*, in innumerable war films, including the BBC's Falklands drama, *An Ungentlemanly Act*, in which a Royal Marine, instructed by his OC to surrender to the Argentine forces occupying Port Stanley, apologetically blurts out, "Fuck off, sir!" It is as hard not to admire this obdurate bravery as it is to accept its basis.'[15]

It is 'not without strain', then, that Hughes moves to the 'larger theatre of mythology', in the notes to 'An Almost Thornless Crown', the second part of 'A Birthday Masque for Her Majesty Queen Elizabeth's Sixtieth Birthday' (*RCD*, *CP*, pp. 808–10), removing the crown from historical to natural time and making it a reminder of the mystery 'that historical time comes second' (Notes, *RCD*, pp. 54–5). Correspondingly, O'Brien notes, and presumably in line with protocol, the poems make little of the individuals involved.[16] Given this anti-historical outlook, O'Brien finds it noticeable that the future plays such a small part in the collection, though the 'resolute pastness' accords with the rural conservatism of Hughes's imagination 'in which modernity features as a kind of infernal Argos catalogue with added politics'. In this view, the affirmations of these poems seem valedictory: 'its imagined personages phantoms from a world long vanished, and its contemporary sources a rich and vulgar family rowing in public'. O'Brien ends by quoting Patrick Kavanagh: 'Gods make their own importance ... but that doesn't mean anyone's listening.'[17]

HUGHES, THATCHER AND NIETZSCHE: JOHN LUCAS

In a critical but judicious chapter of his survey of twentieth-century English poetry, John Lucas makes an important association between Hughes's violent imagery, his notion of 'Englishness', and the politics of a post-Imperial Laureate appointed by Margaret Thatcher's Conservative government.[18] An important premise of Lucas's argument is that Hughes is influenced by ideas about power put forward by Nietzsche (1844–1900), who famously pronounced: 'God is Dead.'[19] Nietzsche attributed what he saw as the decay of modern culture to the Christian promotion of equality, self-abnegation and disdain for materialism, arguing that there is nothing intrinsically better about being poor and submissive rather than rich and masterful. He also suggested that the concept of damnation, enforcing a suppression of passion, led to a suppression of differences in favour of accepted, conventional behaviour. Thus, Christianity deprived people of the will to excel and denied the existence of 'supermen', the higher beings whom Nietzsche saw as possessed of creative, intellectual and physical superiority. Rather than seeing life as ending in the death of the body followed by the afterlife of the soul in heaven or hell, Nietzsche imagined life as eternally recurring, and rather than seeing the material world as a flawed copy of a perfect, non-material world, he argued that this life is the only reality. He saw reality as constantly in flux, but capable of being creatively transformed by the individual will.

Referring to Alvarez's argument (in his introduction to *The New Poetry*) that English poets of the mid-century were unwilling to face extremes or take risks, Lucas, like a number of critics, points out that the exception whom Alvarez cited was Hughes.[20] In contrast to O'Brien's view of Hughes's poetry as focused on the past, Lucas finds that it taps the 'dark, psychic, violent forces latent in modern life'. He cautions, however, that '[t]oday's violence is ... tomorrow's Grand Guignol', and finds that much of the poetry has worn badly. Lucas quotes from an article by M.G. Ramanan, 'Macaulay's Children', which appeared in *The London Magazine* in February 1985.[21] The article considered the impact of the English on Indian life, ending with a suggestion about how post-Imperial English literature might be read by Indians. Ramanan suggests that the 'traumatic experience' of the loss of India resulted in 'an insecure and embattled mental condition' which generated writing that was more and more insular and concerned with the landscape, the 'pikes, otters, hawks and crows' of England 'with merry England gone'. He poses the rhetorical question whether it was any wonder that so English and insular a poet as Betjeman was Poet Laureate, and that post-war English poetry seems to take its bearings from Betjeman's disciple Larkin, and from Hughes, who 'in violent desperation attempts to impose his myths on us and to wrest an identity for England?' Ramanan makes the same distinction between Larkin and Hughes as others, finding Larkin 'soft, Norman French, concerned, nostalgic' and Hughes 'tough, Anglo-Saxon, assertive, imposing'. Larkin represents British gentility, Hughes the British 'masculinity', both of which qualities, Ramanan writes, are appropriate to the imperial character. In spite of these differences, Ramanan suggests, both poets are saying the same thing. He associates the violent imagery of Hughes's poems with authoritarian politics, and Larkin's with the doctrine of 'keep England British'.[22]

Lucas notes that Ramanan was writing before Hughes's appointment as Betjeman's successor, but suggests that Ramanan could have added the point that this appointment, under Margaret Thatcher's government, could be seen as 'further proof of the authoritarian nature of Hughes's politics, which will chime very well with the progressive loss of civil liberties, the malign farce of the Falklands campaign and the almost hysterical, bullying aggression which is an essential element of Thatcher's England'.[23] Lucas admits that this is unfair, but 'by no means absurd', because 'there is something about Hughes's poetry which, both at its best and worst, testifies to a preoccupation with violence'.

PATRIOTISM AND NATIONALISM: PAUL BENTLEY AND TOM PAULIN

Considering the question of patriotism and nationalism, and their extreme manifestation in racism and warfare, Paul Bentley asserts that Hughes's poems are as interrogatory of as they are complicit with such attitudes.[24] Like Lucas, Bentley considers the significance to Hughes and his work of, specifically, the First World War. He suggests that in order to exorcise Hughes's 'biggest ghost', the war, and the shock waves that it sent through the Hughes family, the poet had to allow that ghost to speak. Bentley finds no sense of national or ethnic purity in Hughes's concept of Britishness; that sense is undermined by a sense of the British Isles as a melting-pot of cultures. He quotes from Hughes's notes to 'Rain-Charm for the Duchy': 'the British people genetically the most mixed-up gallimaufry of mongrels on earth'.

Though some of Hughes's lines emphasise the unity of Britain, Bentley finds that the parts which make up that whole are represented as uneasy and precarious; hence, perhaps the need for the Crown which holds the parts together. This vision of the wheel and hub, however, 'can only ever be improvisatory and provisional, to be continually re-negotiated: "a melt of strange metals./To be folded and hammered,/Re-folded, re-hammered"' ('A Birthday Masque for Her Majesty Queen Elizabeth II', *RCD*, *CP*, p. 813).[25]

Bentley sees a message to Queen Elizabeth II from her Laureate in the notes, which inform the reader that the term 'the ring of the people' was used by the Black Elk, a Sioux shaman, whose prophetic vision of the ring of his people broken foreshadowed 'the disintegration of the

Sioux nation as an independent moral unity'. Yet, Hughes reminds us, Black Elk's concept of the ring of the people embraced not only the Sioux, but ultimately all peoples of the earth (Notes, *RCD*, p. 55).[26]

The wholeness of a nation symbolised by its Crown may represent something desired but unachieved in Hughes's writing. One of the best accounts of the 'imaginative and vital interior' of Hughes's poetry as an unsettled and volatile terrain is also an assessment of Hughes's achievement up to and including his Laureate poems. 'Ted Hughes: Laureate of the Free Market?' was given by Tom Paulin as the 1990 Kenneth Allott Memorial Lecture at the University of Liverpool, and is included in his collection of essays *Minotaur: Poetry and the Nation State* (1992). For Paulin, Hughes's appointment as Laureate apparently aligned his poetry firmly and indisputably with the British state, but also revealed that, like Yeats and Blake, Hughes is impelled by unresolvable contradictions in his allegiances, aims, character and outlook: 'A patriot who dislikes the British Empire, a domineering Anglo-Saxon Protestant drawn to a relaxed Catholic Celticism, a monarchist fascinated by the molten energies of the free market.'[27] For Paulin, Hughes is not a nature poet in the sense of writing about pastoral Arcadia; he is aligned with the hunter-gather celebrating the wilderness and a time before history. Even so, Paulin reminds us that nature poetry is a form of social commentary in disguise. 'It may face the campfire and the darkness of the cave, but its back is to the daylight.' The natural forces celebrated in Hughes's poetry are metaphors for historical struggles: the Reformation, 'Industrial revolution, First World War' which, Paulin suggests, 'echo and combine in Hughes's radically unsettled imagination'. For all Hughes's 'professed hostility to technology, many of his poems are laments for Britain's decline as a great manufacturing power'. The 'animist vision of machinery' in Hughes's 'Mill Ruins' (*Remains of Elmet*, *CP*, p. 464) resembles a poem which, for Paulin, is one of Hughes's masterpieces, 'Tractor' (*MD*, *CP*, pp. 511–13). Paulin argues that, like one of Hughes's earliest literary models, Kipling, Hughes expresses 'a distinctively British belief in the creaturely nature of heavy industry'.[28]

Paulin suggests that Henry Williamson's novel *Tarka the Otter* (1927), which Hughes read when he was 11 years old, was not only central to Hughes's imagining of the animal world and vocation as a poet, but also crucial to his whole existence, and he discusses in detail Hughes's sympathy for the right-wing reactionary politics of the author of *Tarka*, Henry Williamson, expressed in Hughes's memorial tribute.[29] For his writing, Williamson drew on his memory of the 'stable, happy world of some of the big old estates, where discipline, courtesy, tradition, order, community and productive labour flourished in intimate harmony with a natural world that was cherished'. This memory shaped his rejection of 'the worst side' of democracy: 'the shoddy, traditionless, destructive urban emptiness that seemed to him to be destroying England, in its ancestral wholeness and richness, as effectively as the work of a deliberate enemy'. Paulin suggests that the 'insistent feudalism' of Hughes's *THitR* might be read as a protest against the materialism and consensus politics of the Britain of Harold Macmillan, or that it could express a 'desire to recover an earlier grasp of power and sovereignty'. He asserts that Hughes would agree with Hazlitt's remark in his essay on *Coriolanus* that the language of poetry 'naturally falls in with the language of power'.[30] Paulin finds that Hughes's mind moves instinctively from nature to monarchy; he would like to revive the age of chivalry; in his poem 'September' (*THitR*, *CP*, p. 29) he represents a pair of lovers as doomed monarchs who might have come from Burke's *Reflections*, and, like Burke, he is not afraid to use 'kitsch' language 'in the service of monarchy'.[31] Quoting from 'When all the birds' to 'Soft as the Thistle's Crown' ('The Honey Bee and the Thistle'), Paulin adds that for Hughes, 'salmon, prize bulls, falling leaves, bees and thistles are naturally royal'.[32]

Paulin finds that Hughes thinks 'in terms of splits and polarities – salt-bleached warriors against the "elaborate, patient gold of the Gaels"' – and his imagination is part Celtic, part Teutonic. The warrior energies are 'prolonged, distorted, changed to a constrained boredom in the neologism "prolongueur," as their wild blood is channelled into Calvinism'. In this view, Hughes has constructed a myth of eternal war between the 'German/puritan/masculine' and the 'Celtic/Catholic/feminine'.[33] In spite of this, Hughes is not a hybrid but an autonomous loner: 'His outlook has in many ways the solitary, committed toughness and risky certainties of the self-employed, and his unique ability to locate a North American type of wilderness poetry in England endorses, however unconsciously, Thatcher's famous remark when she was Prime Minister that "there is no such thing as society".'[34] Paulin's depiction of Hughes's poetic persona as homeless and dispossessed is unusual, as most critics are keen to site Hughes in the countryside of Yorkshire and Devon, and to cite those locations as sources of powerful images in his poetry.

For Paulin, Hughes is an intensely uncomfortable writer; he is 'driven and earnest like a street preacher' and there is a sense of strain underpinning his 'lunging, extempore lines' which is a form of homelessness.[35] Paulin writes that it is as if Hughes's poems are 'cries from the dawn of the English working class, that relatively recent formation which was created out of declining social groups'. Even as Hughes speaks for the 'surge and stress of that process', he 'tries to escape into a dreamtime before history', so that his 'aesthetic primitivism embodies this wounded search for a primordial wholeness'.

Paulin finds in Hughes's work an 'entrepreneurial energy' and 'puritan striving' which work together to produce Hughes's 'dream of an ideal vernacular'.[36] Hughes's mature style, in this view, comes from his admiration for 'the backyard improvisation' of Shakespeare, in which dialect is taken to its limits. Paulin links Hughes's admiration for Shakespeare's 'all-off-the-top-of-the-head inventiveness and authenticity' of language, which has an air of being forged from whatever verbal scraps happened to be on hand, in a crisis, for an urgent job, with Hughes's admiration for his father-in-law, Jack Orchard, described in *MD* as belonging to a tradition of farmers who are equal to completing any job and handling any crisis, and who improvise repairs and solutions with whatever old bits of metal are to hand (*MD*, *CP*, Appendix 1, p. 1210). This unstudied inventiveness, whether of speech or the making and mending associated with farming, is, Paulin asserts, the opposite of alienated labour, and suggests the economy of war, or of the hunter-gatherer. This connotation he finds reinforced by Hughes's drawing for the cover of *MD*, a bull which echoes the styles of naïve art and cave paintings.

Hughes's poem 'A Motorbike' (*Earth-Numb*, *CP*, p. 547) represents, for Paulin, Hughes speaking for the 'freebooting private sector, with its hostility to state interference and control', a protest against 'what Hughes has termed "our psychotic democracy", "our rationalist humanist style of outlook"'.[37] *MD*, Hughes's 'most assured, most perfect work', as 'improvised verses' in a journal form, is aligned with puritan discourse, as well as with the improvisation of Shakespearean English. Paulin suggests that the collection elegises the North Devon farming life of the 1970s, 'deeply satisfying, self-reliant', which was soon to become 'jittery, demoralized, industrial servitude' (*MD*, *CP*, Appendix 1, p. 1204).

Paulin finds that Hughes has a sense that the English language has degenerated from the 'buzz and rap' of Elizabethan speech to 'the crippled court-artifice' of the Restoration and the 'shrunken, atrophied, suppressive-of-everything-under, bluffing, debonair, frivolous system of vocal team-calls which we inherit as Queen's English'. This sense, Paulin finds, makes Hughes identify with the struggle of regional vernacular against standardisation and state centralisation. Paulin reads Hughes's images of caged animals as expressive of that struggle, and suggestive of Hughes's desire to overthrow existing power structures.

The stoat in 'Strawberry Hill' that emerges '"thirsting, in far Asia, in Brixton" symbolises 'the opposition of Asian or Afro-Caribbean English to garrison standard English' (*L, CP*, p. 63).[38]

Though Hughes's poems may seem to express a desire to return to an imagined primal natural world, Paulin asserts that they really give vent to the forces which have created capital. Always in process rather than complete, they express that '"everlasting uncertainty and agitation"' which the *Communist Manifesto* (1848) defined as 'the distinguishing features of the bourgeois epoch'.[39]

Reviewing the *Letters of Ted Hughes* in 2007, Paulin went further into the subject of 'market', arguing that the Hughes of the letters is 'in many ways a literary entrepreneur who always "sells" poems to magazines, and whose reputation ... attracts "lucrative commissions"'.[40] He finds a glaring example of 'the entrepreneurial nature of Hughes's imagination' in a letter from Hughes to Olwyn Hughes (10 February 1963). The letter refers to Hughes's accidentally driving over a hare which he then sold to a butcher's in Holborn for 5 shillings. Hughes records that he spent the money on roses; he got four, 'smashed two, & gave 2 to Assia'. Paulin notes that this is a moment that should be isolated as a short poem in prose, and likens it to something by Hardy, the master of 'prolepsis and superstition'.[41]

TALES FROM OVID: MARINA WARNER AND MELVYN BRAGG

The first major collection of articles on Hughes's work to be published in Britain after his death, *The Epic Poise: A Celebration of Ted Hughes*, had been conceived as a celebration to be presented to him on his seventieth birthday, in 2000. Its editor, Nick Gammage, suggested that it could 'serve a double purpose: a birthday gift and an invigorating new route into the broad span of his work for readers who perhaps only knew him through the well-known anthology pieces'.[42] At the time of Hughes's death, many of the articles had been finished, but 'there was an overwhelming feeling among [the contributors] that, although the book could no longer be the birthday gift for which it was intended, it should go ahead with its complimentary [*sic*] purpose: a celebration of Ted Hughes's achievement'.[43] The essays that Gammage commissioned were to be celebrations rather than critiques: 'intensely personal responses to his [Hughes's] work, full of incisive insight and enjoyment'.[44] One of the three sections of the book is devoted to poems composed for Ted Hughes, and another to personal recollections of

him. Part One, 'On the Poetry and Prose of Ted Hughes', contains more
than forty short pieces, many of which are anecdotal: the author's first
encounter with the catalyst of a Hughes poem; the particular resonance or significance of a phrase or image. Some of these are wonderfully evocative, others moving and poignant in their desire to tell the
story, and thus touch the consciousness, of the poet who once and for
always touched them by delving deeply into his own consciousness but
who is now lost to any expression of gratitude and wonder. Melvyn
Bragg's essay on *TfO* (1997) is unequivocally enthusiastic of 'the best
present I have ever bought myself',[45] and scornful of the 'etiolated critics whose swotted degrees' make them see themselves as 'arbiters of
good writing' and who have sneered at Hughes for his profligacy and
magnificent unfashionability.[46] They, Bragg asserts, are 'mere midges',
whereas Hughes is a great poet, and at his best equal to the very greatest, even, in *TfO*, challenging Shakespeare. Bragg offers his readers a
guarantee that if they read *TfO*, they, like him, will be 'awash with awe
and newly alert understandings about the deep springs of our culture'.

Because Hughes's *TfO* is 'the cave of Ali Baba', Bragg focuses on the
first few pages, delighted in the cosmological opening of the *Tales*. 'All
the world seems to be in Hughes's Ovid, from the description of the
Beginning, which vies with Hawking and Genesis, to the profound
psychology of the violent passions of the gods and their subjects.'[47]

In the same collection, Marina Warner, writing of the 'fierceness'
of Hughes's poetry, finds that Hughes's encounter with Ovid has
'beaten, purified, and annealed his own fierceness to a new, intense
radiance'.[48] She suggests that it would not be saying too much to see
Hughes as having found in Ovid 'a twin soul, someone with whom
he could expose his own terrors and passions unguardedly, through
whom he could speak without sounding a note of anachronistic ata-
vism'. Hughes's tone is less urbane than Ovid's, his lines less measured,
and his comedy more ghastly, but the poetry is 'thrilling' and has the
'magic capacity to strip the listener/reader of all defences and catch us
up in the tale as a child carried on the rhythm of a line of verse to stare
with wide eyes, whispering "and what then?" as the story unfolds'.

Warner surmises that had Hughes not been gravely ill, he would
have brought his metamorphoses back full circle 'from the ectoplas-
mic origins evoked at the beginning', since Ovid's 'Pythagorean credo
of cyclical transformation and renewal would surely have summoned
Hughes to his most Prospero-like enchantments'.[49] Nonetheless, near
the end of the volume he gives us his 'magnificent rendering' of the
story of Tereus. For Warner, the appalling story of rape, mutilation
and planned murder, in the myth of Tereus, Philomela and Procne,

becomes a story of mercy and redemption, as the sisters are saved from becoming victims of further violence and Tereus from becoming the perpetrator of further violence, in each case by a redemptive transformation; Philomela into a nightingale, Procne into a swallow, and Tereus into a hoopoe.[50]

As an example of Hughes's reworking of Ovid, Warner gives the section from 'He came after them' to 'dashing into a battle.' (*TfO, CP*, p. 1036). She notes that Hughes changes actionless or passive constructions into movement. 'The vivid and impassioned simile of Hughes's last two lines with their hammering of the word "battle" expands three very simple, even dull, words of Ovid's ("facies arata videtur") into a hectic, heightened image of a man berserk.'[51] Hughes's 'English diction syncopates the sonorities of the Latin, catches the hexameter's long breath', but the tone is not all loud; the final stanza of Hughes's version illustrates that Hughes could modulate the 'screams and bellows' of the myth's mayhem to 'a mood of redemptive elegy' in lines that are not in Ovid's *Metamorphoses* 'except as ghosts flitting between them'.[52]

TALES FROM OVID AND *BIRTHDAY LETTERS*: JON STALLWORTHY

Two of the *Epic Poise* essays on Hughes's later work represent both personal and professional approaches and are both admiring and analytic of Hughes's lasting achievement. Jon Stallworthy's essay suggests that the doubling of *dramatis personae* so vividly apparent in *TfO* is a structural principle of *Birthday Letters* and, indeed, of a great deal of Hughes's poetry. Tom Paulin, listening to the literary echoes in the phrase 'your roundy face', breathes new life into the sometimes tired trope of intertextuality.

Stallworthy's essay, 'With Sorrow Doubled', opens with an examination of Hughes's use of the myths of Echo and Narcissus. He writes that the 'curse of the circling (or doubling) tongue' is in the myth 'transmitted to Echo like a fatal disease, so that when she falls in love with Narcissus and he, separated from his companions, calls to them: "Where are you?/I'm here", she cannot speak for herself or do other than reply: "I'm here," and "I'm here" and "I'm here"'[53] (*TfO, CP*, p. 915.)

A similar fate befalls Narcissus. A would-be lover, feeling 'mocked and rejected' (much as Juno had felt mocked and rejected), prayed. [Stallworthy quotes from 'let him, like Echo ...' to 'love granted it' (*TfO*, p. 78).] Narcissus, contracting 'a form of Echo's disease', sees the face of a beautiful boy in a pool, and believes his love reciprocated. [Stallworthy quotes from 'I stretch my arms.' to 'through my tears' (*TfO, CP*, p. 921).]

Stallworthy finds that this linguistic doubling, reflecting the dramatic situation, has a 'cruelly ironic aspect'.[54] Whilst it seems to offer a perfect union, it actually signals the reverse: an unfulfillable yearning and imminent death. This story is itself echoed in the tale of Arethusa, who, finding a stream that makes a flawless mirror to reflect poplars and willows, dives in (*TfO, CP*, p. 912). Chased by the river-god Alpheus, Arethusa is rescued by Diana, and tells her tale to Ceres, ending 'This is my story' (*TfO, CP*, p. 914). That in itself, Stallworthy notes, is echoed in *BL*. Quoting from 'You are ten years dead.' to 'Your story. My Story' ('Visit', *BL, CP*, p. 1049), Stallworthy suggests that this 'sorrowful doubling' reappears as a structural principle, perhaps '*the* structural principle' of *BL*.[55]

In Hughes's account of their first meeting, he and Sylvia Plath are shown already twinned, and opposed, by the universe; the conjunction of the planets shown in the horoscope cast by Hughes and confirmed, in his imagination, by 'Our Chaucer'. They become one another's mirror-image when she marks his face to match hers ('St Botolph's', *BL, CP*, pp. 1051–2). For Stallworthy, 'the doubling intensifies' a few poems further into *BL*. In '18 Rugby Street' lexical repetition and syntactic doubling are the principles of the sentence structure, and behind the poet's exclamatory joy is an echo of Donne's 'Elegy XIX' (*BL, CP*, pp. 1055–8).[56]

There is more doubling in 'Your Paris', a city with two faces (*BL, CP*, pp. 1065–7), and the lovers read each scar 'With an eerie familiar feeling'. In '9 Willow Street' the husband and wife are 'Siamese-twinned' and each festers a 'soul-sepsis for the other'; each is a stake 'Impaling the other' (*BL, CP*, pp. 1087–90). In 'The Bird', Stallworthy finds a more sinister image of doubleness, the double totem of the German eagle 'Bleeding up through your American eagle' (*BL, CP*, pp. 1092–3). 'Black Coat' is also full of doubles [Stallworthy quotes from 'that double image' to 'just crawled'] (*BL, CP*, pp. 1108–9).[57] Quoting from 'I did not feel' to 'He slid into me', Stallworthy writes that here the doubling or twinning or substitution becomes 'father/husband'. These 'enemies', he notes, meet again in 'A Picture of Otto', this time as 'doppelgängers in the hellscape of Wilfred Owen's "Strange Meeting"' (*BL, CP*, p. 1167).[58]

Stallworthy finds a third structural pairing in the poems 'A Dream' (*BL, CP*, pp. 1119), 'The Minotaur' (*BL, CP*, p. 1120), 'The Table' (*BL, CP*, pp. 1132–4), 'Dream Life' (*BL, CP*, pp. 1135–6), 'The Bee God'

(*BL*, *CP*, pp. 1140–2), 'Blood and Innocence' (*BL*, *CP*, pp. 1151–2), 'Night Ride on Ariel' (*BL*, *CP*, pp. 1155–6), 'The Cast' (*BL*, *CP*, pp. 1158–9) and 'The God' (*BL*, *CP*, pp. 1163–6), seeing in these poems the daughter descending into the father's grave or his rising to join her.[59] A fourth pairing, in 'Dreamers' (*BL*, *CP*, pp. 1145–6), is of the husband and another woman (also, Stallworthy notes, of part-German ancestry). Stallworthy quotes from 'The dreamer in her' to 'and I knew it' (*CP*, p. 1146), and notes that these pairings, 'each with its mimetic repetitions, are reflections of the central one, the fatal conjunction of the I and the You; and are, of course, subsidiary to it'. Stallworthy sees each of the pairings operating on two planes, 'that of space and that of time: here and now, there and then, as at the end of "The Blue Flannel Suit"' [Stallworthy quotes from 'Now I see' to 'open coffin'] (*BL*, *CP*, pp. 1085–6).

This complex web of doubling and echo, Stallworthy concludes, leaves us with one thing to be grateful for: 'that, unlike so many poets who fall silent in their later years, Ted Hughes went out in the wake of two of his most moving and memorable books'.[60]

HUGHES, HOPKINS AND CLARE: TOM PAULIN

Tom Paulin's piece in *Epic Poise* examines one of the same poems as Stallworthy, '18 Rugby Street', but with a narrower focus. He finds part of the excitement of reading Hughes's work is its 'urgent conversation with a whole series of authors'.[61] Quoting from 'And now at last' to 'crueller, "boneless"' (*BL*, *CP*, p. 1057), in which Hughes uses the phrase 'roundy face', Paulin notes that the adjective 'roundy' stayed with him. It brought to mind an anecdote of Seamus Heaney's: 'how a schoolkid in County Cork began an essay on the swallow by writing: "The swallow is a migratory bird. He have a roundy head." The move between best-behaviour, standard English and intimate spoken dialect – between the official and the warmly oral – is touching.' Paulin quotes Hopkins's 'As Kingfishers Catch Fire':

> ■ As kingfishers catch fire, dragonflies draw flame;
> As tumbled over rim in roundy wells
> Stones ring; like each tucked string tells, each hung bell's
> Bow swung finds tongue to fling out broad its name.[62] □

For Paulin, linking the two poems means that 'a void also opens up – stones are falling down the roundy well with a sound like plucked

catgut knocking against the serried stones that rise up from the darkness'. He observes that Hopkins uses the word 'faces':[63]

■ for Christ plays in ten thousand places,
Lovely in limbs, and lovely in eyes not his
To the Father through the features of men's faces. □

Here perhaps, as in 'a certain type of heightened imagination', not
only individual words or phrases are alluded to, but the whole of the
poem. 'Hopkins's triumphantly religious sonnet, which has "roundy"
in its second line and "faces" in its last, is compressed into the "roundy
face" which triumphs over the pejorative alternatives – "rubbery" and
"boneless" – for her face.' For Paulin, then, the phrase is redemptive
and unique. He quotes again from Hopkins:

■ Each mortal thing does one thing and the same:
Deals out that being indoors each one dwells;
Selves – goes itself; myself it speaks and spells,
Crying What I do is me: for that I came. □

Hopkins's remark to Robert Bridges illustrates the value he places on
the individual: '"Every poet, I thought, must be original and originality a condition of poetic genius; so that each poet is like a species
in nature (not an *individuum genericum* or *specificum* [that is, not an
individual birth]) and can never recur."' Thus, Paulin says, there is 'a
great tribute to Plath's genius concealed in that tender phrase, "roundy
face", just as the tenderness of the adjective is in John Clare's "The
Village Minstrel": "Welcome red and roundy sun/dropping slowly in
the west"'.[64] The word 'roundy', Paulin asserts, 'belongs to dialect, to
the spoken language that so inspired Hopkins, and which informs everything Ted Hughes wrote'.[65]

In the poem 'Daffodils' (*BL, CP*, pp. 1125–6), Paulin catches another
'moment from Hopkins'. Quoting from 'We worked' to 'Opened too
early' (*CP*, p. 1126), in addition to a 'tense, stretch Degas-image', he
finds a reminiscence of a passage from Hopkins's journals in which the
poet writes about bluebells.[66] Both Hopkins's prose and Hughes's poem,
Paulin contends, 'involve flower stalks and jostling shocks' and remind
him of the work of the painter Stanley Spencer. He sees this as an
'intensely English vision with a clear, cold, quietly redemptive light'. It
has an almost subliminal religious iconography: 'hurdle, sheephooks,
crook', which 'informs the glistening sense of transcience' in Hughes's
'Daffodils' with 'a tough, flexible permanence like a hurdle being
leant against'.

Paulin finds a third 'sighting' of Hopkins in Hughes's poem 'The Beach' (*BL*, *CP*, pp. 1143–4), in which he discerns an allusion to Hopkins's image of paintings of the Crucifixion.[67] 'The pain is there' in Hughes's lines, 'but invisibly the uplift in Hopkins is there too'. This kind of allusiveness has 'a fresh-peeled, sappy, present-moment direct-ness' as Hughes's imagination catches up a line or phrase or whole poem, so that 'it lives again and imparts energy to the verse'. Hopkins, for Paulin, 'lives on in Hughes's writing', which is 'an invocation and a celebration which exalts a whole community of writers and readers – past, present and to come'.

Paulin's close reading of poems from *BL*, both scholarly and invigor-ating, avoids one of the problems facing critics of Hughes's later work. Whilst many of the poems dramatise states of mind or resemble diary entries (as in the *Moortown* sequence), Paulin shows that the respective narrative I's need not be completely and exclusively identified with Ted Hughes, nor must the biographical content be the central interest in the work.

HUGHES'S REPUTATION

Sarah Churchwell argues that the critical reception of *BL* presented a new view of Hughes; instead of the demonisation of him as a con-trolling misogynist who silenced Plath, he was remoulded as a 'nobly silent' martyr to the clamour of 'aggressive' feminists.[68] Tracy Brain marks the irony of this, 'given the fact that Hughes is not silent about feminism' in *BL*.[69] She notes that although the word 'feminist' does not appear in BL, several of the poems 'allude to feminist aggres-sion and misinterpretation of Plath's work'. Brain argues that 'Blood and Innocence', 'Brasilia' and 'The City' all represent academics, fans, biographers and feminists as relentless, over-zealous misreaders 'blind to the real Plath', who are interested only in their own theo-ries.[70] Hughes's 'The Dogs Are Eating Your Mother', Brain finds, works 'though a specific analogy between academic feminists and "dogs" or "hyenas"'.[71] Quoting Amber Kinser, she accepts that some might see this as in keeping with 'over-simplified and pejorative representations of feminism', but adds that a more fair reading would look at 'The Dogs Are Eating Your Mother' 'not as engaging with feminism as a set of ethical and political ideas, but rather as a dramatic representation of a particular set of events'.[72] In this view, the analogy between femi-nist academic and dogs and hyenas is 'associative, depending on the reader's knowledge of the controversy concerning Plath's gravestone'.[73]

HOWLS AND WHISPERS **AND** *CAPRICCIO*

Also published in 1998, Hughes's *Howls and Whispers*, in contrast to *BL*, had no broadsheet serialisation, no shock-horror reactions, and few reviews, yet Diane Middlebrook writes of the collection that 'Hughes had reserved [these] eleven poems from the manuscripts that became *BL*, as a winemaker sets aside the choicest vintage for special labelling.'[74] *Howls and Whispers* was privately printed in a limited edition of 110 copies, the first ten of which constituted a deluxe edition which included three watercolour drawings by Leonard Baskin, a second suite of the etchings, a copperplate and a folio of the manuscript.

In *'Howls & Whispers*: The Averse Sephiroth and the Spheres of the Qlippoth',[75] Ann Skea notes the Cabbalistic significance of the number 110 in representing the combined powers of 11 and 10 and 1 and 0; the whole number, representing the powers of 11 multiplied tenfold. Tracing Cabbalistic symbols in the poems, Skea writes that Hughes 'takes the Path of Wisdom (which is also the Path of the Serpent)', a path taken by all human beings who become aware of their spiritual selves; a route of self-awareness and growth. He 'ascends the Sephirotic Tree from the lowest sphere of Malkuth [the number 10] to Kether [the number 1] at its crown'. In doing so, he visits each Sephira in reverse order to that in which the 'Lightning Flash from the Divine Source transmits its energies down the tree'. Skea points out that Hughes firmly believed in the power of poetry to evoke energies both positive and negative, a calling forth which she refers to as the magical aspect of Cabbalistic ritual. She argues that Hughes practised Cabbalistic poetic rituals with great care, particularly in dealing with the 'Averse energies of the Cabbalistic Tree'. She suggests that perhaps until the later stage of his life, Hughes did not feel ready to deal with the Averse energies 'to which he would be exposed on this journey', but that in *Howls and Whispers* he recognised and worked with them.

Elizabeth A. Stansell finds that *Howls and Whispers* picks up several of the themes of *BL*, especially the representation of 'Hughes and Plath being thrown together by the universe and fulfilling a tragic destiny, always together in spirit even after death'.[76] She adds that *Howls and Whispers* 'operates on the central notion that the dead often are not truly dead, at least from the perspective of the living'. She quotes from 'Paris 1954', in which she sees Hughes observing himself on a visit to the city, before he met Plath, 'blissfully unaware' of the scream that the poem shows is already seeking him out, and coming closer, in 'the likeness of a girl' (*Howls and Whispers*, *CP*, 1173–4).

Although published eight years before *BL* and *Howls and Whispers*, Hughes's *Capriccio* has been discussed in concert with them, as a precursor of or first act in the revealed drama. Jo Gill finds the evocation of Assia Wevill's presence and influence in *Capriccio* unsettling in several ways. She notes that Hughes's letters to Leonard Baskin and Seamus Heaney suggest that there was no conscious plan or programme behind the compilation of the poems in these works, and concludes that Hughes presents himself as 'impelled by some larger force or influence outside himself and his immediate muses'.[77] That impelling force may be 'esoteric' and/or the force of history.[78] The opening poem of the 25 in *Capriccio*, 'Capriccios', hammers home the message of the 'relentless force of astrological and occult powers' through its repetition of the date of Friday the thirteenth, which 'sounds like a knell through the text' (*Capriccio*, *CP*, p. 783). That sense, for Gill, is reinforced by the reappearance of the poem, retitled but in near-identical form, in *Howls and Whispers*. Gill notes that the second *Capriccio* poem reads the death of Wevill as 'a fait accompli', rhyming 'fait' with 'fate' ('The Locket', *Capriccio*, *CP*, pp. 783–4) and the third, entitled 'The Mythographers' (*Capriccio*, *CP*, pp. 784–6), casts its subject as both Lilith and Nehama.[79] 'Denied agency, she can only play out the role for which, in this narrative's terms, she is destined.'[80] That destiny is not represented as brought about by the agency of the poems' narrator; Gill finds no direct relationship between the speaker and the addressee. Influence, she writes, 'is mediated by language'. She sees the speaker of the poems reading and rereading 'his "other" in an increasingly fraught attempt to make sense of their shared past'.

Terry Gifford describes the publication of *Capriccio* as Hughes clearing himself of the 'freight' that he carried from the relationship with Wevill.[81] Tom Paulin's comments about Hughes's entrepreneurial instincts seem to be supported by Gifford's observation that the limited edition of fifty copies sold at $4000 each was probably intended for only the 'keenest and richest collectors and libraries'.[82] Gifford suggests that perhaps Hughes 'was testing the water' for *BL* but 'in the most tentative, and lucrative way', and he sees the repetition of the first poem from *Capriccio* as the last poem from *Howls and Whispers* perhaps suggesting 'the overlap in relationships'.

Carol Bere, in 'Complicated with Old Ghosts: The Assia Poems', sees *Capriccio* as important beyond its interest as a collection of 'Assia' poems: it is 'a significant, well-realised narrative sequence in its own right' which also shed lights on the *BL* poem 'Dreamers' and that sequence as a whole.[83]

Bere asserts that while it is tempting to see the sequence as biography or autobiography, she is writing about *Capriccio* as a 'blend or mosaic of ancient myths, historical and contemporary events, some actual facts of the relationship – and, more to the point, as a fully realized poetic sequence'.[84] She notes that the title of the sequence is on the surface misleading, since a *capriccio* is an 'improvisational, lively, joyful free-form musical work'.[85] Baskin's illustrations, however, would quickly dispel those connotations. These suggest that the 'archaic Italian definition of *capriccio*', '"head with hair standing on end"' in horror, or the related derivation *raccapriccio*, meaning horror or shudder, are closer to the story told in this sequence.[86]

For Bere, the 'overall mood of the sequence is finality', and the opening poem announces this in 'a death foretold'.[87] Connections between *Capriccio* and *BL* are implicit in references to Friday the thirteenth, a day marked in '18 Rugby Street', the day Plath left for Paris and the birthday of her father. Like other commentators on *Capriccio*, Bere notes the sense of fatalism that hangs over the sequence. In the poems, she writes, people are subject to the 'seemingly erratic, unmotivated events of life', and the 'magnetic force of desire' has 'implicit potential for self-destruction'.[88] Bere sees the *Capriccio* poem 'Folktale' (*Capriccio, CP*, p. 788) as in some ways the horrific dark side of the 'vision of joyous union' in the poem 'Bride and groom lay hidden for three days' which was to be the triumphant culmination of *Crow*, but was delayed until publication of *Cave Birds*. Whereas 'Bride and groom' was to be the outcome of the question put to Crow 'Who gave most, him or her?', 'Folktale' insistently reiterates speaker and subjects' selfish desires: 'he wanted', 'she wanted'.[89]

Bere concludes that that *Capriccio, Howls and Whispers* and *BL* could be seen as 'fragments of one long sequence' or as separate, though interrelated, sequences that 'speak to each other across separate frames'. The contiguous arrangement of the 'Assia' and 'Plath' poems in Hughes's *New Selected Poems* frames the groups with the poems 'The Other' and 'The Error', reinforcing, for Bere, both the significance of the interrelatedness of the two women, and the notion that the shadow of Plath was a major force in Wevill's death. The reappearance of 'Capriccios' as 'Superstitions' (*Howls and Whispers, CP*, pp. 1183–4), for Bere, indicates Hughes's representation of the unpredictable and unpremeditated nature of events, and his creation of a circular pattern which suggests the 'impossibility of fulfilment or transformation of completed myth'.[90]

For Bere, subtle shifts in the narrative voice of *Howls and Whispers* make the poems 'cut closer to the vein' and reveal more of Hughes's 'painful unresolved feelings' about the death of Plath than many of the poems of *BL*.

SIR GAWAIN AND THE GREEN KNIGHT: SEAN O'BRIEN

Fitting as a final comment on Hughes's later work, touching on his abilities as a storyteller and dramatist as well as poet, is a statement by Sean O'Brien about Hughes's adaptation of an extract from *Sir Gawain and the Green Knight*. This was included in a *Guardian* review of Hughes's *CP*, in which the extract, originally published in Hughes's and Heaney's *The School Bag* (1997), appears. O'Brien's review of the collection is mixed; he finds Hughes's work uneven, the collection 'frequently impeded and distracted by lapses of taste and mistaken ambition', but *Gawain* as representative of Hughes at his best.[91]

O'Brien notes that a number of allegorical readings of *Gawain* are possible, but that Hughes's poem ignores them, rendering a straightforward dramatic scene of a mysterious man sharpening an axe and awaiting his victim. This, O'Brien writes, is 'a piece of dramatic writing, in three dimensions, an event in the imagination of writer and reader alike' which is best appreciated 'on its own terms'. In Hughes's rendition, 'weary abstraction stays in its coffin. The work of Hughes at full power – and there is a good deal of it – engages with the world in this direct, properly dramatic sense, and survives the buffetings of this essential but unlovely book.'

As has been seen, the responses to Hughes's work as Poet Laureate were not universally positive, and *Howls and Whispers* and *Capriccio* attracted less critical attention, but with a few exceptions critics acclaimed *TfO* and *BL* as in many ways the culmination of Hughes's poetic career. Final, posthumous, assessments of that career are discussed in the conclusion of this study.

CONCLUSION

Overviews of Hughes's Achievement

The death of Ted Hughes was followed by a flurry of posthumous summaries of his career and assessments of his achievements. The *Guardian* included the news of Hughes's death on its front page,[1] and obituaries and tributes were published in both British and international newspapers and periodicals. Authors paying tribute in British and Irish newspapers included Katherine Viner in the *Guardian*; John Redmond and Alan Sillitoe, also in the *Guardian*; Peter Forbes in *The Financial Times*; Sandra Barwick in the *Daily Telegraph*; Boyd Tonkin, Ruth Padel and Lachlan Mackinnon in the *Independent*; William Scammell in the *Independent on Sunday*; A. Alvarez in The *Observer*; Glenys Roberts in the *Daily Mail*; John Carey in the *Sunday Times*; Heather Neill in the *Times Educational Supplement*; John Bayley and Anthony Thwaite in the *Times Literary Supplement*; and Rosita Boland in the *Irish Times*. American writers who published at the same time included Marjorie Miller in the *Los Angeles Times*, Sarah Lyall in the *New York Times* and Marina Warner in *Time*. *Le Monde* also featured an article by Geneviève Brisac.

Although there was some disagreement in these articles about those works for which he should be best remembered, most writers agreed that *BL* and *TfO* were a final flowering of Hughes's genius, and that by any standard Hughes was a great poet.

The unsigned *Times* obituary of Hughes notes that it has been said that all great works of literature either find a new style or dissolve an old one, that is, that they are special cases.[2] The author declares the poetry of Hughes to be such a special case, on the basis that its 'forcefulness and animal vitality' had 'injected new life into English poetry'. The rapturous encounters with nature's claws and teeth in *THitR* showed Hughes to be 'the finest English nature poet of his generation'. The obituary records, however, that Hughes was 'oddly neglected in Britain for most of his middle career', and received no literary prize for thirty years, until the *Sunday Times* Award for Literary Excellence, which he received in 1995. The assessment made of *G* is that it is bizarre, and in danger of becoming self-parodic because the encounter with violence in nature 'was becoming an easy embrace', and a *Times* article which described *Shakespeare and the Goddess of Complete Being* as like 'the jumble of an occult bookshop' is quoted. It is reported that criticism was silenced, however, by *M*, whose 'large, lyrical energy' made Hughes's 'fellow poets sound as timid as librarians'. The alternative, 'fierce and mysterious' England, one of the mind yet rooted in English history and language, that Hughes represented in *RE*, established him as one of England's three pre-eminent poets (with Philip Larkin and Geoffrey Hill).

John Kinsella, writing in the *Observer*, declared *TfO* to be Hughes's greatest achievement, though he concedes that the *RE* poems are 'wonderful recountings of absence and the power of lost voices'.[3] Kinsella attributes Hughes's success in translating Ovid to the way that his work represents 'a nail in the coffin of Romanticism', a 'pushing of the sublime into the brutal'. The 'brilliant pastoral' created by Hughes, though 'old-world in taste', was 'entirely new' in speech.

Unsurprisingly, many column inches of the obituaries were taken up with summaries of the events of Hughes's life, in particular the deaths of his wife and his lover and their child (a *Guardian* article is headed 'Life Plagued by Demons').[4] An obituary by John Redmond and Alan Sillitoe, 'Poet of the Spirits of the Land', compares the work of Hughes and Plath, noting that they share an extreme intensity but that Hughes 'worked on a much grander canvas' and is perhaps best regarded as 'a critic of the mainstream of Western culture, particularly of the utilitarian rationalism arising from the Enlightenment'. Redmond asserts that there is no denying Hughes's 'immense significance'.[5] Sarah Maguire, in the same issue, describes *TfO* and *BL* as showing Hughes both 'at the height of his astonishing poetic powers' and as 'displaying a frank and full emotional range'.[6]

A *Guardian* piece on Hughes's death, 'Earth Receive an Honoured Guest', similarly sees Hughes's reputation diminishing from his appointment as Laureate, and his 'poetic stock' residing in his early work.[7] The publication of *NSP* in 1995, the piece suggests, seemed a summing up; for critics, 'the matter was settled' until the 'bombshell' 'sensation' and 'masterpiece' of *BL*. The 'magnificent' poems of that volume ensure that Hughes leaves the world 'with his best work hardly cold from the presses'.

A *Daily Telegraph* article similarly divides Hughes's career into two major phases and a less spectacular middle phase, quoting the poet P.J. Kavanagh's statement that Hughes 'leapt upon the scene, fully armed, in 1957', with *THitR*, and followed this, of late, with 'a sort

of miracle', *Tales from Ovid*, and 'another miracle', *BL*.[8] This echoes
Anthony Thwaite's evaluation in his *Poetry Today* that much of the
force of Hughes's writing comes from the two 'particular clusters' of
the early work: the animal poems from *THitR* and *L*, and to a lesser
extent *W*, and from *C*. These, Thwaite argues, established Hughes as a
'powerful model for his contemporaries and juniors ... No matter what
his later efforts have been, including some very odd manifestations
of his role as Laureate, it is with these earlier works that he has made
his mark.'[9]

The suggestion seems to be that Hughes should be remembered as
the tooth and claw blooding the etiolated urbanity of *New Lines*; for
THitR, *L*, and, perhaps, *W*; for his adaptation of *TfO* and for *BL*. As has
been seen, however, other critics, notably Keith Sagar, Leonard Scigaj
and Ekbert Faas, have found equal merit in, and have traced themes
and preoccupations which unite, many if not all of the collections.

Sagar makes an important point about the difficulty of reading *BL*
and, in a reversal of the received wisdom of most reviews, finds that
volume and *TfO* to be outside the mainstream of Hughes's writing and
indicative of a narrowing of Hughes's creative endeavour. He notes
that though Hughes, having once despised confessional poetry, came
to see it as of great value, 'particularly as auto-therapy', the critical
pronouncement that *BL* is the height of Hughes's achievement 'is as
absurd as it would be to claim that the Shakespeare's sonnets (revela-
tory as they are) are the pinnacle of Shakespeare's'. Sagar finds the
poems splendid of their kind, but neither collection gave Hughes the
creative freedom needed for his greatest work, because each was a
treatment of already existing material.[10] For Sagar, as for anyone who
followed the Plath–Hughes story in its many iterations, the 'plot' of
BL is predetermined. By failing to anonymise the characters, instead
encouraging them to be identified specifically as Hughes and Plath, the
poems, Sagar writes, cast the reader as voyeur, 'however deeply our
sympathies might be engaged'. Sagar objects to the fact that *BL*, as he
asserts, 'sold ten times more copies than any other Hughes book in its
first year' on the basis that the reason was 'not because it is ten times
better as poetry but because there are twenty times as many voyeurs as
poetry-lovers among book-buyers, and a hundred times as many among
newspaper editors'. For Sagar, the poems on which Hughes's reputation should stand are those of the 1970s and early 1980s, works which
'contain the inestimable healing gifts' which are Hughes's 'legacy to
us all'.[11]

In contrast, rather than a healing function, Jeffrey Meyers sees
Hughes's characteristic trope as war poetry. In a 2003 article which harks

back to the opinions of early reviewers, Meyers writes that the dominant outlook of Hughes's work is feral. He sees the effect of Hughes's father's vivid war stories as a psychological wound 'so palpable that Hughes felt he himself had witnessed the apocalyptic carnage [of Gallipoli]'.[12] He notes that although there was no bombing near Hughes's home in rural Yorkshire during the First World War, and Hughes was a non-combatant radio mechanic during his time in the RAF from 1948 to 1950, Hughes inherited his father's 'trauma and survivor's guilt' which, Meyers asserts, continued to torment Hughes's life and to influence his art. Hughes's 'instinctive taste for violence' made war his subject matter and death became his dominant theme in the 'most bloody and horrific poetry since John Webster's'. Meyers aligns Hughes's early encounters with animals, through killing them, with his 'doomed soldiers', who have the 'feral primitivism of the beasts, both hunted and hunting'. 'At war with themselves and with men, these animals have, like predators tearing out the entrails of their prey, a primeval instinct to kill.'

The war poems, Meyers writes, are Hughes's fierce campaign against hypocrisy, oppression and waste of human life. Unlike his father, he could seek relief and consolation in his art, 'propelled by emotion recollected in emotion' (in contrast to Wordsworth's 'emotion recollected in tranquillity'). His poems are cathartic in portraying the effect of war on both 'the guilty survivors and their traumatized descendants'. The psychological wound which war stories inflicted 'hurt [Hughes] into poetry', but his savage indignation helped him to cope. Meyers quotes from Wilfred Owen's preface to his elegiac *Poems*: '"My subject is War, and the pity of War. The Poetry is in the pity"', and concludes that in the aftermath of recent wars, Hughes's poems now resonate more forcefully than ever.[13]

Following Hughes's death, many tributes were paid to him and collected in national and international newspapers. The *Guardian* published a collection on 30 October 1998 and the *Observer* on 1 November 1998 (including some of the same contributors).

In the *Guardian* Douglas Dunn describes Hughes as a poet whom it would not be an insult to place alongside Shakespeare. Malcolm Bradbury echoes earlier critics in labelling Hughes the most important poet of his generation, and one whose work will last for a hundred years. Valentine Cunningham places Hughes with Blake and Milton and in a 'major line of poetic myth-making'. Ben Okri contributed a poem in which Hughes is described as a Titan, with a touch of Prospero, and, echoing Heaney's memorial address, a 'rough Merlin of our age'.[14]

In the *Observer*, Simon Armitage recollects that it was Ted Hughes who got him into writing. Carol Ann Duffy says that she grew up reading Hughes's books for children, and hearing of his death was like hearing that God had died. For her, 'no one on the landscape' could compare with Hughes. For Douglas Dunn, Hughes was a 'full-throated passionate poet' whose passing left a great gap. Alan Brownjohn remembered Hughes as awesome, a 'great chunk of granite', a 'great hunched eagle', but genial and generous. Don Paterson notes that he had had calls from poets asking 'what do we do now?', since Hughes was a poet from whom subsequent generations took their bearings. Andrew Motion ends by attesting that Hughes was 'a great poet and a great exemplary man'.[15]

The *Independent*, on 30 October 1998, published an article by Boyd Tonkin whose title alone suggests the esteem in which Hughes was held: 'The God of Granite Who Could Shatter Stone with Plain Words'.[16] For Tonkin, Hughes had done more than 'anyone since Tennyson to give great English verse a deep public presence' and judged that Hughes's 'impact in the air and on the tongue' far outweighed the honours conferred on him. Tonkin sees *BL* as a 'scorching swansong' which struck the reading public with a force unmatched in English poetry since Byron's *Childe Harold* in 1812. 'In a demystified age' Hughes 'laid bold claim to the titles and ambitions of a tribal bard' and, crucially, 'made good those claims'.

A powerful statement about the impact of Ted Hughes is not an evaluation or assessment at all, but a forceful assertion and testament in a dedicatory poem prefacing Keith Sagar's *Ted Hughes and Nature: Terror and Exultation* (2009):

■ When that oak fell a tremor passed
Through all the rivers of the West.
The spent salmon felt it.[17] □

Terry Gifford recalls that when he and others were asked in 2009 to support the campaign to establish a memorial for Ted Hughes in Westminster Abbey, the Dean of the Abbey asked whether Hughes's work would stand the test of time: would it still be read by generations to come?[18] Gifford notes that in a sense this question is impossible to answer, but cites in support of the campaign that at the 'end of the first decade of the twenty-first century it is probably true to say that Hughes's reputation as a poet has never been higher'; that Hughes is 'often the only post-war English poet considered' in works such as *Writing for an Endangered World* (2001) and *Can Poetry Save the Earth?* (2009); that no course in Modern British Poetry would be complete without Hughes's verse; that between 2006 and May 2010 six works on Hughes's writing and two memoirs were published; that *BL* brought him a new audience; and that *TfO* was awarded literary prizes and became a successful play.

Having provided a wonderfully concise and insightful overview of Hughes's many modes and interventions, Gifford, significantly, praises him not for the conclusions he comes to or the assertions that he makes, but for the questions that he raises.[19] Writing more than ten years after Hughes's death, Gifford states that it has become clear that 'in an always changing body of poetic work, and in a range of other literary modes, Hughes sought to raise questions for readers'. Those questions have become even more urgent: they concern what it might be to be human within our universe; how we might understand our inner life in relation to the forces of nature; 'the moral scope for action within the paths already chosen; how the contemporary imagination might be a force for cultural change; whether we are ignoring alternative forms of knowledge; whether culture is nature', and '[w]hat might be the healing role of literature in considering the problems we have created in our relationship with our environment?'

In this way, criticism can answer the question posed earlier: how and why should we remember, and value Ted Hughes? Hughes and his work continue to be remembered, and criticism of the work continues to be published. As this study is prepared, forthcoming collections of essays on Hughes's work are announced, including Mark Wormald, Neil Roberts and Terry Gifford (eds), *Ted Hughes: From Cambridge to Collected* (Basingstoke: Palgrave Macmillan, 2013), and Terry Gifford (ed.), *Ted Hughes* (New Casebooks Series, Basingstoke: Palgrave Macmillan, 2014). Hughes's work has always attracted different kinds of analysis and it seems likely that a full panoply of critical approaches will be brought to bear on his writing. In particular, perhaps, Ecocriticism, Gender Studies and Postcolonial Theory will provide fruitful insights into Hughes's poetry in the future. New evaluations of Hughes's monumental achievement will surely arrive if and when the existing *CP* is superseded by a 'Complete Works' of Ted Hughes. Further biographical works are likely to follow memoirs such as those by Hughes's brother, Gerald – *Ted and I: A Brother's Memoir* (2012) – and friend, Lucas Myers – *An Essential Self: Ted Hughes and Sylvia Plath: A Memoir* (2010).

Though the year and the season are different, the elegiac poem written after the death of Hughes's father-in-law Jack Orchard, 'The Day he Died' (*MD*, *CP*, p. 533), with its reference to 'a great blank', might equally stand for the sense of the significance of the passing of Ted Hughes himself.

Notes

INTRODUCTION

1. Ted Hughes, *Winter Pollen*. London: Faber & Faber, pp. 8–9.
2. Part of which became the radio play *Difficulties of a Bridegroom*, which was broadcast on 21 January 1963, and a fragment of which was published as *Eat Crow* in 1971.
3. Nick Gammage, Editor's note to Nick Gammage, ed., *The Epic Poise: A Celebration of Ted Hughes*. London: Faber & Faber, 1999, p. xiii. The publisher's profits from the book are donated to Peter Harper's Cancer Research Unit at Guy's Hospital, London.
4. Seamus Heaney, Address given at the memorial service for Ted Hughes in Westminster Abbey (13 May 1999), printed in the *Observer* (16 May 1999) 4.
5. Heaney (1999), p. 4.
6. Leonard M. Scigaj, *The Poetry of Ted Hughes: Form and Imagination*. Iowa City: University of Iowa Press, 1986, preface, p. xxii.
7. W.H. Auden, 'Twelve Songs' IX ('Stop all the Clocks'), *Collected Shorter Poems 1927–1957*. London: Faber & Faber, 1969, p. 92.
8. Joanny Moulin, ed., *Lire Ted Hughes: New Selected Poems 1957–1994*. Paris: Editions du Temps, 1999.
9. Sean O'Brien, 'Time Not History: Ted Hughes' in *The Deregulated Muse: Essays on Contemporary British and Irish Poetry*. Newcastle-upon-Tyne: Bloodaxe Books, 1998.
10. Paul Bentley, *The Poetry of Ted Hughes: Language, Illusion and Beyond*. Harlow: Longman, 1998.
11. Adolphe Haberer, *La lyre du larynx: poétique et poésie moderne*. Paris: Didier Erudition, 1998.
12. Tom Paulin, 'Laureate of the Free Market?: Ted Hughes' in *Minotaur: Poetry and the Nation State*. London: Faber & Faber, 1992. See Chapter 5.
13. James Fenton, 'A Family Romance', review of *Birthday Letters*, *New York Times* (5 March 1998) 7–9.
14. P.J. Kavanagh, *Daily Telegraph* (30 October 1998).
15. Scigaj (1986) p. 3.
16. Keith Sagar, *The Art of Ted Hughes*. Cambridge: Cambridge University Press, 1975, p. 1.
17. Keith Sagar, *The Achievement of Ted Hughes*. Manchester: Manchester University Press, 1983.

CHAPTER ONE

1. Seamus Heaney, Address given at the memorial service for Ted Hughes in Westminster Abbey (13 May 1999), printed in the *Observer* (16 May 1999) 4.

2. Leonard Scigaj, 'Ted Hughes and Ecology: A Biocentric Vision' in Keith Sagar, ed., *The Challenge of Ted Hughes*. London: Macmillan, 1994, pp. 160–81.
3. A. Alvarez, Introduction, 'The New Poetry, or Beyond the Gentility Principle', *The New Poetry*. Harmondsworth: Penguin, 1962, pp. 17–28.
4. Ian Hamilton, *A Poetry Chronicle*. London: Faber & Faber, 1973, p. 165.
5. Antony Easthope, 'The Poetry of Ted Hughes: Some Reservations' in Joanny Moulin, ed., *Lire Ted Hughes New Selected Poems 1957–1994*. Paris: Editions du Temps, 1999, pp. 13–23.
6. Heaney (1999) p. 4.
7. Graham Hough, 'Landmarks and Turbulences', *Encounter* (November 1957) 86.
8. A.E. Dyson, Review, *Critical Quarterly* 1:3 (September 1959) 220, 226.
9. Edwin Muir, 'Kinds of Poetry', *New Statesman* 54 (28 September 1957) 392.
10. D. J. Enright, ed., *Poets of the 1950s: An Anthology of New English Verse*. Tokyo: Kenkyusha, 1955; Robert Conquest, ed., *New Lines*. London: Macmillan, 1956.
11. J.M. Newton, 'Mr Hughes's Poetry', *Delta* 25 (Winter 1961) 6–12.
12. Alan Brownjohn, 'The Brutal Tone', *Listen* 2:4 (Spring 1958) 20.
13. Calvin Bedient, 'On Ted Hughes', *Critical Quarterly* 14:2 (June 1972) 112–13; 107, 105.
14. John Press, *Sunday Times* (3 April 1960); *Rule and Energy: Trends in British Poetry since the Second World War*. London: Oxford University Press, 1963, p. 182.
15. Calvin Bedient, *Eight Contemporary Poets*. Oxford: Oxford University Press, 1974, p. 108.
16. 'Enjoying Words that State and Words that Sing', *Times* (25 August 1960) 11.
17. Robin Skelton, Review of *THitR*, *Manchester Guardian* (4 October 1957), quoted in Keith Sagar, ed., *The Art of Ted Hughes*. Cambridge: Cambridge University Press, 1975, p. 34.
18. Sagar (1975) pp. 34–5.
19. Alvarez (1962) pp. 17–28.
20. Philip Larkin, 'At Grass', *Collected Poems*. London: Faber & Faber and the Marvell Press, 1990, p. 29.
21. Alvarez (1962) p. 24.
22. Alvarez (1962) p. 25. Alvarez's phrase about Lowell's verse, 'walk naked', echoes a phrase in W.B. Yeats's 'A Coat':

■ I made my song a coat
Covered with embroideries
Out of old mythologies
From heel to throat;
But the fools caught it,
Wore it in the world's eyes
As though they'd wrought it.
Song, let them take it,
For there's more enterprise
In walking naked. □

W.B. Yeats, 'A Coat' (*Responsibilities*), *Collected Poems* (1933) rev. edn. London: Macmillan, 1950, p. 142.

Terry Gifford and Neil Roberts point out that Hughes also alluded to these lines in an unpublished poem which appears before a draft of 'Fern' (*W*, *NSP*, p. 61) in a manuscript now in the University of Liverpool library. The authors note that 'Fern' is one of the last of Hughes's poems to be published (in 1969) before the appearance of the Crow sequence. Terry Gifford and Neil Roberts, *Ted Hughes: A Critical Study*. London: Faber & Faber, 1981, n.1 to Chapter 5, p. 255.

23. Alvarez (1962) p. 26.
24. Alvarez (1962) p. 27.
25. Alvarez (1962) p. 28.
26. Brownjohn (1958) p. 22. Lambert Simnel was groomed as a pretender to the throne by Yorkists opposing the usurpation of the crown by Henry Tudor.
27. Thom Gunn is next with seventeen; Larkin has eight; Plath seven.
28. Alvarez (1962) p. 28.
29. A. Alvarez, Preface to the Revised Edition, 'The New Poetry, or Beyond the Gentility Principle', *The New Poetry* (1962); rev edn. Harmondsworth: Penguin, 1965, p. 18.
30. A. Alvarez, 'Ted Hughes' in Nick Gammage, ed., *The Epic Poise: A Celebration of Ted Hughes*. London: Faber & Faber, 1999, p. 207.
31. Alvarez (1999) pp. 208–9.
32. Alvarez (1999) p. 209.
33. J.D. Hainsworth, 'Poets and Brutes', *Essays in Criticism* 12 (1962) 101–2.
34. C.J. Rawson, 'Ted Hughes, A Reappraisal', *Essays in Criticism* 15 (1965) 77.
35. Rawson (1965) pp. 81–2.
36. M.L. Rosenthal, *The New Poets: American and British Poetry Since World War II*. London and New York: Oxford University Press, 1967, p. 224.
37. Rosenthal (1967) p. 225.
38. Rosenthal (1967) p. 227.
39. Geoffrey Thurley, *The Ironic Harvest: English Poetry in the Twentieth Century*. London: Edward Arnold, 1974, p. 173.
40. Thurley (1974) p. 174.
41. Ted Hughes, quoted in Ekbert Faas, *Ted Hughes: The Unaccommodated Universe*. Santa Barbara, CA: Black Sparrow Press, 1980, p. 201.
42. Sean O'Brien, 'Ted Hughes: Time Not History' in *The Deregulated Muse: Essays on Contemporary British and Irish Poetry*. Newcastle-upon-Tyne: Bloodaxe Books, 1998, p. 34.
43. Donald Davie, *Encounter* (November 1956) 70.
44. O'Brien (1998) p. 35.
45. O'Brien (1998) p. 36.
46. Zbigniew Herbert, 'To the Hungarians', *Selected Poems*, trans John and Bogdana Carpenter. Oxford: Oxford University Press, 1977, p. 28.
47. O'Brien (1998) p. 35.
48. O'Brien (1998) p. 37.
49. Thomas West, *Ted Hughes*. Contemporary Writers Series. London: Methuen, 1985, p. 9.
50. Ian Hamilton, *A Poetry Chronicle*. London: Faber & Faber, 1973, p. 165.
51. Hamilton (1973) p. 166.
52. Easthope (1999) p. 13.
53. Antony Easthope, 'Reading the Poetry of Sylvia Plath', *English* 43 (Autumn 1994) 177, 235; Jacqueline Rose, *The Haunting of Sylvia Plath*. London: Virago, 1991, p. 223.
54. Easthope (1994) p. 235.
55. Easthope (1999) p. 13.

56. T.S. Eliot, *Selected Prose*. Harmondsworth: Penguin, 1958, p. 164.
57. Easthope (1999) p. 13.
58. Easthope (1999) pp. 14–15.
59. Easthope (1999) pp. 15–17.
60. Edmund Blunden, 'The Pike' in *The Waggoner and Other Poems*. London: Sidgwick & Jackson, 1920.
61. Easthope (1999) p. 19.
62. Easthope (1999) p. 20.
63. Samuel Taylor Coleridge, *Collected Letters*, ed. E.L. Griggs. 2 vols. Vol. 2. Oxford: Oxford University Press, 1956, p. 459; original emphasis.
64. Easthope (1999) p. 20.
65. Easthope (1999) pp. 21–2.
66. Easthope (1999) p. 23.
67. Keith Sagar, 'Hughes and his Landscape' in Keith Sagar, ed., *The Achievement of Ted Hughes*. Manchester: Manchester University Press, 1983, pp. 2–13, p. 8.
68. Keith Sagar, *Ted Hughes*. Harlow: Longman, for the British Council, 1972, pp. 14–15.
69. Sagar (1983) pp. 2–3.
70. Sagar (1983) p. 4.
71. Paul Bentley, *The Poetry of Ted Hughes: Language, Illusion and Beyond*. London: Longman, 1998, p. 16.
72. Bentley (1998) p. 17.
73. Bentley (1998) p. 11.
74. Bentley (1998) p. 18.
75. Bentley (1998) p. 18.
76. Bentley (1998) pp. 18–19.
77. Bentley (1998) pp. 1–2.
78. Bentley (1998) p. 3.
79. Bentley (1998) pp. 2–3.
80. Bentley (1998) p. 7.
81. Adolphe Haberer, 'Ted Hughes et la transgression imaginaire: Lecture de "Mayday on Holderness"' in *La Lyre du larynx: poétique et poésie moderne*. Paris: Didier Erudition, 1998, p. 211.
82. Haberer (1998) p. 214.
83. Haberer (1998) pp. 223–4.
84. Terry Gifford and Neil Roberts, *Ted Hughes: A Critical Study*. London: Faber & Faber, 1981, p. 68. *London Magazine* (January 1971) p. 8. (Gifford and Roberts's note.)
85. Gifford and Roberts (1981) pp. 68–9.
86. Gifford and Roberts (1981) p. 76.
87. Gifford and Roberts (1981) p. 79.
88. Gifford and Roberts (1981) pp. 62–3.
89. D.H. Lawrence, 'Fish' in *Birds, Beasts and Flowers* (1923), *Selected Poems*. Harmondsworth: Penguin, 1950, p. 88.
90. Gifford and Roberts (1981) p. 63.
91. Gifford and Roberts (1981) pp. 63–4.
92. Sagar (1983) p. 12.
93. Sagar (1983) p. 12.
94. Sagar (1983) pp. 9–10.
95. Rosenthal (1967) note to p. 227.

96. Paul Bentley, 'The Debates About Hughes' in Terry Gifford, ed., *The Cambridge Companion to Ted Hughes*. Cambridge: Cambridge University Press, 2011, pp. 27–39, p. 30.
97. Bentley (2011) p. 31.
98. Ted Hughes, *Winter Pollen*, p. 259. (Bentley's note.)
99. Bentley (2011) p. 34.

CHAPTER TWO

1. For example, *What Is the Truth? A Farmyard Tale for the Young*. London: Faber & Faber, 1984, and *Ffangs the Vampire Bat and the Kiss of Truth*. London: Faber & Faber, 1986.
2. Daniel Weissbort, 'Ted Hughes and Truth: in Search of the Ur-text', *Irish Pages* 3:1 (Spring/Summer 2005) 177–92, 178–9.
3. Weissbort (2005) p. 179.
4. For example in *The Laughter of Foxes*. Liverpool: Liverpool University Press, 2000, pp. 5–12.
5. Terry Gifford and Neil Roberts, *Ted Hughes: A Critical Study*. London: Faber & Faber, 1981, p. 11.
6. Gifford and Roberts (1981) pp. 62–3.
7. Gifford and Roberts (1981) p. 65.
8. *London Magazine* interview (January 1971) 8. Gifford and Roberts's (1981) note.
9. Gifford and Roberts (1981) p. 65.
10. Seamus Heaney, 'Hughes and England', part of a lecture given at the University of California at Berkeley in May 1976. Collected as 'Englands of the Mind' in *Preoccupations*. London: Faber & Faber, 1980; repr. in Keith Sagar, *The Achievement of Ted Hughes*. Manchester: Manchester University Press, 1983, pp. 14–21; 16–17.
11. Heaney (1983) p. 17.
12. Heaney (1983) p. 21.
13. Heaney (1983) p. 15.
14. Heaney (1983) pp. 15–16.
15. Gifford and Roberts (1981) pp. 19–20.
16. Gifford and Roberts (1981) p. 20; Mircea Eliade, *Shamanism*. London: Routledge, 1964, p. 94. (Gifford and Roberts's note.)
17. Keith Sagar, *The Art of Ted Hughes*. Cambridge: Cambridge University Press, 1975, p. 3.
18. Eliade (1964) pp. 510–11. (Sagar's note.)
19. Sagar (1975) p. 3.
20. Sagar (1975) p. 20.
21. Gifford and Roberts (1981) pp. 150–98.
22. Neil Roberts, 'Hughes, Narrative and Lyric: An Analysis of *Gaudete*' in Keith Sagar, ed., *The Challenge of Ted Hughes*. London: Macmillan, 1994, pp. 57–69.
23. Michael Sweeting, 'Hughes and Shamanism' in Sagar (1983) pp. 70–89.
24. Sweeting (1983) p. 77.
25. Sweeting (1983) p. 76.
26. Sweeting (1983) pp. 76–7.

27. Ekbert Faas, *Ted Hughes: The Unaccommodated Universe*. Santa Barbara, CA: Black Sparrow Press, 1980, p. 206. (Sweeting's note.)
28. Robert Graves, *The White Goddess: A Historical Grammar of Poetic Myth* (1946); rev. edn London Faber & Faber, 1971, pp. 9–10.
29. See Graves, 'In Dedication' (1946) p. 5. In subsequent collections and anthologies, the poem is entitled 'The White Goddess' and is slightly revised: 'I' becomes 'we'; 'my' becomes 'our'; and 'Careless' becomes 'Heedless'. See Robert Graves, *Collected Poems*. London: Cassell, 1975, p. 157.
30. Graves (1946) p. 12.
31. Graves (1946) p. 14.
32. Graves, 'To Juan at the Winter Solstice' (1975) pp. 7–8.
33. Graves (1946) p. 422.
34. Nick Gammage, '"The Nature of the Goddess": Ted Hughes and Robert Graves' in Patrick J. Quinn, ed., *New Perspectives on Robert Graves*. London and Cranbury, NJ: Associated University Presses, 1999, pp. 151–3.
35. Ekbert Faas, 'Chapters of a Shared Mythology' in Sagar (1983) pp. 117–22.
36. Review of Max Nicholson, *The Environmental Revolution*, *Your Environment* 1:3 (Summer 1970) 81–3. (Faas's note.)
37. Faas (1983) p. 118.
38. Faas (1983) p. 119.
39. Faas (1983) p. 120.
40. Faas (1980) p. 207. (Faas's note.)
41. Faas (1983) p. 121.
42. Faas (1983) pp. 121–2.
43. Anne Schofield, 'The Oedipus Theme in Hughes' in Sagar (1983) pp. 186–209.
44. Schofield (1983) pp. 186–7.
45. C.G. Jung, 'Psychology and Literature' in *Modern Man in Search of a Soul*. London: K. Paul, Trench & Trubner, 1973. (Schofield's note.)
46. Jung (1973) p. 180.
47. Schofield (1983) p. 187.
48. Jung (1973) p. 183.
49. Schofield (1983) p. 187.
50. Jung (1973) p. 189.
51. Schofield (1983) pp. 187–8.
52. Schofield (1983) p. 188.
53. C.G. Jung, 'Archetypes of the Collective Unconscious' 19 para. 172. (Schofield's note.)
54. Schofield (1983) p. 189.
55. Schofield (1983) pp. 198–9.
56. Schofield (1983) p. 199; Ted Hughes, *A Choice of Shakespeare's Verse*. London: Faber & Faber, 1971, p. 187.
57. Schofield (1983) pp. 199–202.
58. Schofield (1983) p. 204; C.G. Jung, *Psychology and Alchemy*, *Collected Works* 12, p. 50. (Schofield's note.)
59. Schofield (1983) pp. 208–9.
60. Joseph Campbell, *The Hero with a Thousand Faces*. Princeton, NJ: Princeton University Press, 1972, p. 121. (Sagar's note.)
61. Keith Sagar, *Ted Hughes and Nature: Terror and Exultation*. Peterborough: Fastprint, 2009, p. 168.
62. Terry Eagleton, 'Myth and History in Recent Poetry' in Michael Schmidt and Grevel Lindop, eds, *British Poetry Since 1960*. Oxford: Carcanet, 1972, pp. 233–9.

63. Eagleton (1972) p. 238.
64. In *The Story of the Poem*. London, 1971, p. 170. Eagleton (1972) pp. 238–9.
65. Rand Brandes, 'The Anthropologist's Uses of Myth' in Terry Gifford, ed., *The Cambridge Companion to Ted Hughes*. Cambridge: Cambridge University Press 2011, pp. 67–80.
66. Brandes (2011) p. 68.
67. Brandes (2011) p. 71.
68. Marvin Harris, *Cows, Pigs, Wars, and Witches: The Riddles of Culture*. New York: Vintage, 1974, p. 245. (Brandes's note.)
69. Harris (1974) p. 245. (Brandes's note.)
70. Brandes (2011) p. 71.
71. Terry Gifford, 'Hughes's Social Ecology' in Terry Gifford, ed., *The Cambridge Companion to Ted Hughes*. Cambridge: Cambridge University Press, 2011, pp. 81–93.
72. Gifford (2011) p. 86.
73. Seamus Heaney, 'Hughes and England', part of a lecture given at the University of California at Berkeley in May 1976. Collected as 'Englands of the Mind' in *Preoccupations*. London: Faber & Faber, 1980; repr. in Sagar (1983) pp. 14–21.
74. Heaney (1983) p. 17.
75. Heaney (1983) p. 18.
76. Heaney (1983) p. 18.
77. Heaney (1983) p. 19.
78. Heaney (1983) pp. 19–20.
79. Thomas West, *Ted Hughes*. Contemporary Writers Series. London: Methuen, 1985, p. 20.
80. Essay published in *The Listener* (19 September 1963) 421–3, revised in *Writers on Themselves*, BBC (1964).
81. West (1985) p. 16.
82. West (1985) p. 18.
83. West (1985) pp. 18–19.
84. West (1985) pp. 19–20.
85. West (1985) p. 20.
86. West (1985) pp. 20–1.
87. West (1985) p. 21.
88. West (1985) p. 25.
89. West (1985) p. 26.
90. West (1985) p. 27.
91. West (1985) p. 27.
92. West (1985) p. 28.
93. Craig Robinson, *Ted Hughes as Shepherd of Being*. Basingstoke: Macmillan, 1989.
94. Martin Heidegger (1889–1976) was a pupil and assistant of Edmund Husserl, and, in *Being and Time*, used Husserl's phenomenological philosophy to describe human existence, arguing that the extrinsic world cannot be separated from human consciousness; we cannot separate ourselves and our perceptions from external material reality.
95. Robinson (1989) p. 2.
96. Robinson (1989) p. 2.
97. Robinson (1989) p. 3.
98. Robinson (1989) p. 3.
99. Robinson (1989) p. 8.
100. Robinson (1989) pp. 8–9.

101. Terry Gifford and Neil Roberts, *Ted Hughes: A Critical Study*. London: Faber & Faber, 1981, p. 13.
102. Gifford and Roberts (1981) p. 80.
103. Gifford and Roberts (1981) p. 80.
104. Gifford and Roberts (1981) p. 14.
105. Geo Widengren, *Mani and Manichaeism*. London: Weidenfeld & Nicolson, 1961, pp. 49–50. (Gifford and Roberts's note.)
106. Gifford and Roberts (1981) p. 17.
107. Gifford and Roberts (1981) p. 17.
108. Mircea Eliade, *Patterns in Comparative Religion*. London and New York: Sheed & Ward, 1958, p. 216. (Gifford and Roberts's note.)
109. Gifford and Roberts (1981) p. 18.
110. Joseph Campbell, *The Masks of God: Primitive Mythology*. London: Secker & Warburg, 1960.
111. Gifford and Roberts (1981) p. 18.
112. Gifford and Roberts (1981) p. 19.
113. Blake Morrison, '*Wodwo*' in Nick Gammage, ed., *The Epic Poise*. London: Faber & Faber, 1999, p. 24.
114. Morrison (1999) p. 25.
115. Morrison (1999) p. 26.
116. Morrison (1999) pp. 26–7.
117. Morrison (1999) p. 27.
118. Morrison (1999) p. 27–8.
119. Morrison (1999) p. 28.
120. Morrison (1999) p. 28.
121. Ted Hughes, author's note to *W*.

CHAPTER THREE

1. Michael Parker, 'Hughes and the Poets of Eastern Europe' in Keith Sagar, ed., *The Achievement of Ted Hughes*. Manchester: Manchester University Press, 1983, pp. 37–51; p. 51.
2. Neil Corcoran, 'Negotiations: Ted Hughes and Geoffrey Hill' in Neil Corcoran, *English Poetry Since 1940*. Longman Literature in English Series. Harlow: Longman, 1993, p. 115.
3. Corcoran (1993) p. 117.
4. Corcoran (1993) p. 117.
5. Corcoran (1993) p. 117.
6. Corcoran (1993) p. 118.
7. Roy Fuller, *The Listener* (11 March 1971) 297.
8. J.M. Newton, 'Some Notes on Crow', *Cambridge Quarterly* 5:4 (1971) 376–84.
9. Newton (1971) p. 384.
10. Newton (1971) p. 379.
11. Newton (1971) p. 380.
12. Newton (1971) p. 382.
13. David Holbrook, 'From "Vitalism" to a Dead Crow: Ted Hughes's Failure of Confidence' in *Lost Bearings in English Poetry*. London: Vision Press, 1977, pp. 101–63; p. 102.
14. Holbrook (1977) p. 115.

15. Holbrook (1977) p. 117.
16. Holbrook (1977) p. 129.
17. Leonard M. Scigaj, *The Poetry of Ted Hughes: Form and Imagination*. Iowa City: University of Iowa Press, 1986.
18. Scigaj (1986) p. 18.
19. John Carey, *Sunday Times* (24 October 1999) 32. *Crow* was one of Carey's fifty books for the millennium listed in the *Sunday Times* (10 January 1999).
20. Seamus Heaney, 'Omen and Amen: On "Littleblood"' in Nick Gammage, ed., *The Epic Poise: A Celebration of Ted Hughes*. London: Faber & Faber, 1999, pp. 60–1.
21. Heaney (1999) p. 60.
22. Heaney (1999) p. 61.
23. Terry Eagleton, 'New Poetry', *Stand* 19:2 (1977) 78–9; 78.
24. Keith Sagar, ed., *The Achievement of Ted Hughes*. Manchester: Manchester University Press, 1983, p. 11.
25. Sagar (1983) pp. 12–13.
26. Sagar (1983) p. 13.
27. See above, p. 67.
28. Keith Sagar, 'Preface', *The Challenge of Ted Hughes*. London: Macmillan, 1994, p. xxii.
29. Sagar (1994) p. xiv.
30. Graham Bradshaw, 'Creative Mythology in Cave Birds' in Sagar (1983) p. 211.
31. Bradshaw (1983) p. 212.
32. Bradshaw (1983) p. 212.
33. Bradshaw (1983) p. 212.
34. Bradshaw (1983) pp. 212–13.
35. Bradshaw (1983) p. 213.
36. Bradshaw (1983) p. 214.
37. D.H. Lawrence, 'The Fox', a novella published in *The Dial* (1922).
38. Originally published as 'The Escaped Cock', Black Sun Press, 1929.
39. Bradshaw (1983) pp. 214–15.
40. Bradshaw (1983) p. 215.
41. Bradshaw (1983) p. 215
42. Bradshaw (1983) p. 215.
43. Bradshaw (1983) pp. 215–16.
44. Bradshaw (1983) p. 216.
45. Bradshaw (1983) pp. 216–17.
46. Bradshaw (1983) p. 217.
47. Craig Robinson, *Ted Hughes as Shepherd of Being*. Basingstoke: Macmillan, 1989, p. 3.
48. Martin Heidegger, *Poetry, Language, Thought*. New York: Harper & Row, 1971, p. 11.
49. Robinson (1989) pp. 3–4.
50. Heidegger (1971) p. 132.
51. Heidegger (1971) p. 42.
52. Robinson (1989) p. 4.
53. Robinson (1989) pp. 4–5.
54. Robinson (1989) p. 5.
55. Robinson (1989) pp. 5–6.
56. Heidegger (1971) pp. 26–7.
57. Robinson (1989) p. 8.
58. Robinson (1989) pp. 9–10.

59. Robinson (1989) p. 9.
60. Keith Sagar, 'From World of Blood to World of Light' in Joanny Moulin, ed., *Lire Ted Hughes: New Selected Poems 1957–1994*. Paris: Editions du Temps, 1999, p. 25. Sagar's reference to the strong, clear plot of the mythological chapters comes from Ekbert Faas, *Ted Hughes: The Unaccommodated Universe*. Santa Barbara, CA: Black Sparrow Press, 1980, p. 180.
61. Sagar (1999) p. 25.
62. Sagar (1999) p. 26.
63. Sagar (1999) pp. 26–7.
64. Sagar (1999) pp. 27–8.
65. Sagar (1999) pp. 28.
66. Sagar (1999) p. 29.
67. Sagar (1999) pp. 29–30.
68. Sagar (1999) pp. 30–1.
69. Sagar (1999) p. 32. *Daily Telegraph* 31 October 1998, 6. (Sagar's note.)
70. Sagar (1999) pp. 32–4.
71. Sagar (1999) pp. 34–5.
72. Sagar (1999) p. 35.
73. Craig Robinson, 'Creative Mythology in Cave Birds' in Sagar (1983) pp. 210–38, p. 262. (Sagar's note.)
74. Sagar (1999) p. 36.
75. Sagar (1999) p. 38.
76. Sagar (1999) pp. 40–1.
77. 'The Hawk in the Rain'.
78. Keith Sagar, *Ted Hughes and Nature: Terror and Exultation*. Peterbrough: FastPrint, 2010, p. 253.
79. Sagar (2010) p. 263.
80. Sagar (2010) p. 253.
81. Sagar (2010) p. 255.
82. Interview with Tom Pero, *Wild Steelhead and Salmon* 5:2 (Winter 1999) 50–7; 56. (Sagar's note.)
83. Sagar (2010) p. 255, unreferenced.
84. Sagar (2010) pp. 256–7.
85. Joanny Moulin, ed., *Ted Hughes: Alternative Horizons*. London: Routledge, 2004, p. 96.
86. Moulin (2004) p. 97.
87. Moulin (2004) pp. 96–7.
88. Moulin (2004) p. 97.
89. Kevin Hart, 'Varieties of Poetic Sequence: Ted Hughes and Geoffrey Hill' in Neil Corcoran, ed., *The Cambridge Companion to Twentieth-Century Poetry*. Cambridge: Cambridge University Press, 2000, pp. 187–99, p. 192.
90. Hart (2000) p. 193.
91. Terry Gifford and Neil Roberts, *Ted Hughes: A Critical Study*. London: Faber & Faber, 1981, p. 252.

CHAPTER FOUR

1. Margaret Dickie Uroff, *Sylvia Plath and Ted Hughes*. Urbana: University of Illinois Press, 1979, preface, p. vii, introduction, p. 5.

2. Joyce Carol Oates, 'The Death Throes of Romanticism: The Poems of Sylvia Plath', *Southern Review* 9 (July 1973) 512–23.
3. Keith Sagar, *The Art of Ted Hughes*. Cambridge: Cambridge University Press, 1975, pp. 27–8.
4. Uroff (1979) p. 7.
5. Uroff (1979) p. 7.
6. *Writers on Themselves*, ed. Herbert Read. London: BBC, 1964.
7. Uroff (1979) p. 24.
8. Uroff (1979) pp. 25–7.
9. Uroff (1979) p. 26.
10. Uroff (1979) p. 32.
11. Uroff (1979) p. 33.
12. Uroff (1979) p. 35.
13. Uroff (1979) pp. 35–6.
14. Uroff (1979) p. 212.
15. Uroff (1979) p. 212.
16. Hughes referred to Plath's poetry as chapters of a mythology rather than directly confessional or autobiographical in his 'Notes on the Chronological Order of Sylvia Plath's Poems' in Charles Newman, ed., *The Art of Sylvia Plath: A Symposium*. Bloomington: Indiana University Press, pp. 187.
17. Ekbert Faas, 'Chapters of a Shared Mythology: Sylvia Plath and Ted Hughes' in Keith Sagar, ed., *The Achievement of Ted Hughes*. Manchester: Manchester University Press, 1983, pp. 117–22, p. 109.
18. Sylvia Plath, *Letters Home: Correspondence 1950–1963*, ed Aurelia Schober. London: Faber & Faber, 1975, p. 316.
19. Faas (1983) p. 107.
20. Faas (1983) p. 108.
21. Sylvia Plath, 'Johnny Panic and the Bible of Dreams' (1958) in *Johnny Panic and the Bible of Dreams and Other Prose Writings with an Introduction by Ted Hughes*. London: Faber & Faber, 1977; Victoria Lucas, pseudonym of Sylvia Plath, *The Bell Jar*. New York: Heinemann, 1963.
22. Faas (1983) pp. 108–9.
23. Paul Radin, *African Folktales and Sculpture*. New York: Pantheon Books, 1952, pp. 250–3. See also Jon Rosenblatt, *Sylvia Plath: The Poetry of Initiation*. Chapel Hill: University of North Carolina Press, 1979, pp. 43–7.
24. Faas (1983) p. 109.
25. Plath (1975) p. 394.
26. Faas (1983) p. 110.
27. Faas (1983) p. 112.
28. Faas (1983) p. 112.
29. Faas (1983) p. 113.
30. Faas (1983) p. 114.
31. Faas (1983) pp. 114–15.
32. Faas (1983) p. 117; Ekbert Faas, *Ted Hughes: The Unaccommodated Universe*. Santa Barbara, CA: Black Sparrow Press, 1980, p. 213.
33. Faas (1983) p. 117.
34. Faas (1983) p. 120.
35. Owen Leeming, 'Two of a Kind, Poets in Partnership' quoted in Heather Clark, *The Grief of Influence: Sylvia Plath and Ted Hughes*. Oxford: Oxford University Press, 2011, p. 1.

36. Susan Van Dyne, *Revising Life: Sylvia Plath's Ariel Poems*. Chapel Hill: University of North Carolina Press, 1994, p. 40.
37. Van Dyne (1994) p. 19.
38. John Horder, 'Desk Poet', *Guardian*, (23 March 1965) 9.
39. *Letters of Ted Hughes*, ed. Christopher Reid. London: Faber & Faber, 2007, p. 536.
40. Clark (2011) p. 9.
41. Clark (2011) pp. 10–11.
42. Clark (2011) p. 110.
43. Clark (2011) pp. 110–11.
44. Clark (2011) p. 114.
45. Clark (2011) p. 116.
46. Clark (2011) p. 117.
47. Clark (2011) p. 118.
48. Clark (2011) pp. 112–13.
49. Stephen Moss, 'Private Lines', *Guardian* (20 January 1998).
50. Erica Wagner, *Ariel's Gift: Ted Hughes, Sylvia Plath and the Story of Birthday Letters*. London: Faber & Faber, 2000, pp. 24–5.
51. James Fenton, 'A Family Romance: *Birthday Letters*', *New York Review of Books* 45:4 (5 March 1998) 7.
52. Fenton (1998) p. 7.
53. Fenton (1998) p. 7.
54. Fenton (1998) p. 8.
55. Fenton (1998) p. 9.
56. Janet Malcolm, *The Silent Woman: Ted Hughes and Sylvia Plath*. London: PaperMac, 1993, p. 86.
57. Gayle Wurst, 'The (Non)-Americanization of Ted Hughes' in Joanny Moulin, ed., *Lire Ted Hughes: New Selected Poems 1957–1994*. Paris: Editions du Temps, 1999, p. 231.
58. Ian Hamilton, *Keepers of the Flame: Literary Estates and the Rise of Biography from Shakespeare to Plath*. London: Faber & Faber, 1992, p. 295.
59. Wurst (1999) p. 113.
60. Quoted in Malcolm (1993) p. 102.
61. Hamilton (1992) p. 295.
62. Wurst (1999) pp. 113–14.
63. Hamilton (1992) p. 298.
64. Wurst (1999) p. 117.
65. A. Alvarez, 'Sylvia Plath', *Tri-Quarterly* (Fall 1966) 7, 65.
66. Wurst (1999) p. 116.
67. Alvarez (1966) p. 73.
68. A. Alvarez, *The Savage God: A Study of Suicide*. New York: Random House, 1972, pp. 20–1.
69. Wurst (1999) p. 115.
70. Hughes's note to the editor, *Observer* (21 November 1971).
71. *Times Literary Supplement* (19 November 1971) 1448.
72. Hughes to Alvarez, quoted in Malcolm (1993) p. 129; Wurst (1999) p. 116.
73. David Holbrook, *Sylvia Plath, Poetry and Existence*. London: Athlone Press, 1976, p. 19. See Chapter 1 for Holbrook's application of these terms to Hughes's work.
74. Wurst (1999) pp. 276ff. Holbrook's articles include 'Out of the Ash: Different Views of the "Death Camp": Sylvia Plath, Al Alvarez and Viktor Frankl',

Human World 5 (November 1971) 22–39; and 'Sylvia Plath: Pathological Morality and the Avant-Garde' in Boris Ford, ed., *The Pelican Guide to Literature Vol. 7: The Modern Age*. Harmondsworth: Penguin, 1973, pp. 433–49.

75. Wurst (1999) pp. 116–17.
76. *Encounter* 31:2 (August 1968) 35–45.
77. Holbrook and Leon Edel, Letters to the Editor, *Times Literary Supplement* (24 October 1968), 1201 (7 November 1968), 1251; Olwyn Hughes (31 October 1968), 1225 (14 November 1968), 1281. Wurst (1999) p. 117.
78. Holbrook (1976) p. 239.
79. Adrienne Rich, 'When We Dead Awaken' in *On Lies: Secrets and Silences: Selected Prose 1966–1978*. New York: W.W. Norton, 1979, p. 36. Wurst (1999) p. 119.
80. Wurst cites Robin Morgan, 'Arraignment', *Upstairs in the Garden: Poems Selected and New, 1968–1988*. New York: W.W. Norton, 1990, pp. 33–6 and Paula Rotholz, 'For Sylvia at 4:30 A.M.' in Edward Butscher, ed., *Sylvia Plath: The Woman and the Work*. London: Peter Owen, 1979, p. 99.
81. Wurst (1999) pp. 119–20.
82. Wurst (1999) p. 120.
83. Malcolm (1993) p. 93.
84. Anne Stevenson, *Bitter Fame: A Life of Sylvia Plath*. Boston: Peter Davison/ Houghton Mifflin, 1989.
85. Quoted in Malcolm (1993) p. 94.
86. A. Alvarez, 'Your Story, My Story', Review of *Birthday Letters*, *New Yorker* (2 February 1998) 58.
87. Wurst (1999) pp. 120–1.
88. Linda Wagner-Martin, ed., *Sylvia Plath: The Critical Heritage*. London: Routledge, 1988, p. 55.
89. Alvarez (1966) p. 71.
90. For exceptions to this, see Marjorie Perloff, 'Extremist Poetry: Some Versions of the Sylvia Plath Myth', *Journal of Modern Literature* 2 (1972) 581–8.
91. Suzanne Juhasz, *Naked and Fiery Forms*. New York: Harper & Row, 1976, pp. 2–3. Wurst (1999) p. 121.
92. Wurst (1999) p. 124.
93. Quoted in Malcolm (1993) pp. 133–4.
94. Ted Hughes, Introduction, *Collected Poems of Sylvia Plath* (1981); repr. London: Faber & Faber, 1992, p. 15.
95. Perloff (1972) p. 11.
96. M.L. Rosenthal and Sally Gall, '"Pure? What Does it Mean?" – Notes on Sylvia Plath's Poetic Art', *American Poetry Review* 7:3 (May–June 1978) 39–40.
97. Wurst (1999) p. 126.
98. Wurst (1999) p. 131.
99. Ted Hughes, Letter to the *Guardian* (20 April 1989) in Hughes (2007) p. 554.
100. Hamilton (1992) p. 299.
101. Wurst (1999) p. 133.
102. Ted Hughes, 'Notes on the Chronological Order of Sylvia Plath's Poems', *Tri-Quarterly* 7 (Fall 1966) 81–2.
103. Jacqueline Rose, *The Haunting of Sylvia Plath*. London: Virago, 1991, p. 23.
104. Malcolm (1993) p. 86.
105. Wurst (1999) p. 113.
106. Diane Middlebrook, *Her Husband: Hughes and Plath, A Marriage*. New York: Little Brown, 2003.

107. Diane Middlebrook, 'The Poetry of Sylvia Plath and Ted Hughes: Call and Response' in Jo Gill, ed., *The Cambridge Companion to Sylvia Plath*. Cambridge: Cambridge University Press, 2006, p. 157.
108. Plath (1975) p. 243.
109. Middlebrook (2006) p. 157.
110. Middlebrook (2006) p. 170.
111. Middlebrook (2006) p. 171.
112. Middlebrook (2006) p. 171.
113. Wagner (2000) p. 53.
114. Wagner (2000) p. 54.
115. Wagner (2000) pp. 53–7.
116. Carol Bere, '*Birthday Letters*: Ted Hughes's Sibylline Leaves' in Moulin (1999) p. 234.
117. Bere (1999) p. 235.
118. Bere (1999) pp. 235–6.
119. Ted Hughes, unreferenced quotation, Bere (1999) p. 236.
120. Bere (1999) p. 237.
121. In the *Aeneid* Book VI, Aeneas journeys to the underworld to speak with his father.
122. Bere (1999) p. 238.
123. Ted Hughes, unreferenced quotation, Bere (1999) p. 238.
124. Bere (1999) pp. 238–9.
125. Bere (1999) pp. 240.
126. Ian Sansom, '"I was there, I saw it", Ted Hughes, *Birthday Letters*', *London Review of Books* 20:4 (19 February 1998) 8.
127. Sansom (1998) p. 8.
128. Sansom (1998) p. 9.
129. See *Collected Prose of Marianne Moore*, ed Patricia C. Willis. New York: Viking Penguin, 1986, p. 74.
130. Robert Frost, letter to Sidney Cox, *Selected Letters of Robert Frost*, ed Lawrance Thompson. New York: Holt, Rinehart & Winston, 1964, p. 385. Sansom (1998) p. 9.

CHAPTER FIVE

1. *Guardian* Saturday Review (18 February 2006) 22.
2. See for example Alexander Pope's *Dunciad* (1743), a mock-heroic satire which ridicules Cibber and Eusden.
3. Neil Corcoran, 'Negotiations: Ted Hughes and Geoffrey Hill' in *English Poetry Since 1940*. Longman Literature in English Series. Harlow: Longman, 1993, pp. 120–1.
4. Neil Roberts, 'Ted Hughes and the Laureateship', *Critical Quarterly* 27:2 (June 1985) 3–5 (Corcoran's note); Corcoran (1993) p. 120.
5. Corcoran (1993) p. 121.
6. Boyd Tonkin, 'The God of Granite Who Could Shatter Stones with Plain Words', *Independent* (30 October 1998) 3.
7. Programme broadcast on BBC Radio 4 (5 April 1992). Transcript, Clive Wilmer, ed., *Poets Talking*. Manchester: Carcanet, 1994, pp. 148–9.

8. Seamus Heaney, Address given at the memorial service for Ted Hughes in Westminster Abbey (13 May 1999), printed in the *Observer* (16 May 1999) 4.

9. Seamus Heaney, 'The New Poet Laureate' in Leonard M. Scigaj, ed., *Critical Essays on Ted Hughes*. New York: G.K. Hall, 1992, p. 46.

10. Neil Roberts, 'Ted Hughes and the Laureateship', *Critical Quarterly* 27:2 (1985) 3–4.

11. Roberts (1985) p. 5.

12. Sean O'Brien, 'Ted Hughes: Time Not History', *The Deregulated Muse: Essays on Contemporary British and Irish Poetry*. Newcastle-upon-Tyne: Bloodaxe Books, 1998, p. 38.

13. T.S. Eliot, 'The Metaphysical Poets', *Selected Essays*. London: Faber & Faber, 1951, p. 288.

14. O'Brien (1998) p. 39.

15. Stuart Urban, Dir. *An Ungentlemanly Act*. BBC TV 1992.

16. O'Brien (1998) pp. 39–40.

17. O'Brien (1998) p. 40.

18. John Lucas, *Modern English Poetry from Hardy to Hughes: A Critical Survey*. London: Batsford, 1986, p. 193.

19. Fredrich Nietzsche, first used in 'New Struggles', *The Gay Science* (1882).

20. See above, pp. 14–15.

21. Lucas (1986) p. 193.

22. Lucas (1986) p. 194.

23. Lucas (1986) p. 194.

24. Paul Bentley, *The Poetry of Ted Hughes: Language, Illusion and Beyond*. London: Longman, 1998, p. 63.

25. Bentley (1998) p. 119.

26. Bentley (1998) p. 120.

27. Tom Paulin, 'Laureate of the Free Market? Ted Hughes' in *Minotaur: Poetry and the Nation State*. London: Faber & Faber, 1992, p. 252.

28. Paulin (1992) p. 253.

29. Paulin (1992) pp. 255–6.

30. Paulin (1992) p. 257.

31. Paulin (1992) p. 258.

32. Paulin (1992) p. 259.

33. Paulin (1992) p. 266.

34. Paulin (1992) p. 260.

35. Paulin (1992) p. 254.

36. Paulin (1992) p. 260.

37. Paulin (1992) p. 270.

38. Paulin (1992) p. 261.

39. Paulin (1992) p. 272.

40. Tom Paulin, 'Entrepreneurship', review of *The Letters of Ted Hughes*. *London Review of Books* 29:23 (29 November 2007) 17–19.

41. Ted Hughes to Olwyn Hughes, *Letters of Ted Hughes*, ed Christopher Reid. London: Faber & Faber, 2007, p. 29.

42. Nick Gammage, editor's note, in Nick Gammage, ed., *The Epic Poise: A Celebration of Ted Hughes*. London: Faber & Faber, 1999, p. xiv.

43. Gammage (1999) p. xv.

44. Gammage (1999) p. xv.

45. Melvyn Bragg, 'Two Poets Joined by 2000 Years' in Gammage (1999) p. 126.

46. Bragg (1999) p. 124.
47. Bragg (1999) p. 124.
48. Bragg (1999) p. 126.
49. Marina Warner, 'Hoopoe' in Gammage (1999) p. 128.
50. Warner (1999) p. 130.
51. Warner (1999) p. 131. The phrase refers to the long, sharp beak of the hoopoe, suggesting that the bird has the appearance of being armed.
52. Warner (1999) pp. 131–2.
53. Jon Stallworthy, 'With Sorrow Doubled' in Gammage (1999) p. 138.
54. Stallworthy (1999) p. 139.
55. Stallworthy (1999) p. 140.
56. Stallworthy (1999) p. 141. John Donne, Elegy XIX 'To His Mistress, Going to Bed'.
57. Stallworthy (1999) pp. 141–2.
58. Stallworthy (1999) p. 142.
59. Stallworthy (1999) p. 143.
60. Stallworthy (1999) p. 144.
61. Tom Paulin, 'Your roundy face' in Gammage (1999) p. 147.
62. Gerard Manley Hopkins, 'As Kingfishers Catch Fire'.
63. Paulin (1999) p. 148.
64. John Clare, 'The Village Minstrel'.
65. Paulin (1999) p. 148.
66. Paulin (1999) p. 149.
67. Paulin (1999) pp. 149–50.
68. Sarah Churchwell, 'Secrets and Lies', *Contemporary Literature* 42:1 (Spring 2001) 120, quoted in Tracy Brain, 'Hughes and Feminism' in Terry Gifford, ed., *The Cambridge Companion to Ted Hughes*. Cambridge: Cambridge University Press 2011, p. 101.
69. Brain (2011) p. 101.
70. Brain (2011) pp. 101–2.
71. Brain (2011) p. 102.
72. Amber E. Kinser, Negotiating Spaces for/through Third-Wave Feminism', *NWSA Journal* 16:3 (Autumn 2004) 135. (Brain's note.)
73. Brain (2011) p. 102. The name 'Hughes' after the name 'Plath' was removed from the gravestone of Sylvia Plath several times.
74. Diane Middlebrook, *Her Husband: Hughes and Plath, a Marriage*. New York: Penguin, 2003, p. xvii.
75. '*Howls & Whispers*: The Averse Sephiroth and the Spheres of the Qlippoth', Ann Skea's website http://ann.skea.com/Howls1.htm.
76. Elizabeth A Stansell, 'Masks and Whispers: The Complementary Poetry of Richard Michelson and Ted Hughes', *South Carolina Review* 40:2 (Summer 2008) 5.
77. Jo Gill, 'Ted Hughes and Sylvia Plath' in Gifford (2011) p. 60.
78. Gill (2011) p. 61.
79. Gill (2011) pp. 60–1.
80. Gill (2011) p. 61.
81. Terry Gifford, *Ted Hughes*. London and New York: Routledge, 2009, p. 27.
82. Gifford (2009) p. 70.
83. Carol Bere, 'Complicated with Old Ghosts: The Assia Poems' in Joanny Moulin, ed., *Ted Hughes: Alternative Horizons*. London: Routledge, 2004, p. 29.

84. Bere (2004) p. 30.
85. Bere (2004) p. 31.
86. Bere (2004) pp. 31–2.
87. Bere (2004) p. 32.
88. Bere (2004) pp. 35.
89. Bere (2004) pp. 35–6.
90. Bere (2004) pp. 37.
91. Sean O'Brien, 'Essential but Unlovely', review of Ted Hughes, *Collected Poems*, *Guardian* (1 November 2003) 25.

CONCLUSION

1. John Ezard, *Guardian* (30 October 1998) 1.
2. Unsigned obituary, *Times* (30 October 1998) 27.
3. John Kinsella, review of Ted Hughes, *Collected Poems*, *Observer* (2 November 2003) 15.
4. *Guardian* (30 October 1998) 5.
5. John Redmond and Alan Sillitoe, 'Poet of the Spirits of the Land', *Guardian* (30 October 1998) 28.
6. Sarah Maguire, *Guardian* (30 October 1998) 4.
7. 'Earth Receive an Honoured Guest', *Guardian* (30 October 1998) 26.
8. *Daily Telegraph* (30 October 1998).
9. Anthony Thwaite, *Poetry Today: A Critical Guide to British Poetry 1960–1995.* London: Longman, 1985, p. 54.
10. Keith Sagar, *The Laughter of Foxes*. Liverpool: Liverpool University Press, 2000, p. x.
11. Sagar (2000) p. xi.
12. Jeffrey Meyers, 'Ted Hughes, War Poet', *Antioch Review* 71:1 (Winter 2013) 30–9; 30.
13. Meyers (2013) 39.
14. 'Tributes to Ted Hughes', *Guardian* (30 October 1998) 5.
15. 'Tributes to Ted Hughes', *Observer* (1 November 1998) 13.
16. Boyd Tonkin, 'The God of Granite Who Could Shatter Stones with Plain Words', *Independent* (30 October 1998) 3.
17. Keith Sagar, Dedication, *Ted Hughes and Nature: Terror and Exultation*. Peterborough: FastPrint, 2009.
18. Terry Gifford, Introduction in Terry Gifford, ed., *The Cambridge Companion to Ted Hughes*. Cambridge: Cambridge University Press, 2011, p. 1.
19. Gifford (2011) p. 10.

Select Bibliography

WORKS BY TED HUGHES

Poetry collections

The Hawk in the Rain. London: Faber & Faber, 1957.
Pike, illlus. R. Birmelin. Limited edition. Northampton, MA: Gehenna Press, 1959.
Lupercal. London: Faber & Faber, 1960.
Selected Poems: Thom Gunn and Ted Hughes. London: Faber & Faber, 1962.
Recklings. Limited edition. London: Turret Books, 1966.
The Burning of the Brothel. Limited edition. London: Turret Books, 1966.
Wodwo. London: Faber & Faber, 1967.
Animal Poems. Limited edition. Crediton, Devon: R. Gilbertson, 1967.
Gravestones. Limited edition poster poems. London: Exeter College of Art, 1967.
Scapegoats and Rabies. Limited edition. London: Poet and Printer, 1967.
I Said Goodbye to Earth, illus. G. Robbins. Limited edition broadsheet. London: Exeter College of Art, 1969.
Four Crow Poems. Limited edition. Privately printed, 1970.
A Few Crows, illus. R. Burger. Limited edition. Exeter: Rougemont Press, 1970.
A Crow Hymn. Limited edition. Knotting: Sceptre Press, 1970.
Crow: From the Life and Songs of the Crow, illus. Leonard Baskin. London: Faber & Faber, 1970.
Eat Crow. Limited edition. London: Rainbow Press, 1971.
Crow Wakes. Limited edition. Woodford Green, Essex: Poet and Printer, 1971.
In the Little Girl's Angel Gaze, designed by Ralph Steadman. Limited edition broadsheet. London: Steam Press, 1972.
Selected Poems 1957–1967. London: Faber & Faber, 1972.
Prometheus on His Crag. Limited edition. London: Rainbow Press, 1973.
Spring, Summer, Autumn, Winter. Limited edition. London: Rainbow Press, 1974.
Cave Birds: An Alchemical Cave Drama, illus. Leonard Baskin. Limited edition. London: Scholar Press, 1975.
The Interrogator, illus. Leonard Baskin. Limited edition. London: Scholar Press, 1975.
Eclipse. Limited edition. Knotting: Sceptre Press, 1976.
Gaudete. London: Faber & Faber, 1977.
Chiasmadon. Limited edition. Baltimore, MD: Seluzicki, 1977.
Sunstruck. Limited edition. Knotting: Sceptre Press, 1977.
Cave Birds: An Alchemical Cave Drama, illus. Leonard Baskin. London: Faber & Faber, 1978.
A Solstice. Limited edition. Knotting: Sceptre Press, 1978.
Calder Valley Poems. Limited edition. London: Rainbow Press, 1978.
Moortown Elegies. Limited edition. London: Rainbow Press, 1978.

Orts. Limited edition. London: Rainbow Press, 1978.

The Threshold, illus. R. Steadman. Limited edition. London: Steam Press, 1979.

In the Black Chapel, illus. Leonard Baskin. Limited edition. Privately printed, 1979.

Four Tales Told by an Idiot. Limited edition. Knotting: Sceptre Press, 1979.

Booktrout, illus. Ted Hughes. Limited edition. North Tawton, Devon: Morrigu Press, 1979.

Remains of Elmet, illus. photographs Fay Godwin. London: Faber & Faber, 1979. Revised edition published as *Elmet,* 1994.

Moortown. London: Faber & Faber, 1979.

Wolverine, illus. Ted Hughes. Limited edition. North Tawton, Devon: Morrigu Press, 1979.

Selected Poems 1957–1982. London: Faber & Faber, 1982.

River, illus. photographs P. Keen. London and Boston: Faber & Faber in association with James & James, 1983.

Flowers and Insects. London: Faber & Faber, 1986.

A Primer of Birds: Poems, illus. Leonard Baskin. Limited edition. Northampton, MA: Gehenna Press, 1989.

Wolfwatching. London: Faber & Faber, 1989.

Moortown Diary. London: Faber & Faber, 1989.

Capriccio. Devon: Gehenna Press, 1990.

Rain-Charm for the Duchy and other Laureate Poems. London: Faber & Faber, 1992.

Three Books: Remains of Elmet, Cave Birds, River. London: Faber & Faber, 1993.

Elmet, London: Faber & Faber, 1994.

New Selected Poems 1957–1994. London: Faber & Faber, 1995.

Collected Animal Poems. London: Faber & Faber, 1995.

Tales from Ovid. London: Faber & Faber, 1997.

Birthday Letters. London: Faber & Faber, 1998.

Collected Poems. London: Faber & Faber, 2003.

Selected Translations. London: Faber & Faber, 2006.

Letters of Ted Hughes. London: Faber & Faber, 2007.

Prose fiction

Difficulties of a Bridegroom: Collected Short Stories. London: Faber & Faber, 1995.

Plays and dramatic adaptations

Seneca's Oedipus. London: Faber & Faber, 1969.

The Martyrdom of Bishop Ferrar. Limited edition. Crediton, Devon: R. Gilbertson, 1970.

The Story of Vasco (libretto). London: Oxford University Press, 1974.

Spring Awakening. London: Faber & Faber, 1995.

Blood Wedding. London: Faber & Faber, 1996.

Phèdre. London: Faber & Faber, 1998.

Alcestis. London: Faber & Faber, 1999.

The Oresteia. London: Faber & Faber, 1999.

Editions, and prose non-fiction

ed., *A Choice of Emily Dickinson's Verse*. London: Faber & Faber, 1968.

ed., 'Myth and Education', *Children's Literature in Education* 1 (March 1970) 55–70; repr. Geoff Fox, ed., *Writers, Critics and Children*. Oxford: Heinemann, 1976.

ed., *A Choice of Shakespeare's Verse*. London: Faber & Faber, 1971; revised edition 1991.

ed., *Collected Poems of Sylvia Plath*. London: Faber & Faber, 1981.

with Seamus Heaney, ed., *The Rattle-Bag*. London: Faber & Faber, 1982.

A Dancer to God. London: Faber & Faber, 1992.

Shakespeare and the Goddess of Complete Being. London: Faber & Faber, 1992; revised edition 1993.

Winter Pollen: Occasional Prose, ed. William Scammell. London: Faber & Faber, 1994.

ed., *A Choice of Coleridge's Verse*. London: Faber & Faber, 1996.

ed., Federico García Lorca, *Blood Wedding*. London: Faber & Faber, 1996.

ed., *By Heart: 101 Poems to Remember*. London: Faber & Faber, 1997.

with Seamus Heaney, ed., *The School Bag*. London: Faber & Faber, 1997.

Articles in periodicals

'The Rock', *The Listener* 70 (19 September 1963) 421–3.

'Commentary', *TLS* 19 (November 1971) 1448.

'On Images in Crow' and 'A Reply to Critics', *Books and Issues* 3 (1981); repr. A. E. Dyson, ed., *Three Contemporary Poets: Thom Gunn, Ted Hughes and R.S. Thomas: A Casebook*. Basingstoke: Macmillan, 1990.

'The Place Where Sylvia Plath should Rest in Peace', letter to the editor, *Guardian* (20 April 1989).

Interview by Clive Wilmer, *PN Review* 19:3 (January–February 1993) 36–8.

Interview, *Daily Telegraph* (31 October 1996).

Interview with Tom Pero, *Wild Steelhead and Salmon* 5:2 (Winter 1999) 50–7.

Works for children

Novels

The Iron Man: A Story in Five Nights, illus. G. Adamson. London: Faber & Faber, 1968. Published in the USA as *The Iron Giant*. New York: Harper & Row, 1968.

Ffangs the Vampire Bat and the Kiss of Truth, illus. C. Riddell. London: Faber & Faber, 1986.

Tales of the Early World, illus. A. Davidson. London: Faber & Faber, 1988.

The Iron Woman. London: Faber & Faber, 1993.

The Mermaid's Purse, illus. R.J. Lloyd. Bideford, Devon: Sunstone Press, 1993.

The Dreamfighter and Other Creation Tales. London: Faber & Faber, 1995.

The Iron Wolf. London: Faber & Faber, 1995.

Shaggy and Spotty, illus. David Lucas. London: Faber & Faber, 1997.

Timmy the Tug. London: Thames & Hudson, 2009.

Poems and songs

Meet my Folks!, illus. R.A. Brandt. London: Faber & Faber, 1961.

The Earth-Owl and Other Moon People, illus. R.A. Brandt. London: Faber & Faber, 1963.

How the Whale Became and Other Stories. London: Faber & Faber, 1963.

Nessie the Mannerless Monster, illus. G. Rose. London: Faber & Faber, 1964. Published in the USA as *Nessie the Monster*. New York, Bobbs-Merrill, 1974.

Five Autumn Songs for Children's Voices. Limited edition. Crediton, Devon: R. Gilbertson, 1968.

Earth Moon, illus. Ted Hughes. Limited edition. London: Rainbow Press, 1976.

Moon-Whales and Other Moon Poems, illus. Leonard Baskin. New York: Viking, 1976. Revised edition published in UK as *Moon-Whales*, illus. Chris Riddell. London: Faber & Faber, 1988.

Season Songs, illus. Leonard Baskin. London: Faber & Faber, 1976.

The Cat and the Cuckoo, illus. R.J. Lloyd. Limited edition. Bideford: Devon: Sunstone Press, 1978.

Moon Bells and Other Poems. London: Chatto & Windus, 1978.

Under the North Star, illus. Leonard Baskin. London: Faber & Faber, 1981.

What is the Truth? A Farmyard Fable for the Young, illus. R.J. Lloyd. London: Faber & Faber, 1984.

Collected Poems for Children 1961–1983. London: Faber & Faber, 1985.

Moon-Whales, illus. C. Riddell. London: Faber & Faber, 1988.

Collected Poems for Children. London: Faber & Faber, 2005.

Plays

The Coming of the Kings and Other Plays. London: Faber & Faber, 1970.

Prose non-fiction

Poetry in the Making. London: Faber & Faber, 1967. Second edition, 1969. Published in the USA as *Poetry Is*. New York: Doubleday, 1970.

Audio tapes

The Thought-Fox and Other Poems, introduced and read by Ted Hughes. Faber & Faber, 1994.

The Dream Fighter and Other Creation Tales, read by Ted Hughes. Faber/Penguin, 1996.

Ffangs the Vampire Bat and the Kiss of Truth, read by Ted Hughes. Faber/Penguin, 1996.

The Iron Woman, read by Ted Hughes. Faber/Penguin, 1996.

Nessie the Mannerless Monster and *The Iron Wolf*, read by Ted Hughes. Faber/Penguin, 1996.

Tales of the Early World, read by Ted Hughes. Faber/Penguin, 1996.

Ted Hughes Reading his Poetry. HarperCollins, 1996.
T.S. Eliot, *Four Quartets,* read by Ted Hughes. Penguin, 1996.
T.S. Eliot, *The Waste Land,* read by Ted Hughes. Penguin, 1996.
By Heart: 101 Poems to Remember, read by Ted Hughes. Faber/Penguin, 1997.
Crow, read by Ted Hughes. Faber/Penguin, 1997.
How the Whale Became and Other Stories, read by Ted Hughes. Faber/Penguin, 1997.
The Iron Man, read by Ted Hughes. Faber/Penguin, 1997.
Tales from Ovid, read by Ted Hughes. Faber/Penguin, 1998.

WORKS ON TED HUGHES'S POETRY

Books

Bibliography

Sagar, Keith, and Stephen Tabor, *Ted Hughes: A Bibliography 1946–1995.* London: Mansell, 1998.

Criticism

Bentley, Paul, *The Poetry of Ted Hughes: Language. Illusion and Beyond.* Studies in Twentieth-Century Literature Series. Harlow: Longman, 1998.
—— 'The Debates About Hughes', in Terry Gifford, ed., *The Cambridge Companion to Ted Hughes.* Cambridge: Cambridge University Press, 2011, pp. 27–39.
Bere, Carol, 'Complicated with Old Ghosts: The Assia Poems', in Joanny Moulin, ed., *Ted Hughes: Alternative Horizons.* London: Routledge, 1984, pp. 29–37.
—— '*Birthday Letters*: Ted Hughes's Sibylline Leaves', in Joanny Moulin, ed., *Lire Ted Hughes: New Selected Poems 1957–1994.* Paris: Editions du Temps, 1999, pp. 233–42.
Bishop, Nicholas, *Re-making Poetry: Ted Hughes and a New Critical Psychology.* Brighton: Harvester Wheatsheaf, 1991.
Bold, Alan, *'Ted Gunn': Thom Gunn and Ted Hughes.* Edinburgh: Oliver & Boyd, 1976.
Bradshaw, Graham, 'Creative Mythology in *Cave Birds*', in Keith Sagar, ed., *The Achievement of Ted Hughes.* Manchester: Manchester University Press, 1983, pp. 52–69.
Bragg, Melvyn, 'Two Poets Joined by 2000 Years', in Nick Gammage, ed., *The Epic Poise: A Celebration of Ted Hughes.* London: Faber & Faber, 1999, pp. 124–6.
Brain, Tracy, 'Hughes and Feminism', in Terry Gifford, ed., *The Cambridge Companion to Ted Hughes.* Cambridge: Cambridge University Press, 2011, pp. 94–106.
Brandes, Rand, 'The Anthropologist's Uses of Myth', in Terry Gifford, ed., *The Cambridge Companion to Ted Hughes.* Cambridge: Cambridge University Press, pp. 67–80.
Easthope, Antony, 'The Poetry of Ted Hughes: Some Reservations', in Joanny Moulin, ed., *Lire Ted Hughes: New Selected Poems 1957–1994.* Paris: Editions du Temps, 1999, pp. 13–23.
Faas, Ekbert, *Ted Hughes: The Unaccommodated Universe.* Santa Barbara, CA: Black Sparrow Press, 1980.
Gammage, Nick, ed., *The Epic Poise: A Celebration of Ted Hughes.* London: Faber & Faber, 1999.

Gifford, Terry, *Ted Hughes*, Routledge Guides to Literature Series. Abingdon: Routledge, 2009.

—— ed., *The Cambridge Companion to Ted Hughes*. Cambridge: Cambridge University Press, 2011.

—— 'Hughes's Social Ecology', in The *Cambridge Companion to Ted Hughes*. Cambridge: Cambridge University Press, 2011, pp. 81–93.

Gifford, Terry and Neil Roberts, *Ted Hughes: A Critical Study*. London: Faber & Faber, 1981.

Gill, Jo, 'Ted Hughes and Sylvia Plath', in Terry Gifford, ed., *The Cambridge Companion to Ted Hughes*. Cambridge: Cambridge University Press, 2011, pp. 53–66.

Heaney, Seamus, 'The New Laureate', in Leonard M. Scigaj, ed., *Critical Essays on Ted Hughes*. New York: G.K. Hall, 1992.

Hirschberg, Stuart, *Myth in the Poetry of Ted Hughes: A Guide to the Poems*. Totowa NJ: Barnes & Noble, 1981.

Morrison, Blake, '*Wodwo*', in Nick Gammage, ed., *The Epic Poise: A Celebration of Ted Hughes*. London: Faber & Faber, 1999, pp. 23–30.

Moulin, Joanny, *Ted Hughes: Alternative Horizons*. London: Routledge, 1984.

—— *La langue rénumérée*. Paris: L'Harmattan, 1999.

—— ed., *Lire Ted Hughes: New Selected Poems 1957–1994*. Paris: Editions du Temps, 1999.

Parker, Michael, 'Hughes and the Poets of Eastern Europe', in Keith Sagar, ed., *The Achievement of Ted Hughes*. Manchester: Manchester University Press, 1983, pp. 37–51.

Paulin, Tom, 'Your Roundy Face', in Nick, Gammage, ed., *The Epic Poise: A Celebration of Ted Hughes*. London: Faber & Faber, 1999, pp. 147–50.

Robinson, Craig, *Ted Hughes as Shepherd of Being*. London: Macmillan, 1989.

Sagar, Keith, *Ted Hughes*. Harlow: Longman, The British Council, 1972.

—— *The Art of Ted Hughes*. Cambridge: Cambridge University Press, 1975.

—— *Ted Hughes*. Windsor: Profile Books, 1981.

—— ed., *The Achievement of Ted Hughes*. Manchester: Manchester University Press, 1983.

—— ed., *The Challenge of Ted Hughes*. London: Macmillan, 1994.

—— *Ted Hughes: The Laughter of Foxes*. Liverpool: Liverpool University Press, 2000.

—— *Ted Hughes and Nature: Terror and Exultation*. Peterborough: FastPrint, 2009.

Scigaj, Leonard M., *The Poetry of Ted Hughes: Form and Imagination*. Iowa City: University of Iowa Press, 1986.

—— ed., *Critical Essays on Ted Hughes*. New York: G.K. Hall, 1992.

—— *Ted Hughes*. Boston: Twayne, 1992.

—— 'Ted Hughes and Ecology: A Biocentric Vision', in Keith Sagar, *The Challenge of Ted Hughes*. London: Macmillan, 1994, pp. 160–81.

Skea, Ann, *Ted Hughes: The Poetic Quest*. Armidale (Australia): University of New England, 1994.

Smith, A.C.H., *Orghast at Persepolis*. London: Eyre Methuen, 1972.

Stallworthy, Jon, 'With Sorrow Doubled', in Nick Gammage, ed., *The Epic Poise: A Celebration of Ted Hughes*. London: Faber & Faber, 1999, pp. 138–44.

Sweeting, Michael, 'Hughes and Shamanism', in Keith Sagar, ed., *The Achievement of Ted Hughes*. Manchester: Manchester University Press, 1983, pp. 70–89.

Wagner, Erica, *Ariel's Gift: Ted Hughes. Sylvia Plath and the Story of* Birthday Letters. London: Faber & Faber, 2000.

Walder, Dennis, *Ted Hughes, Open Guides to Literature*. Milton Keynes: Open University Press, 1987.

Warner, Marina, 'Hoopoe', in Nick Gammage, ed, *The Epic Poise: A Celebration of Ted Hughes*. London: Faber & Faber, 1999, pp. 128–32.

West, Thomas, *Ted Hughes*. Contemporary Writers Series. London: Methuen, 1985.

Wormald, Mark, Neil Roberts and Terry Gifford, eds, *Ted Hughes: From Cambridge to Collected*. Basingstoke: Palgrave Macmillan, 2013.

Wurst, Gayle, 'The (Non) Americanization of Ted Hughes', in Joanny Moulin, ed., *Lire Ted Hughes: New Selected Poems 1957–1994*. Paris: Editions du Temps, 1999, pp. 27–31.

Works containing material on Ted Hughes's poetry

Alvarez, A. 'The New Poetry or Beyond the Gentility Principle', Introduction to *The New Poetry*. Harmondsworth: Penguin, 1966, pp. 17–28.

—— *Beyond All This Fiddle: Essays 1955–1967*. London: Allen Lane, 1968.

Bedient, Calvin, *Eight Contemporary Poets*. London: Oxford University Press, 1974.

Bradshaw, Graham, 'Ted Hughes's Crow – Trickster-hero or Trickster-poet?', in P.V.A. Williams, ed., *The Fool and the Trickster: A Festschrift for Enid Welsford*. Ipswich: Boydell Press, 1978, pp. 83–108.

Clark, Heather, *The Grief of Influence: Sylvia Plath and Ted Hughes*. Oxford: Oxford University Press, 2011.

Corcoran, Neil, 'Negotiations: Ted Hughes and Geoffrey Hill', in *English Poetry Since 1940*, Longman Literature in English Series. Harlow: Longman, 1993, pp. 112–28.

Dyson, A.E., 'Ted Hughes', *Twentieth-Century Poetry*, eds C. Martin and P.N. Furbank. Milton Keynes: Open University Press, 1975.

—— ed., *Three Contemporary Poets: Thom Gunn, Ted Hughes and R. S. Thomas: A Casebook*. London: Macmillan, 1990.

Eagleton, Terry, 'Myth and History in Recent Poetry', in Michael Schmidt and Grevel Lindop, eds, *British Poetry Since 1960: A Critical Survey*. Oxford: Carcanet, 1972, pp. 233–9.

Gammage, Nick, '"The Nature of the Goddess": Ted Hughes and Robert Graves', in Patrick J. Quinn, ed., *New Perspectives on Robert Graves*. London and Cranbury, NJ: Associated University Presses, 1999, pp. 151–3.

Gifford, Terry, *Green Voices: Understanding Contemporary Nature Poetry*. Manchester: Manchester University Press, 1995, pp. 114–39.

Grant, Allan, 'Ted Hughes', in Maurice Hussey, *Criticism in Action*. Harlow: Longman, 1969, pp. 100–4.

Haberer, Adolphe, *La lyre du larynx: poétique et poésie moderne*. Paris: Didier Erudition, 1998, pp. 210–24.

Hamilton, Ian, 'Ted Hughes's Crow', in *A Poetry Chronicle: Essays and Reviews*. London: Faber & Faber, 1973, pp. 165–7.

—— *Keepers of the Flame: Literary Estates and the Rise of Biography from Shakespeare to Plath*. London: Faber & Faber, 1992.

Hart, Kevin, 'Varieties of Poetic Sequence: Ted Hughes and Geoffrey Hill', in Neil Corcoran, ed., *The Cambridge Companion to Twentieth-Century Poetry*. Cambridge: Cambridge University Press, 2000, pp. 187–99.

Heaney, Seamus, 'Englands of the Mind', in *Preoccupations*. London: Faber & Faber, 1980, pp. 150–69.

Holbrook, David, *Sylvia Plath, Poetry and Existence*. London: Athlone Press, 1976.

—— 'From "Vitalism" to a Dead Crow: Ted Hughes's Failure of Confidence', in *Lost Bearings in English Poetry*. London: Vision Press, 1977, pp. 101–63.

Juhasz, Suzanne, *Naked and Fiery Forms, Modern American Poetry by Women: A New Tradition*. New York: Harper & Row, 1976.

Lucas, John, *Modern English Poetry from Hardy to Hughes: A Critical Survey*. London: Batsford, 1986, pp. 193–7.

Malcolm, Janet, *The Silent Woman: Ted Hughes and Sylvia Plath*. London: PaperMac, 1993.

Middlebrook, Diane, *Her Husband: Hughes and Plath, a Marriage*. New York: Penguin, 2003.

—— 'The Poetry of Sylvia Plath and Ted Hughes: Call and Response', in Jo Gill, ed., *The Cambridge Companion to Sylvia Plath*. Cambridge: Cambridge University Press, 2006, pp. 156–71.

O'Brien, Sean, 'Time Not History: Ted Hughes', in *The Deregulated Muse: Essays On Contemporary British and Irish Poetry*. Newcastle-upon-Tyne: Bloodaxe Books, 1998, pp. 34–40.

Paulin, Tom, 'Laureate of the Free Market?: Ted Hughes', in *Minotaur: Poetry and the Nation State* (1992); repr. London: Faber & Faber, 1993, pp. 252–75.

Perry, S.J., *R.S. Thomas and the Literary Tradition*. Oxford: Oxford University Press, 2013. (Contains substantial material on Hughes.)

Press, John, *Rule and Energy: Trends in British Poetry Since the Second World War*. London: Oxford University Press, 1963, p. 182.

Roberts, Neil, *Narrative and Voice in Postwar Poetry*. Harlow: Longman, 1999, pp. 49–60.

Rosenthal, M.L., 'Ted Hughes', in *The New Poets*. Oxford: Oxford University Press, 1967, 224–32.

Stevenson, Anne, *Bitter Fame: A Life of Sylvia Plath*. Boston: Peter Davison/Houghton Mifflin, 1989.

Stuart, Robin, 'Ted Hughes', in Peter Jones and Michael Schmidt, eds, *British Poetry Since 1970*. Manchester: Carcanet, 1980.

Thurley, Geoffrey, *The Ironic Harvest: English Poetry in the Twentieth Century*. London: Edward Arnold, 1974, pp. 172–89.

Thwaite, Anthony, 'Ted Hughes', in James Vinson, ed., *Contemporary Poets*. London: St James Press, 1975.

—— *Poetry Today: A Critical Guide to British Poetry 1960–1995*. London: Longman, 1985, pp. 54–63.

Uroff, Margaret Dickie, *Sylvia Plath and Ted Hughes*. Urbana: University of Illinois Press, 1979.

Wilmer, Clive, Interview with Ted Hughes, in *Poets Talking*. Manchester: Carcanet Press, 1994.

Articles and reviews in periodicals

Anon., 'Enjoying Words that State and Words that Sing', *Times* (25 August 1960) 11.

Bayley, John, 'Godmother of the Salmon', review of *Rain-Charm for the Duchy*, *London Review of Books* (9 July 1992) 9–10.

Bedient, Calvin, 'On Ted Hughes, *Critical Quarterly* (Summer 1972); quoted in Calvin Bedient, *Eight Contemporary Poets: Charles Tomlinson, Donald Davie, R. S. Thomas,*

Philip Larkin, Ted Hughes, Thomas Kinsella, Stevie Smith, W. S. Graham. Oxford: Oxford University Press, 1974, p. 98.

Brownjohn, Alan, *Listen 2* (Spring 1958) 20.

Davie, Donald, *Encounter* (November 1956) 70.

Dyson, A.E., *Critical Quarterly* 1 (Autumn 1959) 219–22.

Eagleton, Terry, review of *Gaudete*, *Stand* 19:2 (1978) 76–80.

Fenton, James, 'A Family Romance', review of *Birthday Letters*, *New York Times* (5 March 1998) 7–9.

Fuller, Roy, Review of *Crow*, *The Listener* (11 March 1971) 297.

Hahn, Claire, '*Crow* and the Biblical Creation Narratives', *Critical Quarterly* 19:1 (Spring 1977) 43–52.

Hainsworth, John, 'Poets and Brutes', *Essays in Criticism* 12:1 (January 1962) 98–104.

Heaney, Seamus, Address given at the memorial service for Ted Hughes in Westminster Abbey (13 May 1999), printed in the *Observer* (16 May 1999) 4.

Hough, Graham, Review of *The Hawk in the Rain*, *Encounter* (November 1957) 86–7.

Lodge, David, '*Crow* and the Cartoons', *Critical Quarterly* (Spring 1971) 37–42.

Lucas, John, 'The Exclusive Eye', review of *Wolfwatching* and *Moortown Diary*, *Times Literary Supplement* (20 October 1989) 1148.

Meyers, Jeffrey, 'Ted Hughes, War Poet', *Antioch Review* 71:1 (Winter 2013) 30–9.

Moulin, Joanny, 'Cosmologie discrète dans les *New Selected Poems 1957–1994* de Ted Hughes', *Études Anglais* 52 (1999) 435–47.

Muir, Edwin, 'Kinds of Poetry', *New Statesman* 54 (28 September 1957) 392.

Newton, J.M., 'Some Notes on *Crow*', *Cambridge Quarterly* 5:4 (1971) 376–84.

—— 'Mr Hughes's Poetry', *Delta* 25 (Winter 1961) 6–12.

O'Brien, Sean, 'Essential but Unlovely', review of Ted Hughes, *Collected Poems*. *Guardian* (1 November 2003) 25.

Paul, Lissa, 'Inside the Lurking-glass with Ted Hughes', *Signal* 49 (January 1996) 52–63.

Paulin, Tom, 'Entrepreneurship', review of *The Letters of Ted Hughes*, *London Review of Books* 29:23 (29 November 2007) 17–19.

Press, John, review of *Lupercal*, *Sunday Times* (3 April 1960) 182.

Ramsey, Jarold, '*Crow*, or the Trickster Transformed', *Massachusetts Review* 19 (1978) 111–27.

Rawson, C.J., 'Ted Hughes, A Reappraisal', *Essays in Criticism* 15 (January 1965) 77–94.

—— 'Some Sources of Parallels to Poems by Ted Hughes', *Notes and Queries* 15 (February 1968) 62–3.

Redgrove, Peter, 'Windings and Conchings', review of Ted Hughes, *River* and Keith Sagar, *The Achievement of Ted Hughes*, *Times Literary Supplement* (11 November 1983) 1238.

Roberts, Neil, 'Ted Hughes and the Laureateship', *Critical Quarterly* 27:2 (Summer 1985) 3–5.

Sansom, Ian, 'I was there, I saw it: Ted Hughes, *Birthday Letters*', *London Review of Books* 20:4 (19 February 1998) 8–9.

Stansell, Elizabeth A., 'Masks and Whispers: The Complementary Poetry of Richard Michelson and Ted Hughes', *South Carolina Review* 40:2 (Summer 2008) 5.

Stoppard, Tom, '*Orghast*', *Times Literary Supplement* (1 October 1971) 1174.

Tonkin, Boyd, 'The God of Granite Who Could Shatter Stones with Plain Words', *Independent* (30 October 1998) 3.

Weissbort, Daniel, 'Ted Hughes and Truth: in Search of the Ur-text', *Irish Pages* 3:1 (Spring/Summer 2005) 177–92; 178–9.

Witte, J.C., 'Wotan and Ted Hughes's *Crow*', *Twentieth-Century Literature* 126 (Spring 1980) 38–44.

Worthington, Brian, 'The Best Living Poet?', *New Universities Quarterly* (Spring 1980) 199–207.

WEBSITES

dianemiddlebrook.com

'Howls & Whispers: The Averse Sephiroth and the Spheres of the Qlippoth', Ann Skea's website http://ann.skea.com/Howls1.htm

The TedHughes Society Journal, http://www.thetedhughessociety.org/

www.ted-hughes.info

www.uni-leipzig.de/~angl/hughes.htm

CRITICAL WORKS ON SYLVIA PLATH OF RELEVANCE TO TED HUGHES

Brennan, Claire, ed., *The Poetry of Sylvia Plath*. Readers' Guides to Essential Criticism Series. Basingstoke: Palgrave Macmillan, 2000.

Van Dyne, Susan R., *Revising Life: Sylvia Plath's Ariel Poems*. Chapel Hill: University of North Carolina Press, 1994.

Wagner-Martin, Linda, *Sylvia Plath: A Literary Life*. London and New York: Macmillan, 1999.

Index

Printed in Great Britain
by Amazon

29043535R00106